WALKING THEM HOME

A SOLDIER'S JOURNEY IN POSTWAR RWANDA

DERRICK NEARING

◆ FriesenPress

Suite 300 - 990 Fort St
Victoria, BC, V8V 3K2
Canada

www.friesenpress.com

ISBN
978-1-5255-5454-4 (Hardcover)
978-1-5255-5455-1 (Paperback)
978-1-5255-5456-8 (eBook)

1. BIOGRAPHY & AUTOBIOGRAPHY, MILITARY

Distributed to the trade by The Ingram Book Company

Dedication

This book is dedicated to all Canadian soldiers who served in Rwanda and the families who support them.

TABLE OF CONTENTS

Acknowledgements and Credits ix

Preface xi

Part One. 1
The Mission

Part Two. 175
Reflections

Epilogue 203

Glossary of Acronyms/Abbreviations. 209

About the Author 211

ACKNOWLEDGEMENTS AND CREDITS

There are many people who I would like to give thanks to for their help and support during the process of putting my journals together. Many thanks to Dr Paul Munson and Dr Robin Hargadon who helped me to understand and process what I had seen during my time in the military. I am grateful to Marillyn Saffery who, through art therapy, has opened my eyes and emotions and given me a deeper understanding of those things which have affected me far too long. Dr Stefan Boyle who has always been there for me, from my initial diagnosis up to present day his friendship, care and compassion have been invaluable in my healing journey.

I owe a very large debt of gratitude and thanks to those many friends who have helped me along the way, as I was preparing this book over the last two years. There are too many to acknowledge individually, however they were there reading a passage, a chapter or the entire manuscript with positive messages and constructive suggestions for improvement, encouraging me every step along the way. I thank each one of you for the kind guidance and support.

I want to thank those with whom I served in our hospital at the milk factory in Mareru, on all those shifts and clinics, the fellow medics in my detachment and section, the nurses, doctors, physician assistants, medical personnel, and especially to all those soldiers who were in support of us during our mission to Rwanda.

PREFACE

It has been twenty-five years since a Canadian medical mission dubbed "Operation Passage" was sent to assist the government of Rwanda as the war and genocide was concluding. This mission has remained relatively unknown and unacknowledged since then, never fully receiving the attention or acknowledgement it deserved. Since the twentieth anniversary of the Rwandan Genocide in 2014, I had been thinking about publishing the journal I kept during that mission, but at that time was in the midst of medically releasing from the Canadian Forces and dealing with ongoing PTSD, depression and recent loss of several family members.

Five years have passed since then and I have finally distanced myself far enough from those events, taking a step back from a busy career, time to heal and to understand what took place all those years ago. As the twenty-fifth anniversary of this deployment approached, I felt it was time that I should share those daily journals I kept while in Rwanda. My hope is that they will show some of what we went through in trying to assist the Rwandan refugees on their return from the camps in Goma, Zaire after the horrendous Rwandan Civil War and ensuing genocide.

Sitting down preparing to share my journal, memories, and thoughts on the deployment to Rwanda all those years ago, I thought to myself, how does one even begin to attempt an explanation of what happened when we landed in the immediate aftermath of the Rwandan Genocide? Back when I was a much younger soldier, full of innocent wonder about the world, I had a very simplistic understanding of the good and evil that was present. Life was so much simpler to me then; black and white, everything in absolutes. My naïve understanding of the world had withstood an initial shock only year earlier when I had been deployed to Somalia with the Canadian Airborne Regiment. But it would be my time in Rwanda that would forever change my understanding the depths of insanity and hatred humans were capable of and the evil people could carry out on one another.

When I joined the military, it was with a rose-coloured-glass understanding of what we were about as soldiers. The younger me believed that we were the virtuous knights who rode in on white horses, creating calm out of the chaos. I was convinced that we in the military upheld the highest standards that good humans could demonstrate, however, Rwanda was my wake-up call. I quickly learned how unrealistic this way of seeing the world was in the face of the Hutu killing machine and the slaughter of over 800,000 Rwandans in less than a hundred days between April and July of 1994. Another estimated half-million to a million women and children had been raped and/or sexually mutilated by "rape squads" as a genocidal tool of war. With each subsequent deployment after Operation Passage, my rose-coloured glasses were to become a little more obscured, my image of the knight in shining armour increasingly tarnished. Unbeknownst to me, there were also personality and psychological changes taking place within me, changes which I wasn't aware of and didn't understand until my career was concluding, and it was almost too late.

After years of quietly carrying these memories of having been traumatized by what I had witnessed during my career, it was time to let go of the bad and shine a light on the good things I had also been witness to, those things our amazing soldiers do in service for Canada around the world. The weight of what I had seen and done over my career had held me back for far too long. These events and memories were the source of my difficulties with PTSD and depression in all the years after this tour and the main cause of my career ending prematurely. With the writing of this book I felt it was now time to shake off the weight of things past, to speak out about what had taken place and how it affected me. My belief was that perhaps by doing so, I might inspire others to do likewise in coming forward to help themselves heal. From my own experience, I can attest that it's a terrible way to go through life; never letting go or finding peace from those past things that hold us hostage to a time and place in our memories.

With Operation Passage, I would deploy to a country I had no knowledge of, on a mission that would colour the rest of my life; from that first step off the plane on a hot summer's day in Kigali and the days which followed. This country I was being sent to was called Rwanda and I was to be on the vanguard of troops sent. My job was simple, as a medic I was to initially assist with the reconnaissance (recce), to help secure the ground, vehicles, and materials needed to create a hospital facility. Once this was accomplished, 247 soldiers would be deployed from Canada, so we could begin our humanitarian mission: to assist the people of Rwanda in the wake of the genocide they had just survived.

Once the recce was completed, over the days and weeks to come, a diverse group of Canadian Forces men and women would deploy to an abandoned milk factory near the small village of Mareru. We were to be independent of control by the United Nations Mission, Op Lance, already ongoing in Rwanda and commanded by Canadian General Romeo Dallaire. Our mission would consist of a medical platoon from 2 Field Ambulance (Fd Amb), with additional platoons of medical staff from 1 and 5 Field Ambulance Units, located in Calgary and Quebec. This would be the one and only time, I am aware of, when all three Field Ambulances would deploy together overseas in this manner. As well, there were doctors, nurses, physician assistants, laboratory and preventative-medicine technicians, and other medical staff from bases across Canada. A Troop of Field Engineers from 4 Engineer Support Regiment, located at CFB Gagetown, would be sent to support our mission. The Canadian Airborne Regiment would send a platoon of infantry for Defense and Security (D&S). There would be the Service Support personnel such as administration, finance, signalers, Public Affairs, supply, and cooks, many of whom were from 2 Service Battalion CFB Petawawa. This unique group of specialists and soldiers would quickly become a team, with a singular vision, to get displaced Rwandans back to their homes. With little supplies, support or equipment we would quickly establish a walk-in clinic, as well as a two-hundred bed hospital, rehydration and aid stations to provide medical care. All this while encouraging the returning Rwandan refugees along their journey back home from the refugee camps in Goma, Zaire.

Although we did not understand at the time, what we were about to see and do would imprint on all of us who had deployed. We were about to share an experience that most of us could never have imagined, and once seen would not soon forget. We were to witness some of the savagery that had taken place as the genocide concluded, as well as its aftereffects. What we were sent to witness was not only a genocide, but an abysmal stain on the United Nations, and countries all over the world, who turned their backs on this country, their inability to lead, and inaction when leadership and action was needed was evident.

With a massive killing frenzy taking place, the UN having had ten Belgian soldiers killed, the UN Commander, Canadian General Romeo Dallaire, was left hopelessly to beg an impotent UN Security Council for help. All his communiques fell on deaf ears, signalling to the Interahamwe[1] that it was ok to proceed with the killing, that the world would willingly sit on its hands and watch as the genocide unfolded.

Operation Passage was quickly assembled with minimal preparation or situational awareness of what equipment or supplies were needed once deployed. The soldiers I deployed with were sent into the middle of a cholera outbreak, at the end of a chaotic war, with little planning or cultural under-standing of what we were being sent into. For my part, I was sent over with only one day's notice to be with the reconnaissance, securing a place for our mission to operate from when our main group arrived. Once established, over the next three months, we would aid the refugees returning to Rwanda from Goma, Zaire after the war, in a sense *walking them home.*

The story of Rwanda begins for me in the summer of 1994 on Monday, July 25th, while I was completing a medical course at the National Defence Medical Centre (NDMC) in Ottawa, Ontario. I was unaware that events were about to take a turn which would forever alter the path of my life. A change would take place during and after my time in Rwanda, I could have never anticipated or been prepared for. Sent at the conclusion of the genocide that had unfolded in Rwanda the three months prior to us being sent, I was about to be inserted into the middle of its aftermath. My life was to be changed in ways I could have never imagined, a transformation slowly and insidiously crept into my life; first as small personality changes, then as anger, depression and PTSD. This PTSD and depression would not come to its full

---

1   A Hutu paramilitary organization

fruition until many years later while I was serving on tours in Afghanistan; tours that would serve to finalize my mental-health decline and lead to the end of my career.

As you read, please be aware that these are the recollections from my journal and personal letters, which are accounts of many difficult memories and incidents from the Operation Passage Mission. Within these pages I write about many graphic and difficult situations we found ourselves in daily during our time in our hospital and out in the local community. I have resisted the temptation to alter or lessen the impact of what I saw during my time in Rwanda for the reader. I would like for whoever reads this to feel and see what I saw, so that they may better appreciate how a soldier can descend into PTSD and other mental health challenges. The people described within the pages of this book are real, however, there are times when I may use only rank, title or pseudonym and forgo names, I have done so in order to protect those who may be in my journal and wish not to be identified or those members still serving.

The 19th century philosopher Soren Kierkegaard once said, "Life can only be understood backwards; but it must be lived forward." When I read this quote, it made sense to me with the benefit of 20/20 hindsight and the needed distance from these events, I finally made sense of things I could never have figured when first deployed to Rwanda and for many years after my return. I have come to understand that it is with the passage of time we gain clarity and understanding about the past. It is only now that I can sit and calm myself enough to reflect upon, and appreciate, what unfolded during this deployment. I have come to understand that when we are in the middle of an intense moment of our lives, such as ours was in Rwanda, that we cannot fully comprehend, or appreciate, these pivotal events in our lives as we are moving through them. It is only with the passage of time and distance from these events, that they can be "understood backwards"; that we gain much needed perspective and understanding.

With this awareness, I wanted to be careful not to be overly critical of situations and events from that time, since this book is a retrospect view of my many experiences and emotions at the time, emotions I was trying to process, while under extreme stress. This writing is in no way meant to point fingers or be unforgiving towards anyone, much of the book's content is what I had written in my journal as things were unfolding daily. It reflects my personal perception of things as I was living them daily at the time, all my anger, frustration, sadness and hopelessness of the situation, we all found ourselves in, made their way through my pen and onto the journal pages. I cannot emphasize enough that no matter the country, mission, unit, or operation, all of us who were there, were doing the very best we could in a very difficult situation, while seeing things which would forever alter our lives. The consequences of this mission to Rwanda would leave as its legacy, life-long mental health trauma and personal difficulties on many of us who had deployed. It would affect individual and family lives afterward, immediately upon our return and into present times. Mixed in with this are those uplifting stories of care, hope and compassion to those Rwandan's who needed us to be there at that time in their history . . . this is my story.

PART ONE
THE MISSION

Walking Them Home

A never-ending stream of humanity marching,
step by step, mile by mile, day by day,
from where once they drank with the dead.
All human dignity given up after a bloody war,
the long walk back to blood-stained homes.

Still they walk, walk, walk. . . walk on.

The living walking past the dead
tossed aside, a genocide's human waste,
witnesses to naked remains of a killing orgy.
Victims of a world's accepting nod,
graphic reminders to the madness of war,
war without purpose, war without care.

Still they walk, walk, walk. . . walk through.

I wonder their thoughts on that long walk home.
I wonder their lot all those months in Goma.
I wonder if they think about the ones they lost.
I wonder if they will ever stop walking,
walking a distance never to be measured.
Each painful step their price for a world's impotence.

Still they walk, walk, walk. . . walk home.

Derrick Nearing, MMM, CD

July 1994

Monday, 25 July

I had only arrived in Ottawa two weeks earlier to begin a three-month medical course at the National Defence Medical Centre (NDMC). For myself, having returned a year earlier from a deployment called, "Operation Deliverance," with the Canadian Airborne Regiment (CAR) to Somalia, I realized that there had already been small changes to my personality. I had noticed that things felt different within me on returning, but I thought they would level out and go back to normal, that I just needed a little time for adjustment. I had mentioned my feelings to a couple people and was told not to worry, that it was only "a little culture shock" from my first time in Africa. But these personality changes were to carry on, like a slow burning fuse, which I had no understanding of at the time.

Being in the military with the hectic the pace of what we do, day in and day out, I didn't have very much time to reflect or dwell on the deployment to Somalia, as not too long after my return, I was sent off on a six-month long medical course, then in the middle of this was sent to Rwanda. In the military, we continuously train as there is the need to maintain a high level of fitness, currency with weapons and tactics. As Medical Assistants there is a requirement as well to continuously train and be current in the most up to date protocols and medical procedures. It's a never-ending cycle of pre-deployment training, then deploying for six to eight months at a time, followed by post-deployment leave and an opportunity for a couple months' normalcy prior to the start of the pre-deployment phase all over again. With the level of hectic activity through-out one's career, there is little time for frontline soldiers to process events and tours as we are continually moving and looking forward; we must always be prepared for the needs and taskings in front of us.

Things were going well with my medical training in Ottawa when unexpectedly, on 25 July at 11:00 hrs, I was told to hand off the patients I was caring for on the ward and head down to the classroom for an urgent meeting with our course director, Capt. McIntosh. I wasn't sure what was going on as I transferred care of my patients to the head nurse, I headed down to see what we were being called for. As I walked down the stairs from the fifth floor to the basement classroom, I met some of the other guys from my home unit, who were also on the course, and they had been told to report to the classroom as well. As we arrived at the classroom, there were just the four of us from 2 Field Ambulance. Capt. McIntosh had been directed to tell us to clear out of National Defence Medical Centre (NDMC) and return immediately to CFB Petawawa, the home of our unit 2 Field Ambulance (2 Fd Amb). There were no details explaining the urgency for our return or what was taking place, we were only informed it was of the utmost that we return as soon as possible. As I drove back to CFB Petawawa, I felt rushed, probably due to the uncertainty in not knowing what was going on or why we were suddenly being called back to our unit. I kept running scenarios through my mind as to why we were being recalled so quickly. Why had no one told us what was going on before we left Ottawa? It was about a two-hour drive back to Petawawa and as I drove, I kept thinking to myself about what it could be? I was very curious as to what was happening.

By the time I got back to Petawawa, there was no point in going to the unit as it was now 18:00 and no one would be at the unit. I would have to wait until tomorrow to find out what was going on.

Tuesday, 26 July

Reporting to work the following day at 0645, I went down to the Evacuation Company building where I worked at CFB Petawawa. We affectionately called this century-old building "The Stables." The reason for this name, was that it was a World War One horse stable, now used as our Evacuation Company and Ambulance Platoon building.

I went to the canteen where everyone was gathering in anticipation of the upcoming unit briefing. There were the others who had also returned the day prior from Ottawa along with me, waiting to find out what was going on as well. As we spoke and wondered what was taking place, I discovered that we were going to Rwanda for refugee relief within the next fourteen days. With the possibility of being deployed so fast and knowing nothing of Rwanda, where it was or what we were going to do specifically, I felt a butterfly of nervousness and excitement in my belly. With a fourteen-day window to prepare, there would be time to organize some of my personal administration while waiting to deploy.

The first order of business was a briefing for the entire unit where we were told of the situation on the ground in Rwanda. We were informed that on April 6th, there had been a plane shot down over Kigali. It had been carrying Rwandan President Habyarimana and Burundi's president, Cyprien Ntaryamira, there were no survivors from the crash.

The operations officer went on to tell us that once this event had taken place, the UN general on the ground in Rwanda, a Canadian, General Romeo Dallaire, who had predicted mass genocide since early April, had been watching a terrible genocide unfolding, while the world sat by and watched this grotesque killing orgy. We were told of the early morning killings on April 7 of moderate Hutu prime minister, Agathe Uwilingiyimana. Her ten Belgian UN Peacekeepers, acting as her bodyguards were also killed in a gruesome manner. With this taking place, along with the political impotence of the UN General Assembly, as well as the world's reluctance to intervene, the bloodbath began. The Interahamwe set up roadblocks all over the country and then the slaughter of the Tutsis and moderate Hutus proceeded with impunity. The UN Security Council decided not to act, and from the safety of their New York offices far from the slaughter, ordered Gen. Dallaire to abandon his post, which he refused to do. Once this all fell into place, in Rwanda it was seen as a green light to push down the gas pedal and speed up the killing. The Interahamwe killed all the moderates first, who were trying to make the Arusha Peace Accord work between the Hutus and Tutsis. Then the slaughter progressed to the educated; lawyers, doctors, teachers, accountants, priests, and nuns, along with anyone else who could mount an educated argument to the people. With this mass killing a political vacuum was immediately created and the military inserted extremist Hutu leaders to fill it.

We learned that during the three-month period that followed the downing of the plane, an estimated 800,000 Rwandans were massacred. The Interahamwe sent rape parties of HIV-infected men from the north of the country, to the south and those from the south up to the north, so they would not know their victims and would freely rape and kill with a brutal callousness not seen since the Second World War. The Interahamwe continued their fighting as both the genocide and war continued, coordinating with one another as the country was sent spiralling into madness. As we sat there listening to the day's briefing our eyes were opened as to what we were about to embark upon, and reality settled in that this would not be a cake walk.

By the time the medical and support personnel were assembled and sent over three weeks later in late July, the RPF[2] controlled the entire country. A country of nearly seven million people prior to this genocide now had lost forty percent of its population as almost three million people either had been killed or had fled to neighbouring countries. Most of the Hutus had fled Rwanda into the jungle, to refugee camps in Zaire, Uganda, Burundi, and other neighboring countries. Our job would be to try to entice these people back into the country from these refugee camps and to help them. They had all walked out of Rwanda when this war had begun. Now our job was to help them walk back by setting up rest, water, and food points and medical aid stations from Goma, Zaire back into their towns, villages, farms, and cities all over the Rwandan countryside, so they could tend to their crops and get Rwanda back on its feet.

Once the briefing was complete, the rest of the day we had a departure assistance group (DAG); this is where all the checks and balances are done to make sure that as a soldier you are financially, medically, and physically prepared and ready for deployment. There are three stages to this and they are colour coded: Green means you have no issues or concerns and can deploy immediately to anywhere in the World; Yellow means you have a few things missing such as immunizations, a passport, or an automatic payment not in place and will need twenty-four to forty-eight hours to sort this out; and finally, there is Red, which means the issue you have, whether financial, medical, or administrative is such that it is long term and may take months to get sorted out, so you would not deploy.

After being processed at the DAG, I was Yellow on three items and had to wait until the next day to get these small problems corrected. After work, I returned to my apartment and packed my military kit. We didn't finish the DAG process until 18:30, and after this I was told to report to headquarters,

---

2   Rwandan Patriotic Front

that the Regimental Sergeant Major (RSM) and the Commanding Officer (CO) Anderson, wanted to speak with me.

I went up to the headquarters building and was taken to see RSM Doyle and Lieutenant Colonel Anderson, where I was told to have a seat. Then the RSM looked at me and said, "Nearing, is your kit packed and ready to go?"

I did not even think about it for a moment and without hesitation answered, "Yes, RSM!"

He went on to ask, "Do you have any financial or administrative issues that could prevent you from deploying?"

I looked at the CO and then at the RSM and again said, "No, Sir!"

"Good," he said. "Go get your kit ready, you're heading to Rwanda in two days on the reconnaissance (Recce) party to get ready for a mission called Operation Passage."

All I said was, "Yes, sir!" but while saying this I was thinking, *where is Rwanda and what's going on there?* I had never heard of this country, but to go there on such short notice was so very exciting at the time; the unknown, the danger, the excitement. *What is there?* I thought.

Our tour would be dubbed "Operation Passage" to signify what we were tasked to do; provide safe passage and medical care to all those who walked back into the country.

With the briefing, over, I went back to my apartment with thoughts racing through my head. There was so much to do and prepare for it was all a little overwhelming, coming so fast. I tried to sleep, but I lay in bed bouncing around; my mind racing, wondering what was going to happen and running all these scenarios through my head.

Wednesday, 27 July

With the briefing and situational awareness of what we were heading into completed, it was now time to quickly prepare for my deployment, and so today was very busy. I had to go to the pay office and get organized there to clear up one of the Yellows on the DAG, then to the military police building to fix up my security clearance, and finally my passport had to be couriered to Hull, Quebec for urgent processing. So, all three of the Yellow issues from yesterday were now taken care of and I should be good to go.

I went back to the orderly room at the headquarters building to see Sgt Sue Stark, with my DAG sheet signed-off and giving me a nod, I was made Green and ready for deployment, which meant I was good to go at any time now. I had first been told that we had two weeks to prepare for deployment, then yesterday I had been told I was on the recce and to be prepared to move in forty-eight hours. Now suddenly, I was being told that the plan was for me to leave tomorrow night. I was feeling pressured because of all this activity and my mind was racing with the speed at which things were unfolding. It was an extremely busy time.

I went over to 1 Royal Canadian Regiment Unit Medical Station (1 RCR UMS) today and saw a few of the medics there. I told them what was going on with this rapid deployment and asked if they could help me out. I was trying to sort out all that had to be done prior to deploying on such short notice and my mind was spinning, trying to figure out what drugs and supplies I should have for the recce. I asked if I could get some stuff from the pharmacy for my medical bag and they told me no problem, so the boys stocked me up with antibiotics such as erythromycin, penicillin, cipro, and others as well as Tylenol, Motrin, other over-the-counter medications, and some IVs and dressings. I took as much as I thought I could carry. I didn't really care if my medical bag was a little on the heavy side because I wasn't sure of what we were going into on the recce. After what had taken place at the end of my last tour in Mogadishu, Somalia, with us being attacked, I wasn't taking any chances. The medics at the UMS were great and once I had my medical bag packed up, I thanked them for all their help and headed back to 2 Fd Amb.

On the way off base I stopped at the barbershop and grabbed a quick haircut, went home, washed, and got ready to leave for Trenton at 14:00. I was beginning to make lunch when the phone rang, I was told to return to the unit soon; we were now leaving at 13:00. I also had to pick up some small personal items at the store on base and write some post-dated cheques to take care of my rent while I was away. Not sure how long I would be away, I wrote twelve cheques to the landlady and informed her as to what was going on with my sudden deployment.

Got to the unit with all my kit ready at 12:30. Everyone was there from the unit for the recce; Lt. Col. Anderson, CWO Doyle, Capt. Linford, WO Frank. There were also two members of the CAR, Capt. Simpkin and WO

Hartnell, who were coming on the recce to assess the Defence and Security (D&S) needs. We packed our kit onto the bus and then were off to Trenton. I began to feel the enormous pressure of the pace of the last forty-eight hours since first being ordered to return to Petawawa. I needed to slow things down, it was already a little too much and I could feel it. On the trip down to Trenton I sat there by myself, hoping that I hadn't forgotten anything.

I remember worrying about whether I had locked the door or if the stove was on. I never even got to talk to my roommate Jean Claude about anything, and he was going to be gone to Bosnia by the time I returned from this deployment.

I began to feel extreme pressure and stress, suddenly experiencing high anxiety because it was all too much. It was coming too fast and all at once, and we were being rushed into action, too much, too rushed. I sat there and thought to myself. *This is crazy.* I was away on a medical course only two days ago and then called back. I wasn't even sure why they needed me back with all the medics who were at the unit. There were lots of excellent soldiers at the unit. I wished someone else could have been chosen and had more time to be ready.

I began looking back at the last three years since I'd joined the military and I thought, *I haven't had time to breathe since arriving in Petawawa, with courses, multiple taskings, the tour to Somalia with the Canadian Airborne Regiment, my recent military medical course, and now this, Rwanda!* The high tempo over the last few years since joining is catching up on me.

As we rode on the bus to Trenton, I sat at the back listening to the ebb and flow of excited conversations between the others on the recce party chatting with the excitement of going to Rwanda and wondering what we would see and how things would unfold. They talked and chatted as we rode off from Petawawa. I didn't say too much to anyone all the way down. I wasn't really in the mood to talk because of the speed and unplanned way in which this mission was being thrown together on the fly, then I started thinking back to only twelve months ago when I was returning from Somalia. I sat there looking out the bus window as we zipped past the trees, winding our way down the highway to Trenton, thinking back; back to everything I had experienced overseas last year and trying to pull out pearls of wisdom from my Somalia experience, running scenarios through my mind about weapons, food, vehicles, what to do, what was expected, and my place on the food chain on the recce party. After a while into the drive I felt a little overwhelmed, so I just lay down at the back of the bus on a couple of empty seats and tried to sleep, quieting myself for the long journey ahead on the flight and into the unknown once I returned to Africa.

We arrived at Trenton and the plane was delayed about an hour, as our passports hadn't arrived yet. Finally, the driver arrived from Ottawa with our passports, with this we were off for a twenty-seven-hour-long plane ride to Nairobi, Kenya. It was déjà vu all over again, with having only been here a year or so earlier in Trenton on the way to Somalia.

As the plane headed down the tarmac gaining speed for take-off, I felt a nervous excitement within me building. After an eight-hour flight, we landed in Germany for a quick stop-over and fueling and then onto Kenya, finally arriving at 20:00 in Nairobi. We were a little jet-lagged, but we sorted ourselves out at the airport, getting our equipment and going through weapon security and Kenyan Customs to get our passports stamped. Then we were off to the Intercontinental Safari Club Hotel. I had been here many times last year when deployed with the Canadian Airborne Regiment and knew the area and the city well, but as for tonight it was time to have a quick bite, then grab a shower and a night's sleep, tomorrow would come quickly and we needed to be rested for what lay ahead.

Thursday, 28 July

On my first day back in Africa I couldn't sleep and awoke at 03:55, so I just got up, dressed and was ready to go for 06:00. I went down to the lobby and checked out, but no one else showed up for checkout until 07:00.

There were a couple guys missing from our group and the RSM directed me to find them. I knew them both as I had been deployed with them before. The guys were still in their rooms when I went to get them. I knocked on their door and when they finally appeared a few minutes later, with their "friends" from the night before hanging off them, I told them it was time to go and that they needed to get downstairs. As they accompanied the two girls down to the lobby, they bid them farewell. Myself, it wasn't my cup of tea, but I really didn't care who did what. This was the RSM's arc of fire and he would have to sort this out, but I didn't think it a big deal overall.

We finally got everything sorted out, loaded up the bus, and headed to the Nairobi airport to meet our Canadian Hercules CC130 aircraft, which would be taking us to Kigali, Rwanda. I loved the Hercules aircraft and knew that with the four engines there was a lot of redundancy built in, redundancy we had to rely on a few times when deployed to Somalia only a year earlier. At this point I didn't know too much; I was a Leading Seaman (LS), and decisions were made a lot further up the chain of command than with me, so for now I watched as Capt. Linford discussed us being manifested onto the aircraft. After receiving the wave to come over to the plane, we loaded all our equipment on board. Sitting down in the side seats along the length of the aircraft, we buckled ourselves in and with this we were off to Rwanda…or so I thought.

Rwanda, although I had only heard of this country a couple of days ago, in just a few short days I was now fully aware of what we were going into. The feeling of going into the fire on such short notice was exhilarating. What was there, I wondered, and what would we be doing? I could feel the adrenaline quickly building inside me, and I was rapidly getting revved up and biting at the bit to get over there now.

On the final leg of our flight to Kigali we landed in Entebbe, Uganda. We got off the plane at the Entebbe airport as they needed to load some equipment onto the plane, and there was another group of soldiers we were picking up. Some of the guys went for a quick cigarette, while another group stayed close to the plane. As I scanned around, it was at this point I knew this was serious. After getting off the plane, we were kept at the end of the runway and slowly encircled by Ugandan soldiers, all of whom had automatic weapons and looked at us menacingly or with contempt. The Ugandan soldiers watching us looked very suspicious of us and aggressive; they had their weapons at the hip, level with the ground. Their eyes were bloodshot and faces stoic, with a serious look on them. There was no contact from them as they corralled us at the end of the runway. I was extremely uncomfortable, just a feeling, and at this moment the gravity of this deployment began to settle in as I realized this trip wasn't going to be a walk in the park.

I sat there quietly, just wanting to board the Hercules aircraft and get out of there. Once we fueled up, we finally boarded the plane around 11:30.

taxiing down the runway for our take-off, and with this, left Entebbe in the rear-view mirror. However, the tension of this moment, whether real or imagined, set me off as it brought back memories of Somalia. I could feel the adrenaline already coursing through my veins, with my heartbeat increasing and my mission-focus sharpened for the job ahead.

On our way to Kigali I looked out the window of the plane watching Entebbe get smaller and smaller as we flew away. I felt relieved to be out of there. In only a couple hours, however, we would be landing at the Kigali airport.

When we got there, land we did. It was a hard landing, but nothing I hadn't experienced before, with a few bounces off the tarmac. Hitting the runway in a CC130 like a skipping stone on the water, once again I could feel the adrenaline suddenly kick into another level. It felt like when a car is being jump-started; you get your buddies behind the car and they run and push, fast, faster, faster. . . and then you let the clutch out as the car gives a sudden jerk and the engine starts. Well, that's how it felt hitting the runway today for me. I got jump-started for the mission.

As we deplaned off the ramp, the exhaust and fumes from the engines was showering us. I looked to the forward through the aircraft's propellers, feeling the power and sound from them as they chopped the air. Through the haze of heat, fumes, and jet fuel, I caught my first glimpse of the Kigali International Airport. It was a big airport with a newer terminal to my front, but it seemed somehow desolate and empty even with the military aircraft activity on the single runway. For a moment I stood there taking it all in, looking around to the left and right of the terminal building in front of me. It was a beautiful day and not at all what I had expected for heat after my last tour in Africa when deployed to Somalia. It was a nice temperature and not the blistering heat of the desert. As I continued looking around, I caught the faint smell of something that broke my focus for a moment. I knew it was a familiar odour, something I had smelt before, and my brain began digging into the memory banks of my last deployment to Africa. Suddenly, I heard a yell, and my momentary daydream was broken as the flight engineer hollered at me to get out of the way. I grabbed my backpack and shuffled to the side of the ramp, while the plane's loadmaster rolled off some supplies for the UN contingent. As quickly as that, they closed the tail ramp of the aircraft and were off, taxiing down the tarmac, headed back to Nairobi.

As the plane left, the fumes were suddenly mixed once again with that familiar smell wafting past my nose; that distinctive smell I hadn't recognized earlier. Now it hit me, and I recalled what it was, decaying bodies. Unless you have ever had the experience, it's hard to explain a stench such as this. It's kind of like sweet perfume mixed in with rotten meat.

Unexpectedly, the memories and anxiety from my earlier tour returned to my stomach and once again I became tense. With the din of the aircraft's engines now in the distance, the smell and heat from the engines were cooling off, and as I looked towards the terminal, I could see the airport was busy with activity.

We walked toward the terminal and were greeted by two UN officers sent to meet us from their headquarters. After a brief introduction, we were taken by bus to the Amahoro Stadium to get a briefing of the situation on the ground, settle in, and begin to coordinate our mission from there. I knew from the briefings back in Canada, that although on a UN mission, that the Headquarters and Signals Regiment under command of the UN, they were directed by the Vice Chief of Defence Staff (VCDS) at our National Defence Headquarters (NDQH) back in Canada, to support our recce in any way they could when we hit the ground. I figured that this was a good thing and that we were off to a good start. With them showing up here to meet us, I assumed it would be smooth sailing from here.

Within moments of arrival I began to get this overwhelming sense of déjà vu. I could still smell that familiar, rotten-flesh smell. It was surprisingly familiar, a sweet but sickening smell in the air. Then my brain figured it out very quickly; it was that same smell from when I'd exhumed a body in Somalia only a year earlier while on tour. During that time, I had to assist in the exhumation of a young man named Ahmed Aruush, who had been killed in our compound. For the moment, I went back to that day a year earlier, the day we went early in the morning to exhume the remains. We were in the grave digging the sand out as the walls kept collapsing in on us. The heat, the crowd protesting our exhumation of the body, and the events around this, they all came rushing back, and then it was as if I had never left Africa. Here I was having a flashback on the recce for Rwanda, with tunnel vision and heart rate so high I could hear a rhythmic thumping in my eardrums; whoosh. . . whoosh. . . whoosh. With this I could feel the fight or flight instinct beginning, and I wanted to run.

As the butterflies in my belly quivered and my focus became sharper, it was amazing to me how quickly I got back to basics with an aggressive and protective mindset rapidly awakened. I had to slow my breathing down to control the overwhelming feeling inside. I don't think anyone around me noticed, but I could feel it and had to calm down.

As we were driving down towards the stadium, the city itself looked quiet, right now. You could see some damage to the city but not as bad as when I landed in Mogadishu a year earlier, where all the buildings were full of holes from the forty years of civil war.

The weather was cool and wet on our arrival in the late afternoon as we drove through the city. From what was being said around me, the days here are not that hot, but comfortable. I noticed pockets of smell from dead bodies we drove through, saturating the air along the way. You could see wild dogs running around; big, overfed, vicious bastards, fat on the souls of the dead. Then there were large birds, which looked like our black crows in Canada, except they had white chests on them. I think they are called pied crows. They're very large birds and they looked well fed, once again probably on the human remains. They were picking meat off the bodies that still littered the streets around Kigali.

Finally arriving at the stadium, we unloaded our kit and were greeted by a couple of the UN soldiers, also Canadian, from the Canadian Division Headquarters and Signal Regiment (CDHSR) out of Kingston, Ontario. Most of the troops for this contingent are also arriving en masse from Canada the same time as us, preparing to take over the United Nations Assistance Mission for Rwanda (UNAMIR) or "Op Lance." I also heard that our mission is independent of the UN and that we are some sort of Canadian Humanitarian mission requested by the United Nations High Commission for Refugees (UNHCR). Anyway, here we were.

As we got off the bus, it was a surreal scene with all the UN vehicles parking in front of the stadium; mounds of garbage here and there scattered about; and Rwandans, who had survived in the stadium during the genocide being led away to other UN shelters set up around the city as the stadium was being emptied. As we unloaded the bus, we were greeted by a Warrant Officer (WO) and told to grab our kit and follow him in. We would be shown the place we would be staying in while conducting the recce.

We were taken to the place that would become our temporary home for the next week while we were conducting the recce. We settled in at the front of the stadium, upstairs on the mezzanine balcony overlooking the entrance. I found it a little strange that at least they wouldn't have offered better accommodations to my CO and RSM, but perhaps I was reading too much into it and they were just getting sorted out themselves. We set up our beds and equipment and then got orientated to the old soccer stadium. What a sight, it was terrible, extremely disgusting with dirt and human waste, and there were still a couple of refugees sitting on the benches. They looked shell-shocked in clothes that were so dirty with sweat from having worn them for probably the last couple of months. Their clothes looked oil-soaked, hanging off their emaciated bodies.

I felt for them, what they must have gone through here. I guess at one point, from what I am told, during the war the stadium here was used as a protected UN site, which housed between 10,000 –12,000 Rwandans at one time, who were looking for protection during the four-month-long war and stayed the duration. Inside, the main stadium is filthy; the place is full of human waste. Outside the stadium, there is a shallow grave with about a hundred souls in it. The building itself has been destroyed and everything is in terrible shape.

The UN troops who were here in the middle of April and May at the height of the war and couldn't hold down their positions, (how could they with their small numbers?) eventually left to focus on protection and the guarding of large groupings of those Rwandans at risk.

I put my rucksack and medical bag down in the main entrance where we were to be located and went downstairs to the entrance of the stadium field at ground level. I walked straight ahead to the centre of the field and as I looked over the stadium where the refugees had sought shelter from the killing and the protection of the UN, I thought to myself that this is where I will be working from during the next week or two while on recce before the rest of the medical personnel arrive.

On my entering the stadium and walking onto the field, the stench of human waste and death assaulted my senses immediately. The smell was immediate, and the old clothes left behind were all over the seating area and onto the field. The UN was trying to re-establish its footing from the aftermath of the genocide and was clearing out what was left by those who had sought refuge and shelter in the stadium during the war.

I walked to the centre of the stadium's playing field and stood there, beginning to pan, starting with looking to my right and slowly turning around, a little at a time, taking in the immensity of what I was seeing, and imagining what had taken place and what it must have been like during these last one hundred days. Looking around the stadium I was overwhelmed. As I continued turning, I noticed that on the seats, aisles, and floors were old clothes, empty plastic bottles, and waste everywhere as far as the eye could see.

I saw some of those who had been held up here the last couple months slowly being guided to the front and taken away to refugee housing and care by some of the UN soldiers. I continued turning, still scanning up and down the seats as I did, completing the full circle. I turned to the stadium entrance behind me from where I had first entered completing the circle, when I suddenly locked eyes with an older woman sitting in the stands. She was just sitting there, looking straight ahead, almost catatonically. If I hadn't seen her blink, she could have been a statue. She must have been in shock and looked so fragile after all she had been through. I couldn't imagine what she had seen, and if I could I didn't think I would want to. As I scanned her up and down, she looked as if she was barely living. There was no possible way I could ever imagine what had happened to her during these last months in the middle of the killing frenzy.

Her eyes seemed locked with mine as I began walking toward her. I wanted to offer help, to comfort her, but then one of the UN soldiers entered from the side of my view and spoke to her in French, gently taking her by the elbow and helping her to stand. He walked her out to the front entrance, where a transport truck was waiting to take her along with the others to a temporary camp. All this time she stared at me with that empty look; the look of seeing what we could never imagine. That was the last I ever saw of her after that day; however, she has since visited me many times since then in my thoughts and dreams.

> *It would take many years of sleepless nights to understand this lady as she sat there in silence staring in the distance. But as I went on more tours to Bosnia and then twice to Afghanistan, as I saw more people affected by events they were immersed in, I began to understand the silence of war, the silence of survival, the silence of determination, and the silence of desperation. In the end, after all my tours and loss of faith in the military, I developed my own*

silence; silence to mute the disappointment of those who were supposed to protect and lead me, silence in the sadness of eventually losing my career to PTSD, silence to protect myself from me and with this my identity. Whether the language spoken was Somalian, Rwandan, Bosnian, or Pashtun there was an adaptive purpose to the silence I saw on all my tours with those displaced and caught in the middle of the killing. Later, once I had my own metamorphosis, I then joined them in silence, and it would take me years to find my voice again.

I think entire populations we are sent in to help have often suffered for centuries, long before the current situation we are sent to bear witness to. Prior to modern times, it was the colonialists who enslaved these people of Africa, the Mediterranean, and the Middle East. After many years I have concluded that their silence is perhaps the only way they can cope, and that by no means should this silence be counted as their surrender or acceptance. From my last deployment to Somalia a year earlier, I had grown a healthy respect for the strength in their silence. When screening patients in Africa, sometimes they spoke so softly it was inaudible, however, looking at their injuries spoke louder than any words might. In their voices, though, was a quiet dignity, which punctured my heart with compassion. When I buried a small child in Rwanda, his mother never spoke, but in her eyes was a steely determination for survival and will to live for the rest of her children. Although she had just lost a child, she still had many other children needing her love and support, and her drive to live was palpable.

My first day in my new home was overwhelming and a fast-paced period of readjustment, mentally as well as physically. Only twenty-four hours earlier I was in CFB Trenton on a warm Canadian night, waiting to load a plane, and now, here I was back in Africa. I wanted to get on with the mission and see what the future might bring.

For now, it was time to get ourselves acclimatized to the weather and shake off the jet lag quickly, so we could proceed with the recce.

Friday, 29 July

I slept on and off all night that first night, not sure if it was the excitement of being here or the dread of having been in Africa before and knowing what's to likely to come. I don't really feel well either. I feel congested and have a little headache, probably still jet lagged.

There was only one vehicle available to us for the recce on this day, and I was left behind at the stadium while the senior members on the recce drove to Goma, Zaire for a refugee coordination meeting with all the Non-Governmental Organizations (NGOs), so we could be allocated a piece of real estate to set up our field hospital.

Today, while the others were gone, I was the lone agent from my group here at the stadium with little to do. I decided to walk around the stadium for a while, exploring the bowels of the building by myself, checking every door to see if it was unlocked and if so, what was behind it. I was thinking I might find bodies, a cache of kit, or just something interesting to see. As I turned the handles, most doors were now locked with the incoming UN troops gaining control over the stadium and slowly securing the area, but a few were still open. I got into one and found a compass and a UN shoulder brassard on the floor. My mind started to wander, wondering if this belonged to any of the Belgians who had been killed or one of the other militaries who had been here.

I left these things where they lay and moved on, walking up the passageway to the top of the open-air stadium, and then taking the steps all the way to the top seating area. I walked around the perimeter to the scoreboard, there was a little flight of stairs to the back of it and in there was a small room. There was some human waste along the stairs, but thinking nothing of this, I went up to see what was in the room…and it was horrible, disgusting. I can only imagine that with over 10,000 people or more in the stadium for months during the genocide, that eventually the septic system got full, and then they started in one corner of this tiny room and strategically worked their way back to the door, kind of like when you paint a floor, only it was them defecating from one corner of the room over to the doorway! Then they worked their way out and began to do this all over again behind this room in an open area, and then down the stairs. Words cannot explain how disgusting this was to witness; how hard to imagine that it had come to this, but what else could they have done?

I went back to the ground floor and on the way down to the area where we were staying, I spoke to some other soldiers busily working. One of the first people I'd met was a Canadian officer with the UN, and I went over and tried to engage him in small talk. For the most part I was thinking, we were both Canadians and both overseas in a foreign country, so I assumed he would be friendly and not mind a little small talk. Well, with most Canadian soldiers I had met while deployed this was my expectation. However, this Canadian officer didn't seem all that eager to engage with me. As he looked at me up and down with my black beret, he noticed I wasn't wearing the blue UN one. I began telling him I was here from 2 Field Ambulance's Canadian humanitarian mission, Operation Passage, and not deployed with the UNAMIR contingent. When I said this, he seemed to almost immediately disengage and shut down the conversation with me. I was thinking to myself, *what is up with this guy?* I usually never think this way, especially of other Canadians when we are deployed, but my mind went there. With the abruptness of his interactions with me, it was obvious he didn't want to talk or engage with me and he began to walk away. So, I turned to walk away too, thinking that I had never seen this behaviour from another Canadian before while deployed. I thought that maybe it was just a period of adjustment with some of the things many of these soldiers may have seen since arriving here, and the business of trying to get their own tour underway.

Continuing my walk around the stadium, I soon met another UN Canadian senior non-commissioned officer (Snr NCO) from the UNAMIR tour. As I began to speak with him, I quickly got a similar reception as during the earlier encounter, especially after telling him I was with 2 Field Ambulance. He just shut down the conversation, and then actually just turned and walked away from me. *What's up with these guys?* I thought again. I wasn't sure what to think about the passive-aggressive attitude towards me once I mention Operation Passage to them. I got the feeling it was as if they felt we shouldn't be here.

It wouldn't take long for the dots to connect, and I began to understand the reluctance to engage with those of us on the recce. Some in the UN group are certainly not making our recce party feel welcome; we are being treated as if we were from another country and not fellow Canadians. It was as if we were taking their rations, equipment or resources, and it was becoming obvious that we were a bother to them, and they had no time for us. I remember from our briefing back in Canada before leaving on the recce, when we were informed that as soon as we landed, all the support we needed would be available. The UNHCR had asked Canada to provide medical support and water purification capabilities not under control of the UN. However, the Chief of Defence Staff had ordered the Canadian unit in country on the UN tour in Rwanda to support our group with water, food, accommodations, ammunition, and vehicles until we could get the recce completed and establish our own supply chain.

Supporting us for a few days here on the recce shouldn't be a big thing, but it certainly felt that way with my first two encounters here in the stadium today. I knew right then and there that our reliance or ability to depend on the UN would be a struggle if this was to be our treatment during those times to get the resources we require. We need their support just to get the recce completed but if not, I could be resourceful when called upon and help to get what we needed on order to get the mission done.

I was really not understanding what had just happened I had always thought that a Canadian was a Canadian, whether home or abroad and that we had each other's backs. But I didn't get the warm and fuzzy from those first encounters with our "Welcome to Rwanda" yesterday at the airport or from these first encounters in the confines of the stadium.

I went back to the area in the balcony where we were staying and sat down to read. While I was sitting there reading my book, a Warrant Officer from the Canadian contingent approached me, asking if I could help since I was going to be around today and didn't look too busy. We talked for a few minutes, he seemed like a very nice guy and friendly, it was nice to finally talk to someone pleasant after my initial encounters with others here in the stadium. I told him no problem as I asked what he wanted me to do. He had a key ring in his hand and asked if I could take a couple of the UN troops, who had been cleaning the stadium, downstairs to clean out a couple of rooms in the front of the stadium, that would be very helpful and much appreciated. I went downstairs to a locked room next to the ticket booth, I had been told the incoming UN troops weren't sure what was in the rooms on the lower bowl around the stadium. I unlocked the door and turning the handle to go in and see what had to be done, noticed the door was stiff and wouldn't budge. Initially the door wouldn't open, so I put my shoulder to it and gave it a good hit, as I leaned into the door it sprang open, I stumbled forward and almost fell on my face into the room. The others followed behind me as we had our shovels and brooms, then begun to clean up the shit and corruption around the floor, when suddenly I saw in front of me rats everywhere coming from under the garbage. They were pouring out from underneath the garbage we had disturbed, running up the walls, down the walls, across the ceiling, and on the piles of garbage and furniture, all over the place. One of the soldiers with me closed the door as the rats were running around my legs. We started kicking them off the walls, walking on them and snapping their necks, and then I took a shovel and started whacking them. I felt like I was in some terrible horror movie, we must have killed rats for what seemed to me over a half-hour, though in reality it was probably only a few minutes. In the end when all was done, I had rat blood and guts all over me.

I was emotionally and physically exhausted from this short adrenaline burst. Looking over at the two fellows with me, I smiled as they smiled back, then suddenly we all burst out laughing. For sure it was an adrenaline moment; a release of the nervousness and pressure from the experience we just had. We then cleaned up the rat bodies and threw them out with the rest of the garbage and locked the door as we left the cleaned room.

I grew up in a the small coal mining town of New Waterford, Cape Breton and lived next to a coal mine, so I saw rats as a kid and had no fear of them, occasionally there would big rats, but these bastards here in the stadium came from the area out front of the building, where they had been feeding on human bodies in the shallow mass grave. When we were finished cleaning the room, I had to go and wash because I felt dirty and wanted to get out of my clothes. It felt the same as when I had exhumed a body in Somalia last year. I couldn't stop thinking about this and for a moment, once again, thought I was going to have a panic attack.

After I washed, it was still in my mind and knowing these rats ate humans, I began to think about the spot we'd been given to sleep in, upstairs on the floor in the open balcony. My mind jumped to thinking about the thousands of people who died here during the war and that these rats had fed on many of those who perished. A terrible wave of feelings came over me as I began to have a moment where suddenly I was again digging up the decaying body of Ahmed Arush in Somalia. I never will forget that day and with the events of today, the killing of the rats, have reawakened in me those thoughts about this past event, which I thought I had made peace with.

Later in the evening, my CO asked if I could go down and give some immunizations to a Canadian officer at the UN headquarters. It had been brought up in the Orders Group (O Grp) that there were a few troops arriving, those deployed on short notice from Canada, who still required some immunizations. They had taken the serum with them but had no one to administer it. "Yes, sir!" I said as it gave me a chance to change it up and get out of this stadium, where I'd been working all day, and away from some of the things which had been going on while the others had gone to Goma.

Getting my medical bag, I went down to the UN headquarters. Many of the incoming officers needed a tetanus booster, and some needed an immune serum globulin (ISG) injection. Once this was completed, I had a chance to ask one of the signal guys at the headquarters if I could sneak a short call back home to Canada, to talk with my mom just to tell her that I was ok. He was a corporal, the same rank as myself, and turned out to be a pretty good guy who had no problem with doing this for me.

Despite a few of my initial experiences, for the most part, the troops deployed on the UN tour were very good to me. Always eager to assist when something was needed and helped me along the way during the recce.

As I was speaking with my mother, I began thinking that sometimes I put her through too much. All she did was worry last year when I was in Somalia, and now she's home watching the news on television and wondering if I'll make it out of here. She told me she was worried I could be killed in Rwanda. I tried to reassure her that it's not that bad here and not to worry. Saying goodbye, I told her I would call again as soon as I could.

After finishing my call, I went back to the stadium and got the orders group, or O Grp as it is known. There was not much new to report. From the CO's recce today, the refugees are still moving back into the country from the neighbouring countries and many more are now moving toward Kigali. The only point of interest for me was that I might go by myself tomorrow to do some refugee care, which would be an interesting tasking. Anyway, after this I went to bed.

Saturday, 30 July

I bounced around all last night and on getting up felt like shit. After yesterday's experiences here at the stadium, I need to get where we're going and get on with our mission away from here in Kigali and the UN mission. This place is already getting too silly and I want out of here.

I got up, washed, and got ready for the day in front of me. I'm still not sure of what's going on as far as today's activities. However, I do know that at 08:30 I have to take the CO (Lt. Col. Anderson) and RSM (CWO Doyle) down to the International Red Cross (IRC) compound, with RSM Doyle. I ate a ration pack and made a pot of coffee for all of us.

I drove the CO and RSM to the IRC compound to their meeting, so now my job was to wait. As I sat there, I looked out the windshield and saw the gaggle of non-governmental organizations' (NGOs) vehicles arriving. There are so many groups here trying to help. Some, I think, are here for the publicity, but most are here to help and care for those people injured and displaced during the war. I saw all those vehicles; Americares, ICRC, IMC, UNICEF, MEMISA, MSF, Pharmacy Sans Frontier, and many others. Some arrive in their airconditioned vehicles and brand-new land rovers, while others arrive in old, beat-up Toyotas. I wonder what it's all about; the politics of giving help, good intentions, and the whole business of refugee care. Some are in it for the right reasons while others, I am unsure about.

I thought about this, sitting there at the Red Cross compound for an hour or so, waiting for the CO and RSM, and then I drove them back to the stadium. After they had lunch they left with the rest of the group for a recce to Goma, Zaire. I was left behind because there was no need for me at this point. The rest of the day I was left at the stadium to do not much. Staying away from the areas where the UN troops were, I washed some combat clothing, packed my kit, reviewed what I had and what I was going to do, and kept thinking about getting on with the mission. I saw some guys from the Canadian Airborne Regiment's (CAR) 3 Commando, who had arrived the day prior as part of the UN mission. They were out in front of the stadium, shoring up the defensive positions, barbed wire, and access points. Looking around, I recognized many of the guys, since we had been in Somalia together, and I went over to be around guys I knew from Petawawa.

I knew they would at least talk to me even if they were wearing UN blue berets and I was not.

I went outside and just hopped in line with the group working there, and then I grabbed wire gloves and began setting up razor wire around the outside of the stadium with them and packing in some sandbags for the stadium's defence. The defensive wire was mostly being put up to keep out the people who were looting and had gotten used to entering the stadium unimpeded for far too long.

As I was putting up the wire, I noticed some very large birds walking around. They looked like ravens as they were big and black, but they had white rings around their necks and chests. They were picking at some of the body parts still lying around across the street. I always like birds and growing up as I had homing pigeons and spent lots of time amongst them, but these birds here in Rwanda made me feel as if evil was all around us. I know that's a silly thought, but they were creepy-looking things and flying around feeding off the dead bodies, which were abundant, they reminded me of the rats from yesterday. As I continued putting up the razor wire, I got a few nicks on my arm as it bit into me occasionally, but no matter, in short order we had erected a double-double barbed-wire fence with apron around the front of the stadium's exterior.

At supper time, all outside work was coming to a halt, and we gathered the tools to put them away. A couple of buses pulled up front of the stadium with about 160 more UN troops, who had just arrived from the airport. After they got off the bus, they began to unload their equipment. I felt it getting a little more crowded now. Space would be at a premium and with more UN soldiers here, I would stand out by not being one of them.

Later on, in the evening, Lt. Col. Anderson and the RSM arrived back and said the recce had gone well. After supper the CO spoke to me and asked if I had any antibiotics. I said certainly, I had lots in my med bag, and had made sure before I left Petawawa that I had visited 1 RCR UMS and loaded up with the essentials for the recce. I wondered why he was asking, as all of us in the recce party were well and no one was ill from what I knew. He then told me that the UNAMIR medics had a sick guy who had a chest infection, but his medical kit hadn't arrived yet. I looked at the CO and said, "No problem, sir. I have enough to take care of their troop." I was only a Leading Seaman, but I'd had the awareness before leaving Canada to make sure I brought enough medicine for the recce. The sergeant asked me what I had for antibiotics, so I told him what I had and then gave him enough of what he needed for the soldier, who was suspected to have pneumonia. I was glad to be able to assist as I thought to myself that after being in Somalia, I would never be without the essentials. It was Somalia that had taught me the importance of showing up on tour ready to go to work. I gave the medications to him and he went off to care for his sick soldier.

We had an "O" group at 23:00 and we didn't finish until 24:00. Not much is happening right now, except that the main body will show up on Tuesday. That will be about 140 of our people arriving and only three days to get the recce done. The bathroom that night was getting plugged up with toilet paper with some not understanding that they were no longer in Canada. A little of this was perhaps because of poor water and hygiene discipline, people aren't putting a bucket of water into the toilets to flush them after using them, or for others it could be operational immaturity. There is an etiquette on tour, an understanding that we are all in this together, sent to a foreign country and that our collective comfort, or lack of, depends on each of us doing the small things. Made me wonder what some of them live like back home, they probably shit the bed and kick it out. Some are so lazy at the expense of others.

Sunday, 31 July

I awoke today at 06:00, rolled up my sleeping bag and sorted out my kit so it was all together and ready to go. I just like to have things ready all the time. After this was done, I got washed and ate breakfast with the rest. While sitting there I was asked if I could help out and come boost a couple of vehicles. No problems, I went out and boosted three vehicles and then came back into the stadium to see what was planned for me today. It was a wait-and-see kind of morning, so, wanting to be productive I spent a couple of hours preparing four maps and doing smaller but essential jobs that needed to be done. Afterwards, I ate lunch and found out that I was supposed to take the engineer officer out on the recce, but they had sent someone else from his home unit with him.

Later, after lunch, I did a few runs back and forth between the UNHQ and the stadium for some operational messages. Then the rest of the day I worked on my equipment until our regimental quartermaster (RQ), WO Frank, approached me and mentioned that he and I had to go somewhere later this afternoon. At 17:00, we were going to the Canadian support group (CSG) to pick up a truck for the road move tomorrow to Goma. I'm nervous because of the dead bodies and refugees along the way and the unknown with a war just finishing up, but I'm still excited to get on with this mission. The time came and we went to CSG and got the truck, WO Frank knew a few of the supply guys there, so he talked for a while and shot the shit, good investment of time in networking for future favours and trades.

After we got our vehicle, we went bombing around Kigali and exploring the city, up one street, down another like a couple of excited kids exploring our new surroundings. As we were driving all around Kigali, WO Frank was getting thirsty and saw a sign over a storefront. It was a tavern of some sort, so he told me to pull in here and we can go in and grab a drink. Pulling in and parking, I turned off the vehicle, locked the steering wheel, and got out. We began walking towards the tavern, which seemed quiet. It was early enough, so with no vehicles around we figured no one was there, but it was going to be nice to have a cool drink. As we walked in talking to one another, we looked up and in front of us were about a hundred Rwandan soldiers, all sitting and drinking beer with their AK-47s and weapons by their sides. They stared at us and it was the most menacing look I had ever seen. In an instant, it went from the buzz of conversation we could hear as we walked in, to a pin-dropping silence. Immediately I felt in danger and began to instinctively pedal backwards. As we looked at one another, WO Frank said, "I don't think we're welcome in here, Derrick," and I said, "No shit!"

We began backing out slowly. As we were doing this, I think I shit myself and in my mind I was thinking of what I had to do as soon as I got to the safety of my vehicle; *the steering wheel is still locked, we don't have our long-barrel weapons with us, our sidearms are secured in our holsters, we're screwed if these guys decide to charge after us.* We just kept backing away and extracted ourselves outside. Once we were out the door, we turned around and ran to the vehicle. WO Frank and I began laughing as we were driving away. "That was too close Derrick," he said. I just looked at him and thought, *do you think?* That's all I could think or say. I knew we were very lucky and could have been killed just then.

We got back and secured the vehicle, told our story to RSM Doyle, and had a few laughs in the safety of the stadium. We just finished an "O" group and I found out that I'll be driving up an old Russian five-tonne truck, packed with stores and equipment, to our future home. Then I'll drive back from Goma to do some work at the airstrip getting the troops from Fd Amb as well as getting cargo, so with it being 22:30 I guess I'll go to bed.

Milk factory in Mareru, site of Operation Passage – Photo Chris Cormier

The arrival of the troops – Source unknown

Hospital layout begins – Photo Chris Cormier

Setting up of the hospital - Photo Chris Cormier

Hospital set up complete – Source unknown

First day of the hospital and clinic opening - Photo Chris Cormier

five senses

blindness in the despair of the tent ... too much to see all at once,
in the darkness of night with eyes closed tight, visions invade.

silence ... in the still of night my soul searches for meaning,
no sound except the screaming of my mind alone to itself.

death and misery fill the air ... the decaying smell of desperation,
thick and smouldering, permeating my skin; a deathly cologne.

child's desperate hunger for air ... the touch of lips cannot revive,
silent tears in a mother's gentle caress of still child's face.

taste of death and desperation ... permeates the palate,
my soul hungry for answers as the world sleeps.

Derrick Nearing, MMM, CD

August 1994

Monday, 1 August

We have been in Rwanda for five days and I am getting anxious to get on with the recce to Mareru and up to Goma, Zaire. (In 1997, Zaire was renamed the Democratic Republic of the Congo). I really wanted to get on with this damn mission. We were only in the country a couple of days, but it already it felt that we were spinning our wheels. It was getting tiring waiting at the stadium and vehicles were what was holding us up. There was pressure quickly building as we had to get on with this recce. We had roughly 250 troops who would be showing up within the next week and we quickly needed to have a location secured and prepared for their arrival. I began to feel we were being given the runaround by some of the senior UN troops on the ground; it wasn't taking place at my level, but a little higher up the food chain.

For the most part we were treated well by the front-line troops, however, there was an undertone of hostility towards our group from some of the UN contingent, and I couldn't understand this feeling towards us. During the war, the UNAMIR mission was led by a Canadian general, General Dallaire, and afterwards, the Canadian Division Signals and Headquarters Regiment was now the lead element, with General Tousignant assuming command for what would become UNAMIR II. They are all from Canada as we are, but the way some of the leadership has treated us we might as well have been from another country, or planet for that matter.

I left the stadium and headed to the UN compound to pick up my replacement vehicle; a German three-tonne truck. This was already our second vehicle to use for the recce in two days. The first one broke down only a couple hours after we picked it up on the first day. This replacement vehicle was not much better than the first; it's a piece of shit, runs extremely rough due to its poor condition, and sounds as if it will stall out at any time.

I suspected that no matter what vehicle we were given, it would be a vehicle of lesser quality. The UN were supporting us reluctantly, mainly because General Dallaire was directing them to do so on orders from the Deputy Chief of Defence Staff (DCDS). I hopped into our newest vehicle and turned the key to start it up. It started (a good beginning) and was running. Then, as I put it in gear and began driving away, suddenly I could hear someone's voice yelling from behind the vehicle. As I looked in my rear-view mirror, I could see a couple guys shouting and waving their arms at me. Stopping, I jumped out to see what the problem was and walked to the back of the truck. Behind the truck there was a deep groove in the gravel where the back tires had locked up and were not moving. It looked as if the air brakes were locked on the rear left side. There was a big rut in the parking lot where the tire had dug in when the brakes locked up and the wheel had dragged. What a setback to have this happen.

The mechanics took it away and began working on it, and it took over two hours to have that fixed. We still needed a second vehicle for the recce, so we made our way back to 3 Canadian Support Group (CSG) to wait around for another hour for another vehicle, which never arrived. Capt. Linford was visibly upset, while WO Frank was more relaxed about it all. He was a pretty cool guy who never seemed to get too excited, probably because he had been on a lot of tours already in his career, so he didn't sweat the small stuff.

After two hours, the truck was fixed and ready to leave for Goma, we went back to the stadium and met the CO and RSM. However, here we were once again left with only one vehicle for the recce, so there was no room for me. As I looked around at some of those accompanying our CO, RSM, and operations officer, I thought they were going as tourists, as they had gone the last two days and made assessments of the needs for their part in the mission. There was probably not really a need at this point for them to go again. Regardless, there was no room for me, so once again I stayed behind to find something to do.

Unlike yesterday where I was walking around and volunteering to help, today I made myself grey. It wasn't that I didn't want to help out or do anything, but now there were over a hundred troops who'd arrived here the night before from Canada, and they were getting to work and settling in. With this many on the ground now, I thought to myself, *they don't need cheap labour and I am not going to offer myself up. I have other things that need to be prepared and taken care of for our recce.*

I went down to see the medics on the UN tour I had served with at the field hospital back in Canada. They were set up in the centre of the stadium grounds under a tent facility. We chatted for awhile, and then I saw some of the guys from the Canadian Airborne Regiment I knew, and again I just talked awhile with them. I really didn't do too much today except bum around the stadium to talk to the infantry guys and field engineers I knew. There were a few times I was approached and asked if I would drive to the airport to pick up some incoming people and parcels. I didn't mind doing this as it got me out of the stadium to drive around Kigali and get to know the city a little more.

After supper at about 19:00, WO Frank, Capt. Linford, and I went for a drive down to CSG to check in on a few things like the vehicle and supplies for our trip to Goma. On the way back we were driving around a darkened road, smelling the open fires. These smells from here take me back to my time in Somalia; everywhere in Africa smells like this. I enjoy it and who knows, maybe I'll come back some day as a missionary or some type of non-governmental official. I love Africa and the people for the most part.

We were hearing small-gun fire and noise, which was to be expected in a country with a civil war recently concluded. As we drove, there was a vehicle in front of us going very slowly, so I passed it, and as we did, I noticed it had a couple of Rwandan soldiers with a European woman. She looked as if she was panicking, and I was thinking that this lady's going to get raped. I was ready to stop but then something weird happened. After we passed the vehicle, from behind me, the vehicle's horn began honking and there was a hysterical screaming. We immediately stopped and the woman got out and started crying and mumbling incoherently in French about so many dead bodies up in Goma. Once she was settled down a little, Capt. Linford found out that she was a European reporter or photographer who had just come back from Goma earlier that day. It looked like she was having a stress reaction.

The two Rwandan soldiers were only teenagers, seventeen or eighteen years old at most, but teenagers here aren't really the same as what most Canadians think of teenagers back home. I learned in Somalia to always have your weapon ready, mine was...all the time. Although we were told not to chamber a round, I had one chambered and my weapon ready. I thought these were crazy orders in a country such as Rwanda with the war just finishing up. It was a good way to get killed over here. With hundreds of thousands killed in basically hand-to-hand and small-arms fire, anything over twelve years old with a weapon or machete can kill. At this point I wasn't sure if they would give her up, so I waited to see what the WO and captain wanted to do. Capt. Linford spoke to them in broken French, and it quickly became obvious that we were witnessing a nervous breakdown or stress reaction from the woman, who had been overwhelmed with the sights and smells she had experienced during her time here and especially her trip to Goma today, where I heard there were up to 20,000 or 30,000 dead from cholera at this point. As the Rwandan soldiers followed us closely, we took her back to the hotel where all the reporters were staying so she'd be safe.

Capt. Linford Spoke to a couple of people there and explained what had happened and that she probably needed medical attention due to a possible stress reaction. Still can't figure out how she would get separated from colleagues and then be in a car with two Rwandan soldiers without anyone noticing or caring that she was missing. This was crazy. If this had been another soldier, no matter male or female, with me or the guys in my unit, they would be hard pressed to take her away from our sight, at least in our organization. The people over here are so used to death with the war just concluding and the pure volume of those who were killed in such a short time, they could have just popped her off and no one would ever see her again. It was a strange situation. After we dropped her off at the hotel, the three of us went back to the stadium and I turned in the vehicle, locked it up, and went to the fart sack, around 22:30 or so.

Tuesday, 2 August

I found the first few days difficult with learning our place on the food chain and with where we found ourselves in the middle of an ongoing UN mission. We were flown in only six days ago as a separate Canadian humanitarian mission from the UN. The confusion, however, was that we simultaneously had the Canadian Division Signals and Headquarters Regiment (CDSHR) deployed here with the UN, under command of a Canadian general however under UN control. Meanwhile, our masters back in Canada had directed the Canadian contingent to support us, which was a difficult situation to put them in as they were attempting to get their mission up and running, while trying to support us, and not having all their people or supplies and equipment yet. Within the very first day of our arrival last week, I could feel animosity from some on the UN tour, whom I met at the stadium. I asked some of those deployed with me on the recce party if I was mistaken. They also felt we weren't welcomed by the UN contingent as part of anything to do with Rwanda, and it certainly was not hidden from my CO and all the way down to me.

I think everyone felt this contempt towards us. I think it was a misunderstanding mixed with a view that we were competition for insufficient resources and supplies, especially with limited flights in and out of the country and the scarce equipment and assets that were here in Kigali. I understood this but felt this was the wrong way to express frustration because it should have not been directed towards us. Rather, it should have been targeted at the UNHQ in New York or NDHQ in Canada. By itself, it was the situation we came into as we arrived in Rwanda, with dead bodies everywhere, the smell of rot, and the war between the Tutsi and the Hutu just concluding. That would have been enough for anyone, but I would have thought that being on a mission from Canada, which was requested by the UNHCR, along with the Canadians who were on the UN tour, that it would have made sense for them to be a little more understanding as well as a little more supportive and flexible, so we could get on and help before more died along the area we were to be deployed. Still, it was certainly a difficult time for two simultaneous missions trying to get up and running, with one relying heavily on the other.

Getting up at 07:00, it was the usual morning drill of rolling up my sleeping bag, packing my kit, washing, cleaning, and eating. Later in the morning, Captain Linford and I went to the airstrip to check with the Air Movements section to see if any of our supplies or equipment had arrived. Meanwhile, WO Frank still had some things to do at 3 Canadian Support Group (CSG) as the CO and RSM stayed at the stadium to do some planning and talking about our incoming personnel.

It was getting frustrating not being able to secure two vehicles out of the multitude they had at the UN vehicle compound. Our CO informed the UN coordinators and the Rwandan ministry, that the recce for our humanitarian mission could not be completed until we had some working vehicles we could rely on. Capt. Linford and I arrived at the airport and spoke to the logistics officer in charge of controlling the incoming flight cargo. He informed us that no equipment had been manifested for us today, however, he wasn't sure about anything that may have come yesterday and would have to check. After what seemed like an eternity of waiting for him to return, we found out that nothing had yet arrived, so we decided to take a drive to the other side of the airport. We wanted to drive to the storage area where the loads from incoming flights were to see for ourselves when our equipment would be arriving at the airport.

We headed over to the other side of the airstrip and checked to see if any of our equipment had actually come in. While we were there, I saw some jeeps in a compound. They had been left there by Belgian soldiers on the UNAMIR mission when they'd departed the country, after the Rwandans killed ten of their troops at the beginning of the war. I can't say I blame them for leaving, it must have been a tough situation. The vehicles were all lined up neatly and just left there. The UN had taken charge of them and had guards at the gate, and the area was fenced into control entry to the compound.

As we drove toward the compound where the vehicles were, there were Guyanese soldiers guarding the gate. They looked at us smiling while they saluted Capt. Linford as we drove by, and he saluted back and gave them a wave. It was easy to get into the compound; we were in Canadian uniforms with Canadian flags on them and these soldiers were under a Canadian general. We were obviously Canadian, and they most likely saw us as on tour with them like the rest of the Canadian delegation at the stadium. We drove to the back of the compound and there had to be a hundred vehicles all lined up, row upon row of them, so we drove to the back of the last row in the lineup, where we could work without being noticed and see about getting one of the jeeps running for the recce.

I knew how to hot-wire a vehicle by moving a few wires around, it was easy to tear the wires from the ignition under the dash and do this. I hopped into the first jeep I saw in the lineup, reached under the dash, and pulled the ignition wires out. Then I had to separate them and figure out which one was the "hot wire." I knew the red one was the main one in this procedure and now I had to find the starter wire. I stripped all the wires with my pocketknife and began touching them one at a time to the red wire until I found the starter. With that, once I found this starter wire, I took the other wires and twisted them together to the red one, keeping the starter wire separate. All that was needed in future, anytime I wanted to start the jeep, was to touch the red wire to the bundle of other wires. Giving it a try, I heard a weak turning-over of the engine a couple times; *rrr rrr rrr*. Then it stopped - the battery was dead.

I looked towards the front gate and was getting a little nervous as this felt like it was taking too long. We had enough time to try another vehicle before the soldiers at the front gate might start wandering around the compound to see what we were up to. I kept thinking we needed vehicles to get the recce done, get coordinated, and get ready for the rest of our soldiers coming from Canada in a few days. We really needed another dependable vehicle and quick. I hopped into the next vehicle in the lineup, another jeep, and did the same thing with pulling the wires from under the dash. I was feeling a bit of pressure, I didn't want to get caught in the middle of hot-wiring a vehicle. I twisted the ends of the starter wires and then touched them with the hot wire; *rrr rrr rrr*. But then, without hesitation, the vehicle started and the engine vroomed as I pumped the gas pedal. I looked over at Capt. Linford and we were both relieved and pleased with this, because it meant we would finally have a good vehicle for our task, even if we had to liberate it.

I drove the jeep towards the Land Rover we'd driven in together and dropped Capt. Linford off. The trick now was to drive both the Land Rover and the jeep out of the compound with Capt. Linford and me behind the wheel of each vehicle, while trying to not look too suspicious. Both of us calmly drove our vehicles towards the front gate and the same soldiers who had been at the gate on the way in were still there on guard. As we approached the gate, I could tell they recognized us because they were smiling as they lifted the barrier and saluted Capt. Linford as he drove his vehicle past them. With a big sigh of relief, we drove out of there and returned to the stadium.

When we got back, we were filled with nervous excitement, laughing and giggling like two schoolboys who had just pulled a good one over on their teacher. I couldn't wait to tell the CO and RSM about our new acquisition. I knew they would be pleased with the vehicle and the fact that it was relatively new and in good working order. I was *also* pleased with our trip to the airport and the fact that we were successful in liberating a dependable vehicle.

Capt. Linford went into the stadium to get the CO and RSM for meetings with Gen. Dallaire at the UNHQ building. While I was waiting until the CO and RSM came out, I was wondering what they would think of their new vehicle. As I sat there, pleased with myself and my acquisition, the UN transport officer approached the vehicle. He was looking up and down at the jeep and I knew he saw it was a Belgian UN vehicle. He approached me and began the conversation by saying, "This vehicle is mine and you have stolen it from my compound at the airstrip. Furthermore, who the hell are you to be taking it? You have no right to have taken it and I will do everything in my power to have you charged and to get this vehicle back where it belongs."

I thought to myself, *come on, not again, let us just have a couple vehicles to get the recce done before our people arrive.* I also began thinking that maybe they should have secured their vehicles a little better if they didn't want people just walking into the compound and stealing them.

I looked directly at him and with all the seriousness I could muster, saying that I had just came from the UNAMIR HQ, where I had gotten permission to take it. I said I couldn't remember the name of the person, but he had told me it was ok to borrow it.

The transport officer seemed to buy this, and he calmed down and said ok, but that he wanted the vehicle back as soon as we were finished with it. I told him no problem, and he went back into the stadium. I didn't like not telling the truth, but I am so sick of shit vehicles that continually break down being given to us. With us on the recce group being treated as a second-class citizen since our arrival, and people putting up blocks all the time, I am now into whatever-it- takes mode to get the job done. Beg, borrow, or steal; in the end the mission is more important. Unless I get told otherwise, I will do whatever I have to in order to make it happen.

Parked in front of the stadium and waiting until the CO and RSM came out, I wondered what they would think of their new vehicle. I could see the CO's face; he was all smiles with the new vehicle I had just acquired. RSM Doyle got in and said, "What have you been up to, Nearing? Wait, don't tell me, I don't want to know." Then he smiled too.

I drove the CO and RSM to UNHQ where they went in for a meeting with Gen. Dallaire. As I sat waiting in my vehicle outside the headquarters building, again another UN official approached me; this time a civilian contractor. He informed me that the vehicle was his, that it had been taken from his compound at the airstrip, and that I had no right to have taken it. He also promised he would do everything he could to get me disciplined.

I thought to myself this is the second UN guy already on me for this vehicle in the last hour. What I really wanted to say was that maybe he should have better security at the vehicle compound if he didn't want anyone walking in and stealing them. Instead, I tried to calm him down and added to the story I had told earlier. I told him the UN transport officer at the airstrip, to whom I had just spoken, had said I could borrow it for a few days. I then stated to him that I only needed to use it for a short time and not to worry, once we finished the recce, I'd bring it back right away. I was lying again, I'm keeping this jeep as long as I need to, which just might be the whole tour.

After the CO and RSM's meeting concluded with General Dallaire's staff, we went back to the stadium for dinner. I still had an uneasiness; butterflies in my belly from the morning activities that Capt. Linford and I had been involved in. While eating supper, I told the RSM of all the shenanigans from the morning and that I thought the amount of UN politics involved here and the seemingly endless red tape was incredible.

Later in the afternoon, I drove the CO and RSM around all afternoon to a few coordination meetings with the NGOs, same usual organizations, trying to coordinate. I sat there for a couple hours watching people coming in and out of the government office building, sitting there writing in my journal, and waiting for the CO and RSM to appear from the meeting.

We left the meeting late afternoon and our last stop for the day was back to the UNHQ once again. As we arrived at the compound, there were now Canadian soldiers at the main gate, who had landed this morning; Canadian Airborne Regiment Soldiers to be exact. You could tell these troops were ours, with the distinctive airborne hat badge and maroon berets. I somehow suddenly felt a lot more secure with these guys here. The main bulk of them had only arrived earlier in the morning on a flight from Canada, and they already had taken over the perimeter security at the compound, which housed General Dallaire. They were doing security at the main gate of the UNHQ compound and quickly implemented a firm and necessary security, which had not been there a few days ago when I first arrived. They were checking everyone's ID as they came in and looking inside vehicles, trunks, and cargo holds as they were stopped.

Once we were checked and allowed entry into the compound, the CO and RSM got out and went into the building. I decided to go in as well to see if they had any coffee here. Usually signals guys live on coffee, so I knew there would be some brewing. I secured the vehicle by chaining the steering wheel and went in. After having a coffee, I was waiting by the front door for the CO and RSM and when they came out, I got into the vehicle and unlocked the steering wheel. A British soldier was there watching me and when he saw that I had the steering wheel locked up with a chain, he walked over to me saying that he'd never seen this way of securing a vehicle before, and it was a great idea!

I said to him, "Yes, it's a great way to keep your vehicle from being stolen when you park it." Meanwhile, unknown to him it was a liberated jeep I was driving. As the CO and RSM were getting into the vehicle they overheard what the soldier was saying to me, they smiled and chuckled as I drove away.

Wednesday, 3 August

Up at 06:30. All night long more and more incoming troops arriving from the UN's other contingent countries for the UNAMIR II tour. They were talking in the hallways, laughing and joking around. I understood they couldn't sleep because of the jet lag but shut up or go inside to the centre of the stadium. There were dogs outside barking all night, probably fighting over some dead bodies, doors slamming, no respect for anyone other than themselves. Man, this is annoying. I decided just to get up and dressed, because sleep wasn't going to take place.

At 08:00 I drove the RSM and CO down to the HQ and dropped them off for another meeting. While I was waiting outside the UN Headquarters building where the meeting with Gen. Dallaire and his staff was taking place, another UN official, this time a logistics officer, wearing a major's rank, came out the front doors of the headquarters building. He walked directly over to me and without hesitation began screaming in my face. Once more a UN official was shitting all over me, saying, "You took this jeep without permission or authority from the compound at the airstrip." I could feel he was pretty sure I didn't get the proper permission to have it, because he continued by saying, "I am going to have you charged for stealing from the UN and jailed." Then he went on to add, "I want this vehicle taken back immediately to the compound!"

Wow. This guy was really revved up I thought, talking excitedly and waving his hands in my face and at that point I began thinking to myself that it might just come to blows with this guy. Looking at him as he was in my face, I was thinking, *What the hell can I do to calm him down?* looking directly at him I said in a calm voice, "Sir, I just came back from the HQ and spoke to the civilian contractor who controls the vehicles. He said to keep the vehicle and return it when I was finished with it. I spoke directly with him just yesterday and he told me it was ok to borrow the vehicle."

I looked at the major, who was screaming, and then suddenly he stopped with his eyes darting all around. I sensed he was wondering if I was telling the truth or not. Once again, I spoke in a calm voice and assured him that all was ok with me having this vehicle. I knew if he didn't buy this and made a phone call to the transport compound, I would be found out and shit would hit the fan, but luckily he bought into my explanation, changed gears, and quickly calmed down, saying to me, " Ok, use it for now but I need that vehicle back as soon as you are finished with it. Thanks." With that he walked over to his vehicle and was off.

I was sick of us being treated like second-class citizens ever since arriving here in Rwanda, being given the worst of vehicles they had; old trucks and jeeps that barely worked for use here in the capital, let alone for taking my CO and RSM on a long road recce all over a war-torn country where their safety would be jeopardized. I understood that resources were scarce and they were doing their best to help us, but in some ways I thought this ongoing issue with the jeep I had liberated and the threat to charge me was a controlling manoeuvre, a show of force of who's in charge to put us in our place. I do what it takes to get the job done.

We have tried to do what is right: submit paperwork, ask politely, bargain; but seemingly this has been harvesting few results, so now I will do what's needed to get the recce done, no matter if I have to beg, borrow, or steal. In the end, the mission is the most important objective we have and unless I get told otherwise, I will do whatever I must to make it happen. In only a couple of days we will have 250 personnel showing up and we are expected to have a location, security, and supplies to set up a hospital and start treating locals here in Rwanda.

It was only a few minutes after the transport officer left that the CO and RSM returned to the vehicle to go back to the stadium. I noticed that when they came out, they looked a bit pissed off. The CO is a pretty relaxed guy, but I think he is getting sick of the runaround as well, so I am guessing they missed the meeting because it was moved back an hour to 07:00 and the CO wasn't given the courtesy of being informed of this change. Typical of being a second-class citizen here working with the UN.

We went back to the stadium for a quick break and then were off to the new Rwandan Health Minister here in Kigali to get permission to use the old milk factory site at Mareru. I wasn't there at the meeting, but I guess it was a pain in the ass dealing with the new Rwandan government. Having been here in Africa only last year on tour in Somalia, I know what it's like trying to do anything here. It's always about greasing someone's hands, passing around cash or materials, and playing the shell game, so goddamn corrupt.

When the CO and RSM returned, they told me that we'd finally gotten permission to use the milk-factory site but would have to come back later to get the letter of understanding. Well finally, we accomplished something today! We went back to the stadium to have lunch and regroup, and then I was told to be ready because we were off again in the afternoon.

At 14:30 we left the stadium and went back to the Health Ministry in downtown Kigali to get the letter giving us permission to take over the old milk factory. Then after this, we went to the UNHQ for an hour or so. I sat as usual, had a coffee, and watched CNN for the hour. Pretty bad when I get better updates on CNN than we do from the group at the stadium. It was me and RSM Doyle sitting there waiting for the CO to come out of his meeting with Gen. Dallaire. After this we came back to the stadium for supper.

I had to get ready at 18:30 to take the CO and RSM down from another "O Group". The one thing I find is that there are so many meetings and it's taking so long to get things sorted out, but I understand in the aftermath of war there is confusion and it takes a while to regain control. I get this, but I just want to get on with the task at hand we were sent over to do. We have been here now six days and still are not at our location, there's still nobody here from our unit, there's no kit, and worst of all there are no refugees being treated!

This meeting lasted until 20:00 or so. By the time it was over, and we drove back to the stadium I was beat, so I had a shower and then a cup of tea with WO Frank, Capt. Linford, RSM Doyle, and Col. Anderson. After this I came up to my spot on the floor and went to bed. I must drive to Mareru tomorrow. Good night.

Thursday, 4 August

I thought today was going to be a good one for me, but it would turn out not to be. We packed early in the morning and got ready to go to Mareru, where the milk factory is located. We are going to take over the site as we begin our mission, finally. I was going to be driving the CO and RSM, but now there was a change in plans. At 08:30 the CO needed a drive to the airport where he and the RSM were going to be taken by helicopter to a meeting near Goma. We would then later drive up and meet them at our new location at the milk factory in Mareru. This wasn't too bad, just a little adjustment in plans. As I prepared to go to Mareru, I went to get my vehicle fuelled up at 3 CSG. The helicopter was supposed to land at 10:30 and then it was cancelled until 12:30 but they would still be leaving, and we would still be required to meet them there. So now I had to go back to the stadium as I needed to find a co-driver. I came back to the stadium and there was a young field engineer, who was on the recce as a driver with the engineering officer. They were both out of 4 Engineer Support Regiment Gagetown, so he was also eager to get on with the mission and he spoke to his officer about coming with me as my co-driver.

Once given permission to accompany me, he and I drove up to Mareru and had a good talk all the way up. Having been in the engineers for over twelve years as a reservist in 45 Fd Sqn, I had spent many years on and off with stints at 22 Fd and 4 Combat Engineer Regiment, and I knew most of his sergeants and warrant officers, so we could talk about people we had in common, as well as equipment and stuff I enjoyed seeing and doing as a Sapper myself.

As we drove along the road towards Mareru, there was a never-ending stream of walkers along the shoulder of the road, returning back into Rwanda from the refugee camps in Zaire. They were walking back home to their farms, villages, and towns, walking back to the unknown, to bury the dead, I imagined, and to get on with the business of tending to their crops. Although they had just been through a horrific war and genocide, there was still a dignity I could feel with them; in their walk, in the way they dressed in clean, bright clothes, and in their stoic faces heading back to their towns and cities. It must be difficult as they walk these hundreds of kilometers home in silence with so many around them. All I could hear was the rhythmic shuffle of feet, as I was used to as a soldier marching. There were also the dead bodies on the side of the road along the way; some from a couple weeks ago, while some had only recently been killed. But this didn't seem to bother or slow down those walking; it might as well be garbage by the roadside for all it mattered. I guess that after four months of this horror, you get numb.

For a while the young engineer and I got quiet as we drove. Occasionally, he and I just looked at one another. This was crazy, surreal. In the refugee camps in Goma, we had been told there were a million refugees who had fled, seeking protection there during the peak of the war. Goma, Zaire was a small border town, without proper infrastructure, sewage, food, or water, the perfect ingredients to incubate the cholera epidemic that ensued, in which thousands died as the war was ending and upon our arrival.

We continued driving in the quiet of each other's company. About halfway to the milk factory, the vehicle we were driving started to act up and almost stall out, but we babied it, finally arriving in Mareru. On arrival I had a look at the engine and thought it might be air in the fuel filter, so I purged it and it seemed to run well enough when I started it, so we figured all was good to go! Later in the afternoon, the CO and RSM met us there after their meeting in Goma, and we walked around the compound looking at the site where we were to be located. In the distance I could hear the CO and RSM talk about where things would be placed on our piece of real estate. After everything was completed at around 16:30, my co-driver and I, along with the RSM and CO, mounted the vehicle and headed back to Kigali.

As we drove only about twenty kilometers into the 127km journey, the vehicle stalled. Hopping out of it, I drained the fuel filter, figuring there may have been some air in the system from earlier when I had initially drained it, but this only helped for another ten minutes or so. I did this a few more times until we finally stalled, and I couldn't get it to start again. We got out once more and looked under the hood and as we were under it, I began to worry. We were here in the middle of nowhere without an escort, a second vehicle, or protection, and it was now getting close to 18:00. With darkness closing in I was getting worried; we had the CO and RSM here and I felt exposed. We didn't have a lot of firepower with us and with their rank they were high-value targets.

Just as we were talking about what to do, a Reuters News Agency van with the driver and some reporters pulled up behind us. We explained our situation, and at first the CO told the driver to tell someone at the UNHQ when he got back and have them send help our way, but I spoke up and asked the guy if he would take the CO and RSM with him. They were valuable assets and if we got stuck here one never knows what could happen. I said to the CO and RSM that they could leave the two of us here to watch over the vehicle until they could send help to us once they arrived back at the stadium. The CO and RSM agreed with the plan and went with the reporters. I just thought it was the best plan for the situation. It was bad enough having us stranded here, but if ever something were to happen to lose a colonel and RSM, it wasn't worth the chance. After what had taken place back in April with the Belgians, there was no point in chancing it. Losing one of us here wasn't any better, but if we left the vehicle sitting by itself, it would be gone by the time we returned to recover it.

As it was getting darker out, I kept thinking that if we stay here after dark we are in serious trouble, we will be targets for sure with us riding in a Belgian vehicle here in Rwanda. We will no doubt be killed for this vehicle, perhaps more for what it represents as a vehicle from the former Belgian colonial masters, than for its use as a vehicle. I didn't get a warm and fuzzy sitting out here in the middle of nowhere, especially with all the walking traffic going by. These people just survived a war and had nothing, so to them we must have looked like millionaires.

We needed to do something quick because by the time the CO and RSM returned to Kigali it would be night and we would be very vulnerable. We decided to see what we could do with this piece-of-shit vehicle. I had a pen in my pocket, and while talking we got to thinking about the damaged fuel filter, wondering if it would work having the fuel go directly into the engine, skipping the filter, and running the air out of the system.

We finally made the decision and knew we had nothing to lose. Taking both ends of the fuel line off the fuel filter, and then removing the ink chamber and ballpoint tip of the pen so all was left was the hollow pen, we connected both ends of the fuel line to the pen, bypassing the fuel filter. Starting up the vehicle we found it turned over right away; the engine was getting the fuel it needed to run. We hopped in and drove away as we wanted to get back to the stadium in Kigali before it got too dark. Things seemed to be going well, but after about thirty kilometers the jeep began to sputter, and we weren't sure what was going on. So, we stopped for a moment and reattached the hoses back to the fuel filter. To remove the air in the fuel we had to run it for a few minutes to clear the fuel line, and then we reattached the lines to the pen again. This had to be done a few times as we made our way back to Kigali, but we finally made it to the stadium without incident, and only about thirty minutes behind the others.

As soon as we got back to the stadium and after securing the vehicle, I decided to get it looked into first thing tomorrow morning by the mechanics. Going back into the stadium, I found the RSM and CO, who were waiting for us, and told them that we had returned all was ok. I explained what we had done to make the vehicle work and get back. Despite the vehicle situation, I was feeling good that today's recce went well including the meeting the CO and RSM had with the NGOs in Goma and the visit to the milk factory site where we would be located. We were now finally getting somewhere and today actually got a lot done on the recce and the visit to Gisenyi. It all turned out to be probably the most progress we had made since our arrival.

Friday, 5 August

Up at 06:30, packed up my sleeping bag, washed, dressed, and just relaxed and had a coffee with everyone. After breakfast, the RSM and I went for a drive to the airport to see some of the people who had just arrived two days ago, off to the site in Mareru. It was like old home week for me with some of the guys arriving in country. I saw some guys I haven't seen since I was an engineer. There was Steve Wrathall, Dan McPhee, Kelly MacKinnon, Scotty Clucas, and Kenny Sollazzo. I knew all these guys from Cape Breton. You know, it feels kind of weird seeing all these guys and I'm no longer an engineer. This is probably one of my biggest regrets since enrolling in the regular force as a medic, after having spent thirteen years of my life as a field engineer.

After chatting for a while, we left the airport at 10:00 driving down to 3 ASG to fuel up the vehicles for tomorrow. In the morning we (CO, RSM, and I) are heading up to Mareru and I wanted to make sure we have enough fuel for the trip. RSM Doyle said some smart aleck comments to the two warrant officers there as we fueled. It seems no matter what we do there is resistance, or always the questioning of us and our intentions. I know the UNAMIR tour doesn't have any time for us and doesn't want to support us while we are here. I'm so sick of it myself, it's getting tiring.

After fuelling up the vehicle, we headed back to the stadium. I had some time to myself and so I washed my clothes with what was left of the morning and packed everything, using up that time preparing for tomorrow's road move to Mareru.

When I went to wash my clothes, once again there was no water left. I had to wait for some because the UN guys here at the stadium used every single drop of it again; the engineers can't keep up with the water demands. No water conservation or discipline makes me think of only a year ago in Somalia when we were deployed there and were given only five liters a day to eat with, wash with, and drink for the first months there. These guys wouldn't have made it with the way they waste water here, no water discipline. At 12:00 the RSM and I went down to catch the news on CNN at UNHQ.

As we sat to watch, General Dallaire walked out to the main foyer where the TV was. He came towards me and asked if I was doing all right and how it was going for me. I told him that I was doing well and looking forward to getting the hospital up in Mareru. Every time I come down here and he is around, I have noticed that he always has time for the troops. He cares for them and always has the presence of mind to ask if the soldiers are feeling ok.

I really like his watching out for the troops. He is leaving soon, I hear. I can't imagine what he's been through.

> *Years later I would come to learn and understand how much pain General Dallaire was in at the time, but also to appreciate his immense capacity to care for others in the middle of an unimaginable situation. I will always hold him in high esteem for this.*

The RSM and I watched CNN and not much was going on with CNN, just the usual bullshit. Rwanda is all over the news now. It's too bad it took so long for help to arrive, after the UN and countries all over the world ignored General Dallaire's pleas for help. After an hour or so of watching the news and having a good coffee, RSM Doyle and I headed back to the stadium for dinner.

Later, after we ate, I took the RSM and CO to UNHQ first and then onto the Ministry of Health. I sat in my vehicle, as usual, waiting for them to finish their meeting, not sure of what kind of meeting was going on there. The usual NGO organizations were present again, though. I counted about ten or so sitting there for over the next few hours; Americares, ICRC, IMC, Medicine Sans Frontier, MSF, Pharmacies Sans Frontier, CARE, MEMISA, UNICEF Emergency. They were all in there waiting to be given an area to operate out of and get their missions started. I'm sure that this is being cobbled together as best they can. With the chaos that took place here for three months it's difficult to now instill order on this situation, but this is what's needed.

I saw the doors open to the Health Ministry building and thought to myself, *Thank God!* Finally, after a few hours the meeting was over and it was now 17:00, so it had been three hours long. Once my officers got into the vehicle, we headed back to the stadium for supper. As we drove, the CO began to explain things to me, saying we finally seemed to be making headway after our recce to Goma, Gisenyi, and Ruhengeri earlier in the week. The intent was to draw the refugees on the borders back to the capital, Kigali, and to their villages and farms throughout Rwanda. Since they had left on foot by the millions, then it only made sense that this would be how they returned, so a chain of rest stations was needed. However, some clarification was needed in our Area of Responsibility (AOR). The idea was to place rest stations along the highway from Goma to Kigali every ten kilometers or so along Route Nationale 4 (Rwanda's version of the TransCanada). All these stations along the way were to have first aid, emergency services, oral rehydration stations, and of course our 150-bed hospital in Mareru along the route. This plan would allow them to walk back from all the refugee centres on the borders with Rwanda, slowly supporting them as they travelled by foot back into their country.

But we weren't there yet, there was getting our camp prepared for the rest of the incoming 250 personnel on their way from Canada, who would be joining us in the next day or so. For now, it was back to the stadium for supper, another ration pack. As I got the stove on, the CO said he was pleased with all our hard work in getting the recce completed and had something for us as a treat for all the work to this point. He had bought a twenty-four case of Tuskers beer, so in the upstairs foyer, where we had made our home the last ten days, all five of us had a beer. I really appreciated the thought and knew that Colonel Anderson was a good man, and this was a nice gesture on his part. Still, we all knew this was only the beginning and soon the hard work up in Mareru would begin. I was driving the next day and didn't like to drink at the best of times, so I had one beer, talked for a while with everyone, and then was off to bed at 21:30. I can't wait for tomorrow as we finally get to our site and begin our mission.

Saturday, 6 August

Got up this morning at 06:00 and packed my sleeping bag and kit for the last time here at the stadium. Thankfully, I'm out of here! Today we are going to move up to our location in Mareru at the old milk factory. After we all got up, the first thing was to get one last shower, it would be our last chance for a couple of weeks. I had asked Kenny Sollazzo last night, when I was visiting with him, if he could fire up the showers for us in the morning before we headed out, and true to his word he was up and operating the water and showers for us. I also asked Kenny and another Cape Breton friend, Joe Hardy, to do me a favour and take care of the nurses I knew from the field hospital with a few comforts for their rooms, like a desk and some shelves, and to introduce them to Lt.(N) Sherry Butt and some of the other medical staff at the stadium. I told the nurses that it is always good to know the engineers. I had spoken to Sherry the night before. She had just arrived and didn't know too many people here, so I just wanted to introduce her to a couple of the guys from Cape Breton and make sure she and the other nurses had a familiar contact to speak with, just in case they needed anything as their tour was beginning.

All of us on the recce got a shower, and I could tell that the CO, RSM, Capt. Linford, and WO Frank appreciated that it might be the last for a while. After the shower and shave, I ate breakfast, had a coffee, and then went out and acquired a trailer for our jeep from the UN compound. They won't be needing it for a while now and probably wouldn't mind if I borrowed it, they're so nice to help me out like this on short notice. Once I got the trailer hooked up to the jeep, the RSM, the CO, and I left for Mareru at 11:00, arriving at 14:30. Along the way, the RSM threw candy out to the kids along the roadside, while the CO slept in the back seat. I remember doing something similar on my last tour in Somalia. I would carry candy with me whenever I was moving around the country and if we came upon a group of kids, I could pass a couple out to them. My thought was that there are times when it's better to give candy when food isn't available, it will at least take their mind off their hunger for a little while.

When we finally arrived at the milk factory, I went to the area that had been allocated for my unit and spent a few hours fixing up my bed space area. My section was going to occupy this area; it was the first room off the eating area and about 50' x 50' in size. This would be where they were going to put all the males from 2 Fd Amb. There were a few more similar-sized rooms for the other two units' medics from 1 and 5 Fd Amb's. The area we were being assigned was very dusty, so I swept and washed the entire floorspace. I wanted it to be ready when the troops arrived in the next day or so.

After finishing cleaning out this room, I began on the one across from me where the females would be housed, and then the RSM approached me sounding pissed off and upset. I asked him if everything was ok, and boy was he ever pissed off. He began by saying that he and the CO had been the first to arrive out here five days ago to do a recce, and they'd left behind a few soldiers to get the site cleaned up outside around the compound, but actually not much had been done beyond their own areas. I understand his point and it's true, more should have been done in the past five days as far as cleaning and fixing up this building. But in reality, the area the infantry and engineers had been given wasn't the best and needed a lot of work with the shit and corruption that was there to be cleaned; from blood on the walls, to fecal matter on the floors. Not a nice job to tackle at the best of times, but there's nothing I can say. I'm pretty low on the food chain so all I can do is ready my own areas, and the one across from me where the girls would be sleeping needed to be attended to right now.

When I finished cleaning up the area, I washed my clothes and hung them out to dry, had supper, and began writing in my journal. Afterwards, I waited up for a while before going to bed, sitting with an old engineer friend I was in 45 Field Squadron with, Scotty Clucas, who I hadn't seen in years. We talked awhile and got caught up on things. The last time I had seen him was when I was in tasking with 22 Field Engineer Squadron back in 1989 or so. It was so nice to see him and to catch up; he's a really good person.

Overall, it was a pretty good day as far as seeing some old friends from the 1980s when I was a field engineer with 45 Field Engineer Squadron. It was like an old home week seeing all these guys again. It was also a good feeling to do a good day's work and make some headway. I was glad to finally be at our site and ready to start getting at it. I went to bed at 23:00.

Sunday, 7 August

Had my first night's sleep in the milk factory and was up at 06:30. It felt weird but good to be on our own away from the UN in Kigali. I washed, fixed my bed space, then ate a ration and had a coffee. Today, after breakfast, I was to take the CO and RSM up to the Uganda border to see where our kit was and/or why it was delayed, but instead the engineer officer wanted to drive, so I stayed back.

Presently, there's a section from 3 Commando and the rest of the DNS (Defense and Security) platoon should be here soon. A few of the field engineers and the rest of the field troop should be arriving soon as well, along with a couple of logistics people. There is not much to do here except continue to clean the milk factory up to prepare for the new arrivals coming within the next couple of days. I'm the lone medic and I looked at what was to be done, in what would become our home for the next three months.

Having cleaned where we were to stay for the tour yesterday, I then began by sweeping and cleaning floors all morning in the other areas where the guys and girls from the other two units would be sleeping. I worked at this until noon, and then after lunch later in the afternoon, I picked up some garbage around the building to clean up the area and begin the process of making this our home for the next few months.

At 15:00, I was tasked to take a couple of reporters to Goma. I grabbed Cpl. Ron Stanley, a signaller from CFB Kingston, to bring along as a co-driver. As we drove over to Zaire, the smell of the place was the first thing I noticed. It was the stink of humanity; of rotten bodies and things I am afraid will stay with me the rest of my life. We made our way through Goma and found the place to drop off the reporters. After dropping them off, on the way back we drove by a small place called Gisenyi. I guess before the war it was a resort for the upper crust Europeans to vacation, but the tourists who once stayed here, were now replaced with dead, bloated bodies from the war, floating in the water on Lake Kivu. On the beach there were arms and legs of the dead sticking out of the sand.

I still can't understand what happened here the last four months, but I want to do something to help. I'm not sure what I can do, but something. I've only been here about ten days now, but I'm feeling it already; the pressure of seeing things people back home in Canada would never see or understand. It feels almost as if I never left Somalia, I've already had a couple of times where I felt overwhelmed during the recce, with some of the sights and smells. I will do my best just to be of some use here. I guess that's all I can do not to go crazy with this. I've seen lots of death in my military career already, maybe already a little too much. In Somalia there were Mike Abel and Bob Deets, who both died, and I was in the emergency room when we were trying to resuscitate them. I had to assist in exhuming a body and be involved in the post mortem that followed, and then, at the end of my time in Somalia, for the last week we were being attacked by General Adid's militia, who were trying to breach our area and kill us, so we fought and stayed in a defensive position until we finally left.

I am already sick of this already here in Rwanda and its only been a little over a week, but here I am and now I have to just shut my mouth, put my head down, and push through to finish this tasking in Rwanda, no matter what I feel inside.

When I got back with Ron, I didn't do too much, just took it easy, ate supper, and got a water-bottle shower. Then I had a coffee and wrote another note in my journal. I think I'll read for a bit and try to get to bed early. I'm tired.

Monday, 8 August

Got up today at 06:00 and got washed, ate, and dressed. I swept a couple of floors and then at 09:30 the CO, RSM, and I went to Gisenyi. There was a coordination meeting at the hotel that they had to attend, so I sat in the vehicle from 10:00 to 12:30. Then we went for a drive to a meeting in Goma to see some CARE workers and discuss about getting the refugees to walk back into Rwanda and setting up aid and feeding stations along the Ruhengeri-Gisenyi Highway, which is similar to our TransCanada Highway. As we drove towards Gisenyi, it was crazy. The road was getting thicker and thicker with the mass of people walking back into the country, thousands and thousands of people walking along the shoulder of the road. *Holy shit, this is crazy*, the millions of refugees who left during the war all walked out and now they would have to do the same to get back home from Zaire to their families and villages back in Rwanda.

After the meeting in Gisenyi, we then went up to the airport in Goma. What a shithole. The town is really stinky and dirty. After we crossed the border from Rwanda into Zaire, in the distance I saw a bulldozer and it looked like he was plowing a road. As we got closer, we saw that he was actually going back and forth digging a mass grave. There were tens of thousands of bodies wrapped up in sheets and bamboo mats, and they were being thrown in where the grave was prepared, tossed in like garbage bags. The grave was already packed full of bodies and they were putting what looked like lime over them. I wasn't sure, it could have been anything, but my guess was lime to keep the smell down. Pretty crazy anyway you look at it. I feel like a grotesque voyeur at times when I see things like this, wanting to help, but frozen with the inability to know what to do or how to do it.

After we got there, the CO and RSM went to meet the CARE workers. I sat in the jeep and looked over at the sea of humanity on the airstrip. There had to be hundreds of thousands of people in front of me, it was like watching ants in an anthill. It was a crazy thing to witness, I have never seen this many people in my life. They were on the mountainside, on the roads, and even on the airstrip. I found out that this wasn't even the bulk of refugees, as they had been moved into camps north-west of Goma, and there were almost another million located there.

I watched as a Hercules aircraft approached the airstrip to land, not sure how this would take place with tens of thousands all over the airstrip. The plane had to first fly over the airstrip, a low-level pass over the crowd, which sent them running in all directions. Then he flew back and forth a couple more times to give warning to get off the runway. These passes scattered them, and they scrambled to get off. Then he finally landed and as soon as his aircraft came to a stop, there seemed like thousands of people going towards it. I could see the Zairian soldiers with their automatic weapons at the hip, circling the plane and shooing the people off. *This is crazy!* I thought.

I watched for a while until the CO and RSM emerged. I guess the CO had forgotten his paperwork at the meeting place in Gisenyi, so we had to return to retrieve it prior to returning to the milk factory in Mareru.

When we got back to the milk factory, it became a little overwhelming for me as more new people had arrived; the first group of Op Passage soldiers had finally showed up this afternoon while we were in Goma. It was getting louder and more packed with this group's arrival. The Defence and Security Platoon (D&S) was now complete and the Field Engineer Troop from 4 Engineer Support Regiment had finally all arrived, along with a couple more medics and supply techs from 2 Service Battalion out of Petawawa. With the D&S platoon and engineers' arrival, it was a good indication that the medical staff wouldn't be far behind, and then we could get to work.

The Canadian Airborne Regiment troops were tasked with providing our perimeter security and to control those who were coming to our camp and direct them in a positive manner. We were expecting thousands over the next couple months, so it was essential to have control over our area and over who came in and left. These guys were the best for the job, and I felt secure knowing they were on the watch. The engineers were tasked to provide a reverse osmosis water purification unit, (ROWPU) a valuable piece of equipment so we could self-sustain a clean source of water for our personal use and to assist the Rwanda refugees returning home.

Throughout the tour, the ROWPU would prove itself to be an invaluable resource, purifying up to 50,000 litres of water a day for our needs. Since there was no secure source of clean water in our area, we would be needing as much as they could produce. I thought about how we take water so much for granted back home in Canada, but when I think of things such as washing, cooking, our hospital's patient-care needs, and the thousands of walkers who will be passing our facility in the upcoming months, water is such an important resource to have. The engineers would also be providing other essentials for our safety and the running of the hospitals, such as an unexploded ordinance, (UXO) capability, and electrical and generator capabilities. The UXO capabilities allow the engineers to seek and find unexploded bombs (UXB) and explosive remnants of war (ERW), of which there would be many along the streets and in the mountain jungle that may not have exploded from when they were placed there. For the locals and especially women and young kids they still posed a risk of exploding. I had seen this problem when I was in Somalia; old Russian landmines, decades old and slowly rotting, becoming even that much more dangerous, and still posing a risk to locals. I thought, the worst kids in Canada have to worry about when they walk to school, was being splashed on a rainy day or what they would be doing that day, while here in Africa school kids have to be aware of being kidnapped, raped, murdered, and at a very young age must be able to negotiate UXOs on their way to school. I can't imagine.

I found out that I'm in Tim Ralph's detachment, (Det) for the tour. I'm pretty happy with this as he is probably one of the smartest medics I have met since joining the military and was posted to Petawawa. Tim also has phenomenal natural leadership abilities and knows how to care for his troops, and for this we are lucky to have him as our Master Corporal. I also found the names of the rest of the guys in my Det. Filling out our Det are; Ron Andersen, a solid guy with a witty sense of humour, a very smart medic with a good head on his shoulders; and Chris Shadbolt, another great guy, an intelligent man, who rolls up his sleeves and gets the job done and speaks his mind in a matter of fact and often humorous way, not afraid of hard work. There is also Kelley McLeod. I was with him only last year on a six-month tour to Somalia. He is another excellent medic, who knows what to do and is a good worker, not afraid to get dirt under the fingernails. The final guy in our Det is Kenny Thompson, a very quiet guy with a dry sense of humour and a competent medic, who I enjoy working with. Overall, I feel fortunate as we have a really good Det to work with for however long we are to be deployed here in Rwanda. With Tim's amazing level of medical knowledge, it should be a good go.

Our Det nurse is a captain, Debbie Cook. I hadn't ever met her until just today, but she seems like a nice person. I can tell, though, she is unsure of the field setting, but a lot of these nurses have spent their entire careers in hospitals, so that's not really their jobs to know the field. One thing is for sure, they are professional nurses and know their stuff, and that is far more important than digging a trench right now.

The other Det is being led by Capt. Chris Linford with his six medics. Chris is my supervisor from 2 Fd Amb, the training officer and a good person to have in charge; very competent and knowledgeable. The physician assistant (PA) both Dets would share was WO Claude Tardiff. I worked with him in Petawawa and he is a very hard working and gifted PA, who will take care of the two Dets, which together compose a section.

When I found out that I won't be a Det commander, it disappointed me a little. I believe I'm a good soldier and I've got lots of experience after thirteen years in the reserves and another three years in the regular force, plus being combat-leadership qualified. I feel that I deserved that chance to lead in this operation and I would have done a good job. I guess for now I will have to wait out on that and just be a good soldier, subordinate, and worker. It will all work out because we are all in the same misery here, so life has a way of balancing out.

The rest of the day was pretty boring. After supper I washed my clothes and then found out I was on kitchen duty tomorrow, not sure doing what, because all we have is rations. I will get the stove burners ready and boil the water for the ration packs. Hopefully I don't burn the water and I hope most people are intelligent enough to open their own rations and drop them into it. I was also earlier given a task tomorrow to drive the CO to Goma for another meeting. I think I'll ask Tim to cover for me until I return. It's now 22:00 and I am going to bed.

Tuesday, 9 August

It's 05:30 and I'm up, so I got ready for the day. I went out after breakfast and tried to start my vehicle and the batteries were dead. Seems sudden because the vehicle was running so well. I went back to the milk factory and got Tim Ralph to help me push-start the vehicle with the clutch. Good thing it was a standard because that made it easy to jump-start. Once we got it going, I checked under the hood and first thing that I noticed was that the batteries had been changed. I know the airborne troops needed the batteries for their vehicle, because Cpl. Dave Bono had asked me if he could swap out the batteries before we sent this vehicle back to the UN in Kigali. I told him I needed the battery for now, to let me finish with the vehicle, and that before we send it back down to the UN compound in Kigali, we'd switch the batteries out for the one currently in his vehicle. I really don't mind Dave taking the batteries, the airborne troops needed this vehicle, we are all in this together. We need dependable vehicles here at our camp and I'm not sure if we should rely on the UN for much support, so we can trade off good parts from this one for his prior to its return. I only asked if he would wait a couple more days, because I still have a few things to do. As we close out the recce phase of the deployment, the CO and RSM still require me to take them to a few more places.

The rest of the morning I went for a walk around our compound. It was fenced in and there was a small building on the west side. In the middle there were three buildings in a hollow square and then the milk factory, which had a chain-wire fence all around the perimeter. I kept myself busy for the morning and took it easy. Cleaning up around the main entrance, there were a few of us and we were raking, I piled up all the debris from the immediate area around the milk factory. As everyone was raking and picking up garbage, it was being placed in a bigger and bigger pile, and someone came up with the idea to burn it. It seemed like a good plan at the time, so the debris was lit as we kept adding to it and raking up the compound. The fire got going really well as the flames shot up into the air, and then we began hearing pings and sounds like guns going off from it. It wasn't too long before we all ran for cover. The garbage, now fully on fire, unknowingly contained 7.62 mm rifle rounds, which began to heat up and cook off, spontaneously firing in any and all directions. We all stayed under cover and figured we would have to wait a couple hours until it cooled down, but one of the engineers put on the bomb disposal suit, walked over towards the fire with a fire extinguisher in hand, and sprayed the extinguisher back and forth over the fire, putting it out.

It was still hot, and more cook-offs were very much a possibility, so we all stayed away behind the walls of the milk factory for a while until it cooled down. This would be a laugh for some time and a story to have when we returned home. Fortunately, there was no one injured, which could have easily happened.

At 15:00 Tim and I were tasked to go down to the ROWPU (reverse osmosis water purification unit) area to get a trailer full of water and bring it to the other side of the building. After finishing this I had to take the CO, RSM, and OC Med Coy, who was Lt. Cdr. Landry, over to Goma for another NGO coordination meeting. In Goma, I sat for an hour or so and waited for them to come out, then went back home.

When I got back, I had a quick meal then one of the Airborne guys came to the Unit Medical Station (UMS) we had set up. He was bent over in immense pain and holding onto his side, white as a ghost with tears coming down from his eyes. He had what Dr. Laundry believed to be kidney stones, poor bastard was in a lot of pain. The doctor gave him a shot of Demerol, and he calmed down a bit. Tim, Dr. Laundry, and I took care of him, got an IV started, began some meds, and made him comfortable. Once he was settled with the IV and medications, he was then packed up on a stretcher to be sent off to Kigali by helicopter, to the field hospital there. Good thing was, the debris that had been on fire earlier had cooled down and the cook-offs were finished. A backhoe scraped up that mess and took it away as we called in a helicopter.

Later, when the helicopter landed and we put the stretcher on the back of the Land Rover to get the patient over to the helicopter, I had the idea of putting some chains on the back of the vehicle to fit around the stretcher's carrying handles to secure it in place.

Today everything worked out for the good. It's now 22:00. I think I'll go to bed.

Wednesday, 10 August

Today, Tim, Ralph, and I were tasked to do some water runs back and forth from the lake we were drawing the water from, bringing it back to the milk factory where it gets transferred into large, thousand-gallon holding bladders. From these settling tanks, it is left to sit for a time, so the bigger particles can settle. Afterwards, it gets put through the ROWPU to purify it in order to support the camp and hospital.

I was with my section commander and we were thinking this would be a good day, just driving back and forth transporting water, but that thought quickly disappeared when on our very first run to the water point, we were stopped very aggressively by the Rwandan Patriotic Front (RPF) at an improvised roadblock. They told us to get off to the side of the road because the new president was coming through, and they wanted no one and nothing on the road during this time. With what had just taken place over the last few months, there was still a lot of suspicion between the Hutu and Tutsi peoples. But it was nonetheless very stressful for Tim and me, because the RPF was basically child soldiers armed with rocket propelled grenades and recoilless weapons they were pointing at us. In this place one never knows when a fourteen-year-old, who back in Canada would be doing kid stuff, might just squeeze the trigger, popping a few rounds off and let you have a couple rounds in the head. People back home have no idea of the reality these kids have to live with here in Africa, being forced into war as child soldiers.

A tense sort of start to the day to say the least, however, after the president's convoy passed, we were waved on. We carried on for the rest of the day hauling water back and forth from the lake to our compound, only stopping for a moment for lunch.

We ended the day at around six o'clock, went back to the milk factory, fuelled up the MLVW, and parked it until tomorrow's next tasking. As night turned into evening, our section was getting ready for supper. Then one of the doctors came into the kitchen area and pointing to Tim and me, told us to grab our medical bags; there had been an accident on the highway towards

Gisenyi, and he needed us to drive him to the site and help triage. We ran to our Jeep and as we were driving down towards the accident site, he quickly briefed us that there had been a motor vehicle accident, and someone had gotten hit by a car. A reporter from Reuters News had come to the gate asking if we could send help. Apparently, the reporter thought only one or two people had been hurt and that it should be easy to assess the accident site. However, as we arrived on the scene, we could see that a large crowd of civilians was gathering and viewing the accident scene, as well as RPF soldiers. It was last light and getting dark quickly. There was chaos all around with onlookers panicking and hollering, the injured lying and moaning on the ground, and the bodies of those killed strewn around. Added to this were a lot of very tense and agitated Rwandan soldiers around us.

As I looked around at the situation, I quickly wondered about the five-tonne truck that had rolled over close to the side of a forty-foot embankment. Was the vehicle stable or would it ignite or explode? What the hell were we walking into?

When we began sorting out the accident scene, it wasn't one person hurt as we had been informed, it was a whole truck full of refugees; seventeen injured persons to be exact. With the war just concluding, there was no electricity and no streetlights. There was the smell of local fireplaces and the stink of blood, but more importantly, we couldn't see with the darkness coming on. As the three of us were working feverously, the last of daylight sank into the horizon. Just then, two of our field engineers, MCpl. Rick Melanson and Cpl. Scotty Clucas, from 4 Engineer Support Regiment arrived with a heavy logistics vehicle wheeled (HLVW) truck and they used the bright lights from the vehicle to give us much-needed illumination for the area we were working in.

It was very confusing and hard to control the situation with it so dark at nightfall, people all around, and too many voices. There was noise, talking, foreign languages, aggressive RPF soldiers screaming at locals trying their best to control this situation, confusion, smells, and we were literally unarmed and very vulnerable with no weapons, guns, or security. *What the hell is going on in this crazy place?* I was thinking during this time.

Most of these locals only spoke Rwandan and a few spoke their second language of French. Although my supervisor, Tim, one of the newly arrived engineers, and the doctor with us all spoke French, it was still confusing because of the enormous task at hand and the number of injured and dead. The two engineers assisted with triaging and treating the low-level injuries as well as directing some of the locals to help. They made some improvised splints out of bamboo and placed dressings on many of the wounds.

There were no medical resources except what was in our backpacks that we'd taken with us, no medical equipment, no radios, and no ambulances. We improvised splints from old bamboo shoots, using cargo straps from the HLVW for an improvised stretcher. While Tim and the others worked with triaging and packaging patients, I went up and down the hillside with the doctor, collecting the injured and dragging up the injured and deceased until at last they were all up top on the road where we worked feverishly to do treatments. With having to grab the rest of the injured and bodies and drag them to the triage site, it seemed to take forever. The whole scene of retrieving the injured, triaging, caring for the wounds, and preparing them to move to the hospital in Goma, was going in slow motion in my head.

For some reason, the RPF didn't want us to take the patients down the highway to the city of Gisenyi or over to Goma, Zaire. It would have been only roughly fifteen minutes away, but they insisted we not go to that facility. When we tried to explain how much better it would be to go to Gisenyi or Goma, they maintained an aggressive posture. Watching us while holding their weapons at the hip, the RPF soldiers were adamant that we go to Ruhengeri versus Goma. I was suspicious as to their motives, but they had the firepower and we didn't. Default win to them.

Although we were so close to Goma, now we had to backtrack, because we were directed to Ruhengeri, which was in the opposite direction heading north-east. Ruhengeri added an extra forty minutes or more onto the evacuation time for terribly injured people, who were either in shock or heading there with some devastating injuries and blood loss. Some would probably die before we arrived.

It was crazy, very busy, and dark, with foreign languages being spoken and lots of adrenaline. My mind was racing a thousand miles an hour. As we finished loading and packing the five-tonne stake truck, it sped away. I drove the jeep with Tim and the doctor with me, following the truck speeding down the highway towards Ruhengeri. There was no medic in the back of the truck, because what would they have done in the back of a blood-soaked vehicle with no lights and it not being an ambulance or having any equipment?

I sped along the road trying to keep up, but it was pitch black and there were people everywhere walking back from the refugee camps. Here I was, speeding down the highway and all I could see on the shoulder of the road were silhouettes of people walking as I zipped by them, woosh, woosh woosh, driving so close to the edge of the road and almost hitting some of those walking as I drove. I really don't know how fast I was going, for certain it was too fast for the situation, but I was trying to keep up with the truck to my front. There wasn't a single road light and no lights were in any village and here were these hundreds, if not thousands of people along the shoulder of the road with only the lights from the truck and my vehicle illuminating the road as we sped on. It was scary and to my front was the truck speeding along the route on our forty-minute drive towards the British field hospital in Ruhengeri. At this point, I was really having difficulty keeping up with the truck that the injured were on. On the one hand, I wanted to keep up, but I didn't want to kill anyone in the process. It was making me very uneasy.

When we finally arrived at Ruhengeri and handed over the patients at the British military hospital, there were the twelve patients who were still alive, we had also loaded the five deceased from the accident site. But as we unloaded the deceased, we somehow now had six. There was an extra dead body? His throat was slashed, we could only think that the RPF soldiers had done some vigilante justice on someone from the war, throwing them on the stake truck during the confusion at our expense. We all looked at each other without speaking, knowing that this could have been one of us in the black of night. With no security, no weapons, and no communications, we had been extremely lucky that nothing had happened to any of us.

The back of the truck smelled of dripping, thick, slippery, coagulated blood as I pulled out those who had perished with my rubber gloves on. You could smell the blood even in the compound amid all this confusion and pressure that had been on us for the last hour or however long it was. It was still confusing to me after the handover. I felt disoriented and I hated this feeling. It felt like Somalia all over again with uncertainty and confusion, and for some reason I felt that I'd screwed up and realized more than ever why I didn't want to be in the medical field. I hated this and the uncertainty it brings, I don't like to be in charge of trying to keep someone alive, it isn't what I want to do.

After we'd unloaded all the patients and deceased in the compound at Ruhengeri, the military doctor who had been with us began questioning me as to my competence as if I had done something wrong. He began by asking me if I had been in control while we were at the accident site recovering the injured and dead from the road and the embankment, asking if I ever had done a mass casualty before. He went on to tell me that it didn't appear I was in control or really knew what I was doing during the whole event from beginning to end. He also began to question my driving capabilities as we had driven here to Ruhengeri. I couldn't mount a defence; I didn't know what to say to a major. As I looked at him, I thought to myself, *I did everything fine, why is this idiot questioning my abilities?* At that moment I just wanted to haul off and smash him in the face, but he was an officer and a doctor, I couldn't be doing this, so I reached deep into my soul for control over my emotions and sat on it.

> *After this doctor ran off his mouth, at the very moment he was dressing me down with me staring back at him in silence, he lost all credibility and respect from me for the rest of the tour. I had no use for him now and for the next couple months I would only acknowledge him if he asked me a direct question. Otherwise, when he came into the hospital and I was around, I would go and recheck the patients or make myself scarce.*

With the way he had just treated me, I was in disbelief as I sat there. My internal dialogue began going crazy and I replayed the accident scene the best I could, thinking that he was the one who left the accident site and went up and down the hill looking for injured when in fact, as the senior medical person, he should have stayed on the highway directing the triage and tending to the most injured. He wasn't the one up on top of the road caring for the injured; those who should have been brought to him. When we'd initially left from our compound, it was the two medics who had their medical bags. I believe it was he who never took medical supplies or a back pack and while we were on site trying our best to save lives, he was the one who spoke the least and defaulted to a master corporal who really took charge of the triage and ran the show.

I just sat there, stunned and unable to say anything, just listening and there was not one single positive comment from this medical officer for me at all; no "Good job," "Well done," or "You've been through a lot with this mass casualty and should be proud of your actions," or "That was a lot of stress with that many casualties and only the few of us there." I was only hearing negative comments from this arrogant prick, at least this is what I was hearing in my mind at the time. I was thinking *maybe it's just me*, but at this point I was biting my tongue so hard it was bleeding and telling myself that he had no right to question my performance or anyone's performance for that matter. He should be reflecting more on his own performance and perhaps he wouldn't be quite so quick to criticize.

We stayed a bit longer to help the British medical team and then we finally left at 21:30 for the long drive back to camp on unlit roads. We got home at 22:30, then one of the nursing officers said she wanted to do a debrief; a debrief at 22:30, which was a bit too much for me at the time. I thought, *I don't need a warm and fuzzy hug right now, I need to be left the hell alone.* I was still wired with adrenaline, eyes dilated, heart still pounding, and I needed a couple of hours to calm down from what I had just experienced. I was also still focused on the doctor who'd berated me. As far as the casualties from the accident site we took care of, they were either in the morgue at the Ruhengeri hospital or receiving treatment there, so that's over with. Then I thought to myself that I now must work with this officer for the rest of the tour and today is my first day with him. I figure this is going to be a long tour!

When the nurse spoke to me and talked about a debrief, I looked at her and said in an angry tone, "Please, not now, madame!" It wasn't her fault, she was just directed to conduct a debrief, however, I was just still peaking from my earlier encounter with all that had taken place with the accident and the ensuing mass casualty, as well as the doctor and his disdain towards me. I said to her, "Madame, this makes no sense to do a debrief when you are still full of adrenaline. I need to be left alone to calm down, digest, and reflect on what just happened and especially after a very long day ending with this incident. I just want to go to bed and be left alone!"

But no, the chain of command insisted we do a debrief, so I sat there passive aggressively, listening and just wanting to go to bed. It was approx. 24:00, after the debrief, which only pissed me off after being up since 05:30 and with the day we just had.

What a day, I wish I was still alone on the recce, it was easier dealing with the UN in Kigali at the stadium, dead bodies on the side of the road, and driving around the country in a hotwired vehicle than this nonsense.

Thursday, 11 August

Up and at it at 0630, wash and breakfast, then see what's ahead today. We still don't have everyone here on the ground yet for the tour. We are just getting the milk factory building ready for the incoming troops' arrival and the arrival of our equipment, so we can start to set up the facility and help these people. Tim told me we were tasked to do runs back and forth to the water point at the lake to get water for our ROWPU. Today was already shaping up to be a pretty boring day, driving back and forth to the water point picking up water.

As I went out to check on the MLVW and water buffalo, the four hundred-gallon water trailer, I noticed that at the gate there were more and more people every morning. They are watching and anticipating what we are here for. The guys from the Airborne regiment are now into a routine with their patrol matrix securing the compound. I still feel uneasy with a battalion of RPF just down the street, all we've got around us is a wire fence for what that would ever be worth if they decided to just come in and do what they want.

Tim and I got ready and just went down to the water point and filled up the water buffalo, but when we got back the engineer checked our load of water and said the water source was too contaminated for purification, so that was it for the day. I can understand how it would be contaminated when only a few days ago on the recce I saw so many bodies floating in the lakes and along the shorelines and rivers around here. Now here we were taking it back to camp, purifying it, and using it for washing and cooking. Kind of creepy when I think about it.

After we got back, I wanted to fuel up the MLVW truck, but the fuel bowser was busted with the pump not working. I went to fix the fuel bowser, because we really needed fuel and this was the only source available to us, so if it wasn't working, we were shit out of luck. I was thinking that with the danger level in this country, not having vehicles fuelled and ready to leave at a moment's notice, to me that's criminal as we would certainly die. I noticed that there was a dead head (broken down) MLVW truck, so I started to cannibalize a needed electrical part used for boosting a vehicle, called a slave receptacle. Once I got it off, I could then put it on the fuel bowser and get it working, it wasn't that hard to do. All I had to do was take the exterior cable jumper off the truck and change the one out on the fuel bowser. I started out to do this and was busily and quietly working on it, when one of the mechanics, who had just arrived the day prior from Canada, came over and started telling me to stop what I was doing. He said that I couldn't take that part off the dead head and use it on the fuel truck. I looked at him and asked why not, the fuel truck was broken, this one part from the other vehicle could get it operational again. But according to the mechanic, we needed permission from Ottawa to do this and that there had to be a message from Canada stating that we had permission to do this.

I just looked at him and smiled as I thought to myself, *What the fuck?* I stopped taking the cable off the truck and I must have looked dumbfounded to him, because I was thinking 800,000 people just got killed in close-quarter fighting here over the last couple months, and here this guy was giving me flack over swapping out a slave cable adaptor. This was silly. Holy Jesus Christ! I was staring at this guy and thinking, *What the hell? We are here in a country where almost a million people died. We got a battalion of six hundred or more RPF, who are just down the street, who knows their intent? They may want to overrun us, take our supplies, or rape the female soldiers here. With very little fuel in our vehicles, I think right now it's our survival over the rules and regulations, which might serve us well back in Canada, but right now we aren't in Canada Dorothy.*

This guy was being too much of a policy parrot, going exactly by the rules; black and white thinking, which I despise. Myself, I am right now totally grey and let's do the right thing when the situation dictates, act and get the job done. When someone must spout the rules and regulation in a crisis environment, I'm unsure I fully buy that or would want to follow a leader like this.

What would have happened on the recce if we had waited for permission to get a vehicle that worked? I say action now and forgiveness later.

I guess that I really didn't make a good first impression on the mechanic. I'm sure he is a good guy, but here in Rwanda that might not be enough to keep us alive if we get overrun. To me it was obvious that after my experiences in Somalia, and with being here on the recce in Rwanda for the last ten days, I just might have a sense of what was happening on the ground and the urgency of having the fuel truck fixed.

I said no more, there was no point. I quietly put the cable back on the truck, then put the tools down, and walked away shaking my head. After this little episode was over at 19:00, I didn't say anything to Tim and went and washed my clothes, which were full of blood from last night's mass-casualty adventure to Ruhengeri. The mobile laundry and bath unit (MLBU) hadn't arrived yet, so I grabbed a two-liter bottle of water and washed up before supper.

Tonight, I had a bowl of instant noodles while sitting and talking with Michelle, a very good friend from my home unit. She's a good person, we did our first medical course in the army together. I've always liked her, I think she'll go far; she's fit, smart, and funny. Besides Michelle, there are a few of us deployed here that did Somalia only a year ago, and now here we are back in Africa again; Michelle, Joanne Leadbeater, Kelley McLeod, Francois Cameron, MWO Pare, and me. Not sure if this gives us any advantage over the others as far as knowing the conditions in Africa and that we're used to eating rations after eating them for the entire tour last year. Michelle and I talked for an hour or so then at 23:00 I went to bed.

Friday, 12 August

Got up at 06:00, couldn't sleep anymore. Got dressed, washed, and cleaned my bed space area. Had a ration pack for breakfast, the beans and wieners one. I ate beans and wieners for over half my six-month tour in Somalia, where we were on ration packs the whole tour, and now in Rwanda here we are eating rations again. It's too bad that just down the road an hour and a half or so, the UNAMIR II tour are eating fresh food. We are treated like the poor cousins and not a thought is seemingly ever given to us or about us eating rations all the time. I would give the shirt off my back to help anyone, wouldn't matter who it was, but these people have not thought of helping us or making our time here on tour a bit more bearable.

I was told that yesterday while Tim and I were hauling water, I guess there was a mass grave found by the building where the engineers and Canadian Airborne Regiment guys were living. This had to be one of the grimmest of tasks, but it needed to be completed at the milk factory site before we could begin to build the hospital. The graves were shallow and several medical personnel volunteered to carry out the exhumation and relocation of the bodies, along with some of the troops from the Commandos volunteering to help. While this was begun, a couple of heavy equipment operators from the engineer section, Corporals Boulay and Macker, went to the north-west corner of our compound and cleared the ground in order to prepare the site for a mass grave, which would eventually be turned into the hospital graveyard. Father Bosse, a military Catholic priest deployed with us, was at the site the entire time as the bodies were being moved. Padre Bosse provided spiritual comfort as well as blessing the bodies as they were being laid to rest at their new resting site. He also served as a visual representation to the locals who had gathered along the fence at the back of the compound and were watching the events unfold. His presence was a calming reassurance for all parties involved in this unfortunate but necessary event.

> As the tour progressed, it would be Fr. Bosse along with Sgt. Kenny Nunn, an infantryman with the Canadian Airborne Regiment, along with some of the field Engineer troops, would go on to create a very solemn burial ground with proper crosses for those patients who had passed away while in our care. Even after the gruesome task of moving the mass grave was completed, deceased were still being dropped off at our main gate during the night. We also had patients passing away from illness or terrible injuries inflicted upon them during the war. These bodies as well we would bury at our location over the coming months.

Today was shaping up to be a slow day. Basically, we just did a repeat of yesterday with water runs all day to ensure that the ROWPU had lots of water to purify. That's pretty well it, Tim and I running back and forth getting water all day. After we finished our last water run, and had returned, I wanted to fill up my vehicle and jerrycan and I saw that the pump on the fuel truck was now working and the cable off the other truck had been used. *What a good idea!* I thought. *The parts I was going to cannibalize off the truck yesterday but was told I needed special permission from Ottawa to do.* However, the parts had been exchanged between the vehicles and the fuel tanker was working. Someone must have gotten a message to and from Ottawa since yesterday. I wish I had of thought of this, I could have been recognized for my initiative, but the main thing is that it's now working, nothing else.

I think it's a good thing the tour is finally beginning to shape up. We worked until supper going back and forth from the water point with water, finishing at supper. After we ate, I sat down and wrote these goings on in my journal from today. I'm thinking that it will begin to get better, we just have to get our canvass hospital constructed and get the clinic up and running. It's now 21:30 and I think I'll go to ground soon, see what tomorrow brings.

Saturday, 13 August

Today was a quick start. Not sleeping very well so got up at 06:00, just washed my face and threw on my combats. Then I went out for a cup of coffee and it tasted so good I had another. I like waking up early and being by myself as I get my thoughts organized. It's just a few moments to kind of get my head together and plan the day ahead. I don't like it when I can't have these few minutes to be alone, I feel rushed. With so many people here now, no one will leave you alone. As soon as they see you sitting at a table, they assume you want company. It's not that I don't want company but at 06:00 in the morning I just want to be left alone. I think I'll start sitting in the vehicle compound when I first get up, no one sits there.

The rest of the troops finally arrived late yesterday afternoon and now we can get started and go about building the hospital facility. I hear that we will be a composite unit like we had a couple years ago on exercise in Wainwright during Rendezvous 92, with a medical platoon from each of the three field ambulances. For myself, I think they should mix us all together, but as usual these things are above my pay grade. I saw the layout for the hospital and it's a big facility under tent, looks like around sixty pieces of canvass will be used.

Within the hospital, we will have six wards, with four in use and one empty to rotate the other ones into so we can clean one of the wards every other day to keep diseases down. There will also be an isolation ward in case of serious infections and diseases as well as an area for oral rehydration, a treatment and screening area, and the pharmacy area. Once it is built, this place will be filled with hundreds of patients as they stream back from Goma, Zaire.

I know that this time will not be without its difficulties for me; the mass graves I have already witnessed; patients dying after being chopped up, burnt, or tortured; digging graves; the strain of working long days. But I feel that I am already sort of inoculated from only last year being in Somalia. Not sure if this makes sense, but I will see.

I have begun today to write up a letter requesting that Scotty and Rick be recognized for their assistance the other night at the mass casualty incident we had to deal with. If they hadn't showed up, I don't know what would have happened. Their quick actions in bringing down the HLVW, making splints, and helping us to care for the locals was amazing and should be recognized. It's not only good for them but it gives the people back home something to bite into, so they know what amazing work we do overseas. Anyway, this is something I will do over the next day or two.

Tim and I were also informed that as of today, we weren't doing water runs and another section was going to do it because they wanted to get off camp and go see where we got the water from. What a bunch of crybabies. I don't get it, we are here to do a job and not be tourists, who gives a shit where the water is from? Just give people a task and let it happen. I am sure that with this whole medical composite-unit thing with the three platoons from different units will actually separate us instead of unifying us. We will see the three field ambulances working separately, and because we are from Petawawa and the headquarters is also from Petawawa, we will get most of the shit jobs, mainly because the people in charge of us won't want to appear as if they are screwing around the troops from the other two field ambulances.

We did little all day long. I guess the tents for the hospital won't be all here now until tomorrow, and then we will have to just get it done. It's heading on three weeks now here and we haven't done a single medical thing! It's becoming very frustrating.

Today I finally met the padre who is deployed with us for the duration of the tour. His name is Father Whelan Bosse, and he's a diminutive, French Catholic padre from CFB St Jean, a most quiet and modest man. I introduced myself to him and told him if he needed any help throughout our time here when he was conducting Mass for us troops or going out to the community, to let me know and I would try to help him when I wasn't working in the hospital. We spoke for a while and I had this feeling he was a good person, and I looked forward to helping him over the next few months as he does his work here with us and in the local community.

> *Over the next few months, I would be his driver as permitted.*
> *Together we would visit every church and the Nyundo Cathedral*
> *between Mareru and Gisenyi during our time in Rwanda.*

I enjoy working with people on the spiritual side more than being a medic, because I am not comfortable with the responsibilities we are given in caring for people. I never really wanted to be a medic, but it was all that was offered to me when I transferred. While in the reserves, I was a field engineer for thirteen years and I wanted to do this for the rest of my life, but on transferring to the regular forces, medical assistant was the trade I was given, and I felt stuck in it. There was no use in looking to change trades, but it will be a long career in a profession I really don't feel comfortable with.

Other than a few mindless jobs today cleaning up and then talking to the padre, it was a slow day, monotonous. I got a haircut tonight from an Airborne guy I knew from Somalia, MCpl Trent Holland, an excellent leader. I like being around the guys from the Regiment, they are real and if they like or don't like you, well you are told and that's a good thing, to know where you stand. They don't pretend to like someone if they don't. At tonight's orders' group we were told that everyone needed for the mission has finally arrived now. The good news was that some of the canvass also came in, so I guess tomorrow we will begin building the hospital. It's now 21:30 and I think I'll rack out soon.

Sunday, 14 August

It's now been almost three weeks since our arrival on the recce party. Seems like forever since first landing in Kigali and for the last two weeks we have been waiting for our hospital tents and equipment to arrive from Canada. There have so many problems to this point with the Operation Passage deployment; mainly not enough flights from Canada bringing our equipment. The canvass finally arrived yesterday and so today we would be setting up. As we prepared to set up the hospital, the camp sergeant major (CSM) showed us where it was proposed to be built. He was a good man and I had worked for him for the past couple years and in particular a year earlier in Somalia, so I felt comfortable enough in speaking with him in private. I informed him that from my time on the recce and seeing the lay of the land, I didn't think it would a very good place to locate the hospital. He asked me why and I mentioned that with the low areas, uneven ground, and the fact that volcanic rock isn't very porous we would be set up for flooding should we ever get a rainy period. I thought if it rains, the water will pool in these low spots and would flood out the hospital. However, the plan was already made and the CSM was fixed on this location since this was the plan that headquarters and all the planners had agreed upon and it was too late to change. I said to myself, *What the hell, let's do it!*

Once the template of the hospital was figured out with the length and width of it, we were then shown where the centre was to be placed. From this point we figured out by pacing the ground where the wards, pharmacy, and screening areas would be located and began to lay out the footprint on the ground with the skeleton frame. Building the facility turned out to be a slow and arduous process. Many of the people deployed with us didn't know how to put up purloins and A-frames, or how to string the canvass tent sections together. However, there were three platoons of field soldiers here and we had a bumper crop of physician assistants and sergeants who had filed more time than I could imagine, so it would work out. With hard work and patience we got through it, there were enough of us from field units across Canada to guide everyone. The facility had a main spine down the centre with nine wings off the main one. We didn't have the proper poles to have a seamless transition from the main spine to the wings, but we jerry-rigged it and it would have to do.

After being in Somalia only a year earlier, I know this is just the start today with putting up the facility. It's going to be a long and difficult haul no matter how long we are here once we are up and operational, receiving patients, and beginning our shifts on the ward.

Finally, the field hospital was up and completed. We got the beds in; pharmacy, emergency, and screening room areas all set up; and a separate shower tent to wash patients with scabies. We put a sorting-area out front with an administration area close to the hospital for tracking and paperwork and a secure area by the main gates where the military police (MPs) could do proper control of those entering the grounds. It's been a long day, everyone, but it's done.

We were into the actual tour less than a week now and we had an incident take place earlier today that left many of our people upset and worried that this might be a harbinger of things to come. One of our medics, Michelle Tremblay, was sent out with a field engineer section and airborne infantry section, to provide medical coverage for the day as water was beginning to be drawn from the lake to be brought back to our camp for the ROWPU.

At the site, the water was drawn about a half-hour drive from our main camp. There were only about fifteen of our soldiers all together, and Michelle was doing her medical coverage in case anyone should become injured or ill. The day seemed to start innocently enough. Once the water pumps were set up along the river and water loaded into the tanks on the trucks, Michelle sat down by the river's edge to read a book. As she was reading, she noticed an elderly gentleman walking down the opposite side of the road collapse not far from where she was sitting.

Being a medic, she ran over with her medical bag to render assistance to this man, but then an RPF truck pulled up, stopped, and soldiers dismounted, approaching Michelle and the man she was attending to. Sensing something wrong, the airborne soldiers put themselves between Michelle and the RPF soldiers and asked what they wanted.

The RPF soldiers responded that they wanted to "borrow" Michelle for a while. Many on our tour were operationally immature and hadn't been on many tours, and they just didn't understand that in Africa women are viewed differently than back home in Canada. It was a dangerous place before, during, and this soon after the war, and I don't think our chain of command understood that rape was a possibility. Sadly, very often during the war, local women would be forced into prostitution for soldiers, as the men travelled village to village, fighting their way across the country. The RPF were thinking that we had brought our own prostitutes, and not understanding that this isn't the way we operated, they wanted to "borrow" Michelle.

The airborne troops on the ground were having none of this and told the RPF soldiers they would shoot her before they let them take her, and a standoff ensued until the RPF mounted their vehicle and hurriedly left the area. Immediately, there was a hasty call made back to our main camp requesting to switch with another medic, that an incident had taken place and to send a male medic. The next load of water sent back to the camp had Michelle on board and her replacement was sent on the return trip.

Shortly after Michelle's departure, a truckload of RPF showed up as a show of force at the river where the water was being drawn. They were looking for Michelle and were very agitated. They didn't realize she had been sent back to camp until they saw her replacement, the male medic.

This was a close call to say the least, and if not for the quick thinking and actions of the airborne troops on the ground, it could have turned out much worse. I spoke with Michelle and during the time this was taking place she really wasn't aware of the danger she was actually in, she was a little back from where the airborne soldiers were exchanging words with the RPF, so she didn't hear the discussion that they wanted to take her away. However, once back in the relative safety of our main camp, slowly the gravity of what had taken place began to sink in on her…just how terrible this could have turned out had she stayed and that truckload of RPF troops showed up.

> For the rest of the tour, the chain of command smartened up and didn't expose the Canadian female soldiers to situations like this again. I am unsure of what our chain of command was thinking sending her to the site on that day, over a million women had been raped during the genocide. Perhaps this was operational immaturity or naïveté on the part of our leadership, or perhaps a little of both. Regardless, it never took place again. Rwanda immediately after the war wasn't a country to make mistakes like this in. Sending out females when we were out-numbered, out-gunned, and vulnerable with only a platoon of fighting soldiers was a very dangerous thing to do.

I am just glad that everything worked out and nothing bad happened and she is ok. I was thinking to myself, *what is this place about?* They are so messed up here in this country. About a million people just died here and they need our help and then they pull a shit stunt like this.

I thought back to when I was doing the water runs with MCpl Tim Ralph, earlier in the week before everyone arrived. There was really no reason to change the way we were doing this tasking, but everyone has an agenda. I am all for equal rights and I truly believe that women can do whatever I can do as a male, but here in Rwanda we are not in a controlled environment like Canada anymore. Rwanda is not the place to play games and push certain agendas. In Africa when there are women accompanying the soldiers, they are usually sex slaves and are passed around between the men.

Although this was an extreme example, it was, however, an example of why I was trying to get that fuel truck's broken pump working last week…so we would have fuel for our vehicles in case we ever got attacked and had to make a run for it. The leadership here have to get with it and realize that we are not in Canada any longer. I have tried to give my opinion since getting here three weeks ago on the recce party, and with a few of us having operational experience in Somalia or in the Gulf War, you would think if we said something, perhaps it's because we may have experienced it only a year or two ago. But I am only a leading seaman and need to mind myself.

Later in the afternoon we were given an intelligence briefing, which wasn't of any real use. I had seen most of what they were saying when I was in Kigali at the UNHQ as it was being reported on CNN. Only thing of significance that was mentioned, which perked my ears, was that once the hospital was up and running, we were going to work shifts of eight hours on, eight hours off, then eight hours on. This was to be the schedule every day during the first couple weeks' cycle of working on the hospital ward. I just looked up at those giving the briefing. I didn't get this, and I thought to myself that this was not a very well-thought-out work schedule, that it was probably dreamt up by some officer who will only be working straight days. There was no doubt in my mind that with the twelve detachments here on the ground from 1, 2, and 5 Field Ambulance, there would be no need to drive us into the ground with this type of heavy work schedule and it doesn't make one iota of sense.

However, if the goal was to burn out the troops and create mental fatigue, it's a good way to set people up to be sick, get run down, and develop coping problems. In Somalia a year ago, with only sixteen medics doing taskings, being loaned out to the Commandos, working in the OR, going downtown to work at the local hospital, and doing security and general duty details, we still got even shifts and could sustain a half-decent sleep pattern. But here in Rwanda, with over 150 medical people on the ground, we are told it's a tight schedule with only having this many people on tour? I was baffled. They have created this extreme shift schedule in order to make it work when there are enough people here to staff double the hospital we have, what a joke, madness really. There are more than enough people to have three rotating shifts or two twelve-hour shifts. But then again, I can't say too much at this point or they will think I have an attitude. I probably do, as this is plain stupidity. I think they are setting people up for future issues and that's all I can say.

We thought we were done for the night after working all day on the main hospital, but after supper around 20:00, a speed wobble occurred and we were told we had to stay up all night to get the panniers containing our medical supplies ready for tomorrow's opening of the hospital. Not sure what the issue is with this bullshit, there are three medical units here, so why are we up all night doing this when we must begin the eight on, eight off schedule tomorrow? Why couldn't one of the detachments who are not on shift for a week or two, be tasked with this and let us sleep? Just another example of the senseless organizational fuckery here. We finished around 22:30 or so. At 23:00 I finally got to my bed space and went right to sleep. We will see what tomorrow brings.

Monday, 15 August

Had a couple of coffees this morning, trying to wake up and get my head together. Everything is coming fast, things are evolving and changing as we go along. We are all settled in as a Det and sat together for breakfast and a coffee. I felt good with who's on my team, but I don't doubt how hard this will be over the next couple months. Today we were tasked to do the finishing touches in the hospital, and we were informed that the hospital won't be open now until tomorrow. So, most of what we did today was to complete setting up the remaining couple of sections of canvass and straighten out the inside of the facility by the end of the morning. After lunch we were given a tour of the hospital by WO Tardiff. He walked us around each of the sections and explained how it was laid out, and where things were located. Not really much different than the setup we have in most of our major exercises back in Canada.

After the hospital tour we were supposed to be off for the rest of the day so we could rest up until we start tomorrow, but that was not to be. Instead, we were tasked to Ruhengeri to drop off supplies to the CARE agency, but I knew that we should have gone to Gisenyi because Ruhengeri is where Medicine Sans Frontier (MSF) is located. Anyway, when we got to our destination there was no CARE agency there. We had to drive all the way back to our hospital just to get redirected to where we should have gone in the first place: Gisenyi. What a waste of four hours.

At the end of the day, I washed up, then washed my clothes, ate supper, and relaxed. I spoke to Fr. Bosse today and told him that if I could be of any help that I would be there for him. I don't care if it's in between shifts or on an occasional day off, I want to go and help Fr. Bosse in the community. I'm writing in my journal now and will soon be in bed and asleep, hopefully. It's only 21:00, but I am really tired with the last three weeks of going non-stop since my arrival on the recce, and I think it's finally beginning to catch up on me.

My detachment (Det) was led by a nursing officer and six medics, and we worked alongside another Det of the exact same make up. There was also a physician assistant, WO Claude Tardiff, who was the go-between for the two Dets and provided his high-level medical knowledge and skill set, which might be called upon as we worked with the patients. The two Dets, when combined, formed what we called a section. Within this group of fifteen personnel, we could care for 100 to 150 patients during a shift, depending on the flow of those admitted versus those discharged. Now we began a three-month journey, which would touch the lives of some 22,000 Rwandans in our little hospital facility at the milk factory.

Once we began operation, the days ahead would not be without their difficulties; the mass graves, patients dying, the digging of graves, and the strain of two eight-hour shifts out of every twenty-four-hour cycle. We were placed on this foolish schedule for the first couple weeks, and then we were eventually rotated out for a week at a time to work at local clinics or in our screening and triage area…then once again back into the hospital shift schedule a week later. The schedule was demanding and very quickly I felt a lot of people were overworked and overtired, with no time in between shifts for recovery. On the eight hours off between shifts you were expected to eat, wash, sleep, and if you were lucky make a phone call home. Then you were expected back to your next shift, so in fact it wasn't eight hours off—rather a possible six? Myself, I expressed that twelve-hour shifts would have been better than this. Making matters worse, it would only be the sections who were working in the hospital who had this type of schedule. All the other medical personnel, other than us in the hospital on shift, got a nice sleep while we were working at a burnout rate. On top of this there were the occasions when we would have visitors come up from Kigali and give lectures for hours, which most of us were too tired to listen to or mentally engage in for the time they were being presented. Even if we were in the middle of our eight hours for sleep on the hospital schedule, we were forced to attend these lectures at the cost of much needed, valuable hours of sleep before returning to our work at the hospital. The way we were being managed was unnecessary and repercussions from the sleep deprivation would be revealed only after our return to Canada when the tour was complete and mental health issues began to arise post-tour in the coming months and years later.

Tuesday, 16 August

All last night I just couldn't sleep. I was restless throughout the night thinking about our first day, so I was awake at 05:00 just lying there, waiting to go to work. Unable to sleep, I finally got up and went out to the eating area. It was nice, no one else, no one around, just me alone to myself, me and my thoughts. I was eager to get on with the task at hand of opening the hospital here in Mareru, it seemed to be taking too long, though. I left home three weeks ago, and finally we are going to see our first patients today. Seems sort of like getting to a high school dance and they're playing last dance as you arrive. You're glad you went but wish you had come sooner. But it is what it is, so here we are and my time to myself is gone and everyone is up now and ready for the day.

We went to the hospital with a sense of going to do some good and help the returning refugees out as they filtered back into the country.

When we arrived, I felt a little over the top with some of the stuff we were asked to do. Initially they made us wear white, full-body, nylon-paper jump suits with hoods and a zipper up the front, as well as a surgical mask and gloves. Talk about difficult to work with this on, they were all medium and large sizes and our section members certainly weren't the body types these were made for. I was thinking all day that for the most part I won't get sick unless if I stick myself with a bloody needle. The suits would only help if one of the patients licks me or one the kids flings crap on me. I thought to myself that this is crazy, we are probably scaring the hell out of these people with our getups. In a full body suit with a hood on it and a surgical mask on, we must have looked like something from a sci-fi movie. It's just silly, we are dealing with injured and ill people, not working in a high security laboratory.

Within the first twenty-five minutes, patients were beginning to be admitted, what a rush of humanity it felt like. Suddenly, the hospital was full of sick people. We went from zero to forty patients in the first hour of operation; sick and injured people of all ages. There was a little girl with one of her ears cut off. She was a beautiful little one about eleven or so, just part of the insanity that went on here prior to our arrival. I felt so bad for her and all we could do was to clean the wound and place a dressing on it. There was nothing else we could offer as we had no surgical capabilities. She would be needing extensive plastic surgery if that were even available in this country.

Then there was the man who waited for hours in the lineup with a very deep facial wound from a machete. The wound went from just above his right eyebrow on an angle to the corner of his jaw, with an opening a good two to three inches all the way along the laceration. The wound was too old for suturing, and it would have to be packed and heal slowly from the inside out. A deep and disfiguring scar would certainly be left as a reminder of the madness he survived. As we cleaned it and placed a dressing, he didn't say a word, and I was thinking how this man this must be in pain, and here he was so silent. I can't even imagine the craziness that went on here the last few months.

There were the mothers who brought their very sick kids, hoping that we could do something for them. Although they didn't speak English, their eyes spoke a compassion and love for the children they were holding; words which we could never express. It was plain to see and feel this. Although it was only our first shift of this first day in our hospital, I began to drift in my thoughts and the sound of babies and people moaning already began to overwhelm my senses. I thought to myself that it's going to be a difficult time here in this facility when babies start to die on us.

It was a very busy day, just making sure all the patients were cared for. Most of the patients had bloody diarrhea or scabies and were dirty from the living conditions in the refugee camps in Goma, and now with all the walking back from there. The day went very quickly, though, not from distractions but just from taking care of the very sick and wounded patients arriving here. I was proud of the fact that we had the only medical facility in Rwanda offering 24/7 in-patient care. It was amazing to think of this when at home we think nothing of walking into a hospital any time of day or night.

I noticed very quickly in our first day of operation that when you admit a patient, you are putting up the entire family in that bed space. I think we were all a little proud of our first shift on that first day, knowing that we offered this level of care to those needing help as they returned from Zaire.

After work we had a quick "Orders" group about the hospital. How did we think it went for our first day? How was it going to run? Our shift schedule came up and I mentioned that I didn't like the eight-hour shifts, but this was quickly spoken to and then moved on. There was talk as well that we may be moving by the weekend if things don't improve down south on the Burundi - Rwanda border. Apparently, there is still some fighting going on there and few NGOs are willing to go into this. I would go at the drop of a hat if asked to volunteer, there is important work to do here, but to get in the middle of fighting parties is what we train for and should want to do. I can imagine the type of care we would have to do down there. Only problem is we are not top-heavy with fighting soldiers, and I am not sure a platoon of infantry from 3CDO would be enough to protect us as we did our work. I'm not sure what's happening, but we may end up here for more than two months if this get worse, and it might. Nonetheless, the Orders Group concluded, and we were dismissed until our next shift in eight hours. I need to go to bed soon.

Military police providing crowd control at the gate – Photo Chris Cormier

The ill and injured carried on wicker stretchers – Photo Chris Cormier

Wednesday, 17 - 19 August

It is only now I can catch up on my journal. It's the 19th of August and I've been busy these last three days with the equipment finally arriving and setting up. Now we are into our second day of operation. It's been crazy busy with the hospital and patients, trying to work and sleep and have a minute for myself and everything else in between.

I arrived in country three weeks ago now. The hospital's only been operating a couple of days since everyone's arrival, and I am getting into the flow of the eight-hour shifts. I still think this crazy schedule of alternating eight hours on, eight hours off, for a week at a time is a foolish work schedule really. I can see it is already affecting the troops with fatigue and overexposure to the immense misery and sickness the hospital contains within its walls. I feel this work schedule is wrong and I've looked around and seen that we are getting tired fast.

Tonight, I was on the night shift, which runs from 23:00 until 07:00. Having just completed my hand-over report from the outgoing medic, I was doing my first rounds and preparing to settle in for the evening. Things seemed to be going well, and with all the patients presently sleeping, it seemed tonight might be a slight respite for us, who had not stopped.

A couple of hours into my shift, while sitting on the edge of a bed to check on one of my youngest and sickest patients, I saw he was quietly sleeping in his mother's arms. As I was checking on him, I smiled at the mother and the other children with her. There were a couple of her children lying down in the bed with her and another under the bed. It's just the way it is here in Africa, when you admit one, you admit the whole family. This little sick guy was underweight for his age and his skin was loose fitting all over his little body. He looked very tired, just breathing was an effort for him. While I was preparing to care for him, he turned his head in my direction and his big brown eyes looked up at me. He had a sad and knowing look, and those beautiful, brown eyes touched me for some reason.

I reached over to feel his forehead and face. He was cool, with barely enough energy to move and as he tried to cry, his face and mouth made the motions of crying, only he was so weak that no sound was heard. He was too dehydrated to make even a single tear.

It was during this time when I was about to give him some rehydration fluids through the nasogastric tube that he began having difficulty with breathing. As I was squeezing the syringe to push some fluid into the tube, he stopped breathing altogether. I quickly scratched the bottom of his foot and rubbed his chest, and he responded by taking in a deep breath, looking up at me as he did. Once again, his eyes locked with mine for what seemed the longest of times and somehow, I felt he was trying to tell me something; to tell me that he was weary, that he had nothing left to give in this life of his. Once more he took a deep breath in and let out what would be his final breath. I noticed after this that there was no longer any air movement, and I tried to get him breathing, tried to get his heart beating again, but couldn't. Raising my voice, I called for the nurse to come and assist me. She quickly arrived at the bedside, saw what I had going on with the patient, and told me to go and awake the duty doctor.

I left the child's side to run over and wake the doctor to come over and assess him, and as we both headed back to the hospital, I explained what had happened. When the doctor and I returned, it was already too late. The nurse looked in our direction, giving a subtle shake of her head, indicating that his life was no more, he had died. This would be my first experience with the death of a child, the first of many during my time in Rwanda. It took me a moment to regain my composure and get back on track as I shook it out and calmed myself down to the reality of what had just taken place.

I went over to the milk factory building where the priest with us, Father Bosse, slept and awoke him to have Last Rites done for the child. He told me to give him a few minutes and he would come right over. While the padre was getting dressed and preparing, I went out to an area at the back of the hospital, where we had begun a hospital graveyard, and picking up the shovel I proceeded to dig a small grave for this child.

Once it was completed, I went back to the hospital where the priest had arrived at the child's bedside and Last Rites were given. Watching intently all this time was the mother with her other children present. I began covering her dead child in a cloth, wrapping it around him gently, as if he were asleep and I didn't want to awaken him. Looking down at his face one last time, I saw how calm his face appeared. I suppose he was out of his misery from the life he had been born into; a life of hardship and of little opportunity. After wrapping him in the blanket, I placed him in an empty cardboard ration box, and then placed the box into a thick, heavy-gauge plastic bag and sealed it. This was done so dogs wouldn't be able to locate and dig up the human remains and eat them, which had often been the case during the war.

Placing this little boy in the orange bag bothered me, because of the indignity of burying this innocent child in garbage bags. It just didn't seem right. However, in this terrible situation, it was the best thing to do with the thought of what the wild dogs would do otherwise. The mother, children, and Fr. Bosse all left out the back doors of the hospital to the grave I had prepared for the child, while I followed behind them carrying the box containing the baby.

I knelt on one knee and placed his remains in the grave, and Fr. Bosse then said a prayer, gave some readings, and blessed the "coffin." Once this was completed, there were a few moments of silence as the mother hesitated in leaving. When the silence finally broke, Fr. Bosse spoke to them to move back to the hospital. As they all turned and headed back, I was left to myself and to the job of filling in the grave.

When the burial was completed, I went back to the hospital where Fr. Bosse was still speaking with the child's mother. The woman was looking intently at him as she was speaking to him through the interpreter. She was asking if it would be possible for her to have the child's blanket and some of the food, we had allocated for him. All she wanted was some warmth and a little food as she still had children to care for. I intently watched her face as this woman who had just lost a child, stood there emotionless. There was no time for tears as she was preoccupied with the present, living for today, too busy trying to figure out how her family could survive one more day. I thought to myself that this poor woman had no time to mourn her loss, no time for herself to think of the child she had just lost, who was freshly buried behind our hospital. She had three other kids in tow and who knows what awaited her back home in her village. I didn't know what was in her future, but at this moment I was thinking of this woman's immense strength and her focus on living for today and the task at hand with caring for the surviving kids.

I didn't care at this point what anyone thought or would have said to me about what I was about to do. I went to the storage area and came back with a full box of protein cookies, some bottles of water, and a wool blanket for her and each of the children. I wanted her to at least have something to leave with. She has left so much here with us, too much, and although I could never imagine her pain, witnessing this affected me greatly. I knew some of the other soldiers were now giving blankets and food when families left after these difficult losses, and why not, it wasn't a lot to give in contrast to what they left behind.

What else can you do? What hope can you give in a hopeless situation? After I had said my goodbyes to the mother, she wanted to leave immediately as the morning sun had begun to rise over the mountains. I still had patients to care for, and I still had a couple of hours until the end of my shift. With this task now complete, I cared for my remaining patients and carried on.

We finished our shift at 07:00 and by the time the handover was done, I went back to our sleeping area, exhausted and knowing that I would be going back on shift at 16:00 later in the day. As I pulled the blankets over my head with another long shift completed, I was filled with exhaustion, slowly being pulled into mental numbness and difficulty in sleeping. There were seven hours to sleep before heading back to the hospital to try to bring hope to those we cared for.

I awoke at 13:30 and quickly got ready for our next shift on the ward. This pace is already killing me and, although it is eight hours on, eight hours off, we are only getting at most six hours sleep each cycle if we are lucky. I hope tonight will not be another bad night with more patient deaths. It's a hard thing having mostly children die on us. Everyone has their ways of coping; some get protective around the burial, others get quiet, and some just carry on as if it doesn't bother them, but I think we will have more of our patients die while we are here.

On the 18th of August we were working the back shift, which ran from 16:00 to 23:00, then tomorrow from 07:00 to 15:00, when it became extremely too busy all of a sudden. We went from a walk on opening day, to a full sprint in only a couple days since opening our doors. Many of the patients are sick with dysentery, cholera, or tuberculosis and a few have HIV/AIDS. Then there are the trauma patients with severe machete and burn wounds from the war. We are also having babies being dropped off at the main gate; orphans of the war. We have a couple of babies already. One was quickly named Chip; this was because of a small chip of skin missing on his forehead. The other baby we call Peanut because of his small stature. I think they both have AIDS, especially Chip. He looks very underweight and ill and has a very weak cry when he attempts to cry.

We all want a turn at the care of the babies. I'm unsure why, but I think it connects us with the people here, or maybe it is that they are so innocent and haven't asked for what was done to them. It's a quiet time for us when we get to be rotated to care for them, a time we aren't on the ward with the adults, because we stay off on our own in the main hallway where the babies are located. I think it is good we only do a shift each, rotating through the caring of them. It would be too easy getting attached to them, they're so innocent and vulnerable. We know that they will most likely not live or that we we'll soon drop them off at a local orphanage. It is hard on us knowing this.

By now most of us have gotten rid of the white body suits we wore the first few days of the hospital's opening. There was no way to prevent cross-contamination with taking them off and putting them on. Most of us have gone to making an apron out of heavy-gauge, orange, plastic bags and wearing it around our waist. I don't think the suits did too much to protect us anyway, and it's not sustainable to change into a new suit, or to wear the same one for days at a time, with how often we come and go. We move back and forth to our eating and sleeping area in the milk factory multiple times daily and during the shift, so to put on a new protective suit every shift, or to continue to wear the same one for days on end, only sets us up to spread disease within our group. There is no 100% sure way to prevent cross con-tamination with taking them off and putting them on so often. Many of our people are getting now sick because of working so closely with the patients.

The other issue which has been coming up is that once the hospital was fully functional, we were having an excess of human waste and biohazard materials being created, which if left untreated would cause disease or the wild dogs would dig it up. The engineers had organized and constructed a dump for our garbage and waste when they had first arrived, however, now something else was needed for the biohazard waste. The Preventative Medical Technician (PMed Tech) indicated the only safe way to dispose of this was through an incinerator, but that would take weeks to arrive from Canada. For the field engineers that was no problem; they came up with an idea to build an improvised incinerator. They looked through some of the manuals they had brought with them and together came up with a design for an improvised incinerator, one which would burn at the required temperature to properly dispose of the biohazard materials.

We were fortunate to have the combat arms troops with us and with the ingenuity of these teams, they would help to support us through to the end of the mission.

The last few days feel as if they run one into one another and already, I feel as if I am in a daze and unable to shut down mentally on my time off. We are on the ward for eight hours working with very sick and injured people, then we are off for eight hours, and it feels as if there isn't enough time to wash, eat, sleep, and take a moment to breathe before it's back to the hospital for another eight-hour shift.

This schedule is ridiculous, but the funny thing is, those who came up with the schedule only work during the day. I know they are not running us in this manner because they are mean or cruel. However, I think they have no thought or awareness as to what damage they are causing us here in the hospital tent. We are all beat. We play the music on the ward and try to joke with each other and keep spirits up, joking around with some black humour to deal with the deaths and things we see, but it is not sustainable. The only thing I look for during the last week since starting work at the hospital is once a day at 13:00 when I get to listen to the CBC news on my old transistor short-wave radio. I had this same radio when I was deployed to Somalia. I still have the schedules and the short-wave radio stations for Africa, which I received from CBC last year when I went to Somalia. With these schedules, I can pick up CBC and the BBC and at least hear a little of home and what is going on in my life back there. There are also world radio frequencies from the paperwork that was in the box with the radio. This has all come in handy with leaving for this tour so fast. This transistor radio is my little piece of home to keep me sane and up to date. I listen to the news from back home and try to keep up with things. It's hard but it's important to try to stay current.

It's now Friday, the 19th of August and I am on my third straight day on the hospital ward. I finally got a few moments to sit and collect my thoughts. This schedule is killing me. Today after eight hours of sleep, when we got up and went down to work at the hospital again at 07:00, we were told to leave and come back at 14:00. With this time to spare, I wrote a few letters and I made a cheque out for Canadian Tire and mailed it to my roommate to pay a bill for me.

At 14:00 we headed back down to the hospital and after only an hour we were told that the hospital was still not at full capacity and that one of the Dets would be enough to cover the in-patients. Our team was told to go home, and we did. I think the nursing officers think we are seeing too much and made a command decision about which Det to send home. It doesn't matter who sees what, it's all shit either way. Misery loves misery, whether someone dies on you or you have to see babies die with AIDS.

Not much else happened the rest of the evening, except that I was taken out of my Det to be sent to Kigali with one of the health care administrators, Lt. McCormick, to be her driver. She would be our liaison officer with the UN contingent there. Kind of a joe job really. I know I am being sent down because I was here on the recce and know the city of Kigali, the UN head-quarters, and the stadium. I am not happy either way, but we do as we are told, that's the way the army works. I came on the recce to get things settled before everyone arrived, and now that we only opened the hospital and began seeing patients a few days ago, I am already being given a joe job. There are many others here who haven't been placed in a section yet and would love this tasking, so why not send them?

Lt. McCormick has only been posted to the unit a year or so and still has not cut her operational teeth. I have been given the task of running with her and being her driver. She is a nice person and in Kigali she will be our liaison officer along with WO Frank, who is working the logistics side of the house. I think they will work well together. I can see no reason for me to be here as a designated driver when most of her time will be spent either in the stadium or next door at the UNHQ and I will get sent to work with the UN guys who wear blue berets and I don't.

Tonight a few of the guys from my Det are starting to get sick, low grade fevers and gastro, probably from the conditions and difficulty maintaining hygiene. Presently in our sleeping area, we have a couple guys down with gastro or something like this. One of the other guys asked me if I had any injectable Gravol. I did have lots from the recce, so I drew some up and gave a couple of the guys 50mg Gravol injections into their butts to calm down their stomachs. Gary snarled at me because he said I was rough with giving him the needle and it hurt his arse. He's just not feeling good. Once this kicks in he'll have a good sleep and feel better in the morning. After doing this, I cleaned up my needles into the sharp's container, washed, and put away my med bag. I had a cup of tea and then went to bed to get a few hours before heading off to Kigali tomorrow.

Saturday, 20 August

What a wild day. I was up early, got washed, and had a coffee. Said goodbye to Tim and the rest of the guys from the Det, then ran around trying to get all my stuff together before I left for Kigali with Lt. McCormick. Loaded our kit in the back of the truck and hopped in, then we drove down in the back of a truck. Same scene on the way down as on the way up, looking out the back of the vehicle; thousands on thousands of people walking along the road. Still a few bloated bodies along the way and banana leaf-wrapped bodies here and there.

Arriving at the stadium in Kigali, we waited around for a few hours before we ate until the UN administrator found a place for us to sleep. I noticed some senior NCOs here at the stadium didn't seem too impressed or welcoming with our arrival. I don't give a shit really. We finally were shown our places to sleep, and surprise…I'm back in the hallway again. Nice quarters for guests. I wonder if they do this for the UN contingent troops when they visit or for visiting dignitaries arriving from Canada? After getting settled in my hallway bed space, I went to eat and as I entered was asked if I was UN or a visitor. Then I was told not to eat too much. Holy shit, you'd think they were buying it.

After supper I went to the field in the stadium where the medics were set up and saw Gary Cue, Greg MacDonald, and a few others who I knew from Petawawa. There were others I really didn't know, who were from the Kingston unit medical station and others from units across Canada. Everyone seems to be doing all right, they are going out and inoculating kids at clinics around the city. This is rewarding, doing some good and I think good for them.

So now it's 19:00. I had supper, talked to the guys and gals awhile, and now will probably go down for a beer or a Pepsi with the guys from the

Airborne Regiment with 3 Commando. I served with them only last year in Somalia. What a top-notch group of guys and the Sigs Regt is lucky to have them here for their protection.

Had a Pepsi with the guys, just small talk and them asking how it's going where I am. I told them that my plan is to make myself unnecessary and not be here within the next few days. WO Frank and Lt. McCormick, they can do what they must do without me here, I am a tit on a bull here with no real job or purpose. Not much else happened the rest of the evening, Later Greg MacDonald came and talked to me. He looks good. It's good to see people from home that are friendly and make me feel welcomed. Afterwards I went to my bed space in the front of the stadium, got washed, and then off to bed.

Sunday, 21 August

Up at 07:00, washed, dressed, and went down for a coffee in the kitchen. It was a Sunday routine here in the stadium for the Sigs Regt, and the halls are quiet, nice. I enjoy my own company and being alone especially when I first wake up. As I drank my coffee, I was wondering what the guys were up to at the milk factory. This isn't right to send me down here when I should have been left with my Det right now, especially with the hospital so busy and now my team is a man short. There's a lot of shit going on up there in the hospital and the workload is getting bigger with the increase in patients. This pisses me off, but I will get back, it might take a day or two but it will happen. Once I finished my coffee, I went and found Lt. McCormick and we talked about what tasks we had to do for the day ahead. Then I drove her down to the UNHQ, where she was going to try and see how she could get in with the HQ and work with them to advocate for our Operation Passage people up in Mareru, hopefully to help our group get a voice in the daily operations for food and supplies coming in from Canada and some cargo space on the aircraft.

I just sat in the main area in the foyer of the UN Headquarters and watched CNN while I was waiting for the lieutenant. While I was waiting there at the UNHQ, WO Frank showed up and when he saw me, he came over to talk. As we spoke, he told me that I wasn't really needed here, he would tell them to send me back to the milk factory in Mareru. I was so excited I didn't hide it either and as soon as I saw Lt. McCormick, I told her that I was going to be sent back to Mareru as soon as we could arrange for it. At this point I would have hitchhiked or taken a food convoy, whatever, I just wanted to be out of here by today or tomorrow morning.

After she had a few more meetings here at the UNHQ, I drove her back to the stadium and thanked her for trying to get me back to my Det. She knows it's where I must be, where I want to be. She doesn't need a babysitter, it's an insult to have me at her side if we are to be here for another few months, an insult to both of us.

After this, I just relaxed. A little later in the morning, WO Martell showed up from Mareru to do some business and I mentioned to him that WO Frank said I was no longer needed here. He replied that he would see what could be done to take me back with him tomorrow. The rest of the day I just took it easy and laid down in the afternoon and had a nap. Later I called back to Petawawa and spoke to my roommate to check on my rent and bills to make sure all was ok. Afterwards, I went to the area where the engineers were and spoke to Kenny Sollazzo, Joe Hardy, and some of the other guys here from 4 Engineer Support Regiment and others at the Unit Medical Station. I went for a run at supper, running for five km so it wasn't too bad with the thin air and getting fatigued at this altitude. I think we are at a couple thousand feet above sea level. So now I'll write a letter to my mom and have a coffee. I think bedtime will come early today, so I can get this day behind me and head back to Mareru tomorrow.

Monday, 22 August

I awoke early and packed all my kit. I am out of here today one way or another and on my way back to the guys in my detachment. After packing I got washed and had a coffee with my breakfast of Mefloquine and vitamins. It wasn't a bad way to start the day knowing I'll be back in Mareru later today. I walked Lt. McCormick down to the UNHQ for the last time. She is staying here for the day to work and will get escorted back later. I watched a bit of CNN before leaving. It's amazing how sexy and newsworthy this whole Rwanda thing is. It's all the rage on the news, when just a few weeks ago no one cared or would commit troops to stop the genocide! Funny how this works.

I'll be leaving this afternoon back for Mareru, back to 2 Fd Amb. I guess I could have stayed here in Kigali for a while in the comfort of the Amahoro Stadium, but I can't do this. I understand that Lt. McCormick is glad that there was someone she knew from the unit here, but she's also got WO Wayne Frank, our logistics warrant officer, who is also here from the unit taking care of the logistics side of the house. She'll be fine. I just don't want to sit here and take the easy way out while I'm in Rwanda. No thanks, that's not my style, I'm a worker bee and need to get back and rejoin the guys in my detachment. Anyway, it's only 09:00 and I'm bored to death, I'll drop a line after.

I visited with Kenny Sollazzo for a while, and we talked a little about how this war happened, how I spent thirteen years as a reserve field engineer recce sergeant but had to enroll as a no hook private. Still pisses me off when I think about this, but at the time I needed just to get into the military and have a job to pay off my student loans, so here I am. I met Sgt. Columbus, a mechanic from my unit, he just arrived from the milk factory about 10:30 and has a few things to do this morning, coming back for me later on his way back to Mareru. Anyway, I spent the rest of the morning with WO Frank shopping at the local market, looking for artifacts and carvings, but I really didn't buy anything. There wasn't anything I wanted right now, plus I didn't need the extra weight in my kit.

I went to the kitchen and grabbed a quick bite for lunch and then helped myself to a few more pieces of fresh fruit and groceries to take back to the guys in Mareru, filling my pockets up and taking it in my backpack. We are on hard rations and will most likely be for the whole time we are here, so this will be a nice treat for them. Sgt. Columbus returned after lunch and we then were off to 3 CSG to pick up some supplies, leaving for Mareru immediately afterwards. It was about 15:00 when we left, I finally got back to the milk factory at 17:00.

I went back to where my bed space was in the corner of the warehouse, and my bed was still there, no one had pushed me out yet. Tim and the guys were between shifts, so then I placed a small loaf of bread and the fruit that I had liberated from the UN kitchen in Kigali on each of their beds. Once the guys finished their shift and returned, I spoke to Tim Ralph for awhile, seeing how the last two days went, and he told me about the sudden rainstorm that flooded the entire hospital complex. The day after the torrential rain, they had to stop accepting and screening patients at the main gate, only taking the most seriously ill and injured, telling others less seriously ill they would have to wait. I guess they went in to a quick-fix phase with everyone on the ground all hands-on deck, trying to save valuable medical supplies, equipment, and the pharmacy as well as continuing the care for the inpatients, until the water receded. Then everyone turned their attention to cleaning the wards, which were contaminated with soil and mud and biohazards. The engineers have begun to dig a moat around the hospital to help with drainage for future rain. I guess they were open for business the very next day with lots of work.

Tim spoke about next shift, which is tomorrow morning and what he wants me to do. Then I had a look at some of my mail that arrived. As I checked the mail, I noticed some bills that didn't seem to be getting paid. I had automatic deduction and finally realized that something was wrong with my chequing account. I would have to wait until tomorrow to sort this out with Rejean Michel, one of the administration clerks here with us, who could help me with the bank back in Canada. I decided to call my roommate but couldn't get a hold of him. I know he is getting ready to go to Croatia and is busy with his unit preparing for exercises and their upcoming deployment. There was also a parcel from the Holy Redeemer Convent in Sydney, Nova Scotia as well, dated August 13, 1994. It was from Sister Catherine MacDonald. My mom works there as a nursing assistant, but she never told me about giving my address out to the sisters at the convent. I opened the parcel and within it were some 200 brightly-coloured rosaries. On top of them was a letter addressed to me, I opened it and began reading:

August 13, 1994

Dear Derrick,

Your dear mom is a very special friend of mine. I just got your address from her because I wanted to send some long-overdue rosaries. They are blessed and will bring a special bit of hope for those to whom you may have an opportunity to give them. (Our rosary makers say a prayer for all those who use our rosaries.)

You and your brave comrades are in our prayers. May Our Lady send her angels to help you at all times. A little prayer to your guardian will be a source of courage to you, I know. Our Blessed Lord is near you every time you minister to one of these wounded and perhaps dying as a result of war. It will help you to have lots of courage if you can picture yourself smiling into the eyes of Christ, as you smile, in spite of all sorts of danger, at the one you are helping to overcome pain and anguish. God bless you! I'll send my guardian angel often to intervene. You are with Our Lady's help and protection!

Love and prayers, dear "Angel of Mary,"
your mom's friend, Sister Catherine MacDonald, C.N.D.

P.S. I'll send more rosaries later on. This is all we have on hand, and the rosary makers are on vacation.

This was an unexpected gift, but I was glad to have gotten it and thought I would bring it over to Father Bosse right away. I thought it might give him something to smile about and he would have the rosaries to take next time we went to a local church to do a Mass.

Tuesday, 23 August

I was up at 06:30, got washed, dressed, and had a coffee and got ready for the day. It is good to be back with the guys and to take on some responsibilities again at the hospital. I just hope that if some other tasking such as escorting officers to Kigali comes up, that someone else gets picked! It doesn't make sense that I even went with Lt. McCormick two days ago, especially when I am in a detachment. There are others who are not assigned yet, so one of them could have been designated to accompany her.

We went to work at 09:00 for the shift change and took over a ward, it was just the regular smells, stink, and sickness that we usually see on the ward, nothing has changed in the short time I was away. The first thing I noticed on entering the hospital was a little girl sitting there, up in the isolation ward by herself, with Padre Bosse speaking to her in French. He looked sad and somewhat disgusted. I think this place is wearing on him. The little one was probably about ten years old or so and had Down Syndrome. I went in for a moment to speak with the padre, and I looked under the blanket over her feet and saw that her toes were almost burnt off. It was horrifying. Despite her injuries, she had this beautiful smile on her face and never acknowledged the pain her feet must have been causing her. I asked Fr. Bosse what happened, he said he believed they had stuck her feet in the fire to burn out the evil spirits; they wanted to burn out the Down Syndrome he guessed. I can tell that this has shaken Fr. Bosse's spirit…mine as well. I don't know what to think, this is where some of their ways and beliefs clash with much of the first world thought on medicine and care for the disabled.

I spoke with Padre Bosse for a few minutes and then carried on to my shift on the ward, still in shock with what I had seen.

On the ward it was a busy start to the shift. I had an AIDS patient and I don't think he is long for this world. I also had a couple of patients to administer IV antibiotics to and it's a lot of work just to make sure I give the right drugs to the right patients. One of the girls with the French group from 5 Field Ambulance had a needle stick today I heard. It was with a needle which had been used on a Rwandan patient for an injection. That's scary with the diseases here in Rwanda. I hope she's going to be all right, but it's going to be a long few months for her waiting to be cleared of any infections with the bloodwork.

We finished at 15:30 or so and came back to the milk factory. There were a couple of the guys who asked me if I could cut their hair. So, I borrowed some clippers and cut a few heads of hair. Gary Vienneau wasn't too happy with my job, he joked and called me a butcher. He's losing his hair anyway so I'm just helping him along the way. Afterwards, I took a shower myself to clean off all the hair from all the clipping I did. I ate supper and went to the front of the milk factory where the Sigs were, hoping to get on the Inmarsat satellite telephone to speak with my roommate, to see how he was and if there was any important mail for me. I finally got through this time and spoke to Jean Claude. He said all my bills are in order, so it seems the administration guys here have it all under control.

After I got off the phone with J.C., Tim got our Det all together for an "O" group and told us what was going on with the number of patients we've seen, the number of inpatients we currently have, and the deaths up to this point. He also said that some of the officers and senior NCOs think that we're all having a "nervous breakdown" in our Det, which is bullshit. Myself, I think it is they who are feeling the stress and that they're using us to get a slow-down of these insane working hours. For sure we are all tired and stressed with this schedule and the types of things we are seeing, as well as the work to rest cycle being unbalanced. They should talk to whoever is in charge of this schedule, maybe question them on it and see how they could function after a couple weeks of sleep deprivation. I really don't know why it is not being stopped. Anyway, I guess tomorrow I'm going to Gisenyi with the padre to visit a church and I'll help him out by driving him and being there should he need anything. It's now 23:00 so I'll head to bed.

Wednesday, 24 August

We finished our last shift today in early afternoon then we are off the hospital wards for the next thirty-two hours. It will be good to have this break. After the end of today's shift there was another short meeting, with the two nursing officers we work for. They wanted to talk and check in with us. I guess that people in the command team think we are stressed out and wanted them to have another meeting with us. I don't really think we are; I think it's just dissatisfaction with the ongoing situation here with the shift schedule as well as the distribution of work amongst the three medical platoons. I am unsure of why they really need to ask us why we are stressed out and why they can't see the problem. It makes no sense at all. Those who make the schedule clearly have no understanding of how to organize and work people, especially since they themselves most likely only work the eight hours during the day and are off until next morning. They have a pretty cushy, low-stress job here in comparison to us if you ask me, but for them to start emphasizing that we are having stress issues…get a life and look inward at what we are being asked to do. We were told during the meeting that some social workers and a psychologist, the Critical Incident Stress Debriefing (CISD) team, will be here in the next couple of weeks sometime, so we can all debrief together, hold hands, and feel good about what we've done here so far.

I changed into my physical training clothes then had supper, and just talked for a bit. I wasn't feeling good, so I got a shower and went to bed a bit early. We'll see what tomorrow brings.

Thursday/Friday, 25-26 August

I was actually going to sleep in today, but instead when I got up, I was asked if I wanted to go into the local mountains with the guys from the Commando unit. It was Sgt. Davies group from the 3 CDO platoon that was going up for the morning. He asked if any of us were into doing some exploring around the mountains around here. I was certainly game to see the jungle around our local area. I said sure and went for a walk with one of the sections in the Rwandan mountains around our location.

Sgt. Davies gave us a briefing and some Rules of Engagement (ROEs), I don't remember ever getting any since we got here, but this was good so we knew what to do should we have to fire our weapons. We lined up single file in the compound and then left heading across the street from the milk factory and then south east, where we immediately ascended a steep hill. Once we got to the top, we entered what was left of the jungle. Most of the Rwandan jungle was deforested by foreign countries for its wood. In exchange, these countries built and paved roads through the country. Kind of sad because it chewed up most of the mountain gorillas' range and food.

I thought I was in shape but just walking up the hill had me winded a bit already. It's understandable, though, because we are a couple thousand feet above sea level.

We used machetes to work our way through the jungle. There were stinging nettles running against our legs and they hurt. There were Rwandan kids in shorts following us, but they seemed not to be affected. As we walked, the kids were taking leaves occasionally, rubbing them on their legs, and carrying on. Whatever it is I will take it and use it. Sgt. Davies thinks it must be aloe vera plant.

It was a hard walk, but it's good to know what's out there around the area we live in. As they say, time on recce is never lost. It took five hours in total, out and back. After the walk we came back, washed up, ate, and got some sleep for tonight's shift.

We got up around 22:00 and got ready to go back to the hospital. Everyone looks really tired; the day and a half off really weren't enough. So off we went to work on the ward at 23:00 hours and we worked until 07:00. It was a long, cold night and we lost another baby tonight. Lately I find some of the guys are beginning to take it personally in caring for the patients who die. We are totally involved in all aspects of caring for our patients, especially with the children, and when we lose a patient, especially a child, I can see the guys become quiet. I am so tired of all this misery.

We finished at 07:00 and then went back to the sleeping area. I can't even eat properly because I'm sick of eating canned rations. All we ate were rations for the entire six months I was in Somalia, and here we are now, again eating them. Unlike Somalia, however, there is no excuse for us to be eating like this, when the UN troops in Kigali are eating fresh rations like kings and can't even send a little fresh fruit or bread our way. That isn't what I expect from other Canadians. I understand they are on a UN mission, but we are all still Canadian and should look out for one another. This is something our military should be ashamed of. I don't understand how one unit treats another like this in a theatre of operation, no matter if we are UN or not, it's still a shame. We are supposed to be all one army, all Canadian.

I got washed, used the bathroom, and went right to bed. We had another shift in eight hours at 15:00.

We got up again at 14:00, grabbed a quick wash and shave to clean up before supper, then it was back to work for 15:00. It seems that every day is a Monday. I am losing track of the days and of time…not that I mind doing what we do, but I think there is a better way to do business with the running of the troops.

One of the things noticed as Op Passage has been progressing, was that we're seeing more and more patients with intestinal parasites. A few of the doctors came up with this treatment plan to give every single patient in the hospital Vermox, a drug which causes the chemistry of the body to become extremely toxic to parasites. Once Vermox is taken, the intestinal parasites leave their now-toxic human hosts through any of the body's orifices, escaping the toxic effects of the drug. So here we were now, going to treat every inpatient in the hospital, whether they medically needed it or not.

I had been in theatre a few weeks prior to everyone arriving on the recce and during that time had had opportunity to find a manual of African medicine from Medicine Sans Frontier (MSF). The recommended protocol for treating intestinal parasites in this book was that only if it was causing a blockage in a patient's bowel would you treat…otherwise don't treat.

There were two problems with this plan to treat everyone in our facility. One was that we had about 150 inpatients and in the wisdom of the moment, once all the patients were treated, we were going to increase the inpatient workload incredibly high with the extra need to care for the unnecessary vomiting and diarrhea. The second issue was that intestinal parasites are endemic here in Africa, in the soil, water, and food chain. So, unless you were going to purify the water for the rest of their lives, give everyone in Africa shoes, and use insecticides on the food, we were totally wasting our time and efforts. But even though they were not thinking this through with a common-sense approach, it was decided to treat everyone at our facility at once, and it would be mostly the already-overworked medics and nurses there, who would have to clean up all the vomit and diarrhea and pick up all these disgusting worms the medication would cause to escape. This was an unnecessary stress in an already stressful situation.

In a last-ditch effort to somehow stop the insanity this would cause, I showed one of the nurses in our section the book I had found, pleading my case, and hoping they would take the book and show those who had ordered the treatment of intestinal parasites. I emphasized that it was a book on third-world medicine from Medicine Sans Frontier and it had all the treatment regimens they recommended for sub-Saharan Africa, and information on how to set up triage and tenting systems. It was a wonderful book and certainly of immense value to any organization arriving in Africa. That's why when I saw it, I decided to pick it up, but my words, and my enthusiasm for the techniques and treatment protocols within the book and for the book itself, fell on deaf ears.

As the night began, we were slowly but steadily overwhelmed with the expulsion of helminths from the patients' bodies. It was disgusting. There were tape worms coming out of every orifice the patients had; rectums and mouths. They were sneezing them out noses. We were busy all night long in a futile battle with the worms. The treatment had started a shit tsunami, diarrhea and worms were everywhere, so we were trying to keep up with this as well as doing our regular work with the other patients; medications, dressing changes, and IVs.

I was so pissed off as I had mentioned the MSF book I had found on the recce and my thoughts on this treatment to a couple of nurses and doctors prior to this taking place. I spoke to my supervisor, saying to him that it doesn't make any sense to treat worms, especially if all of our patients have bare feet and will be walking out of here in a couple of days only to get infected again. What a waste of time, of treatment, of drugs—we were busy enough without a shitty make-work project.

The insanity of this was too much, so with the bumper crop of worms, some of us began a "who has the longest helminth" contest, and we would put them into a kidney basin and measure them against one another for length. One of the guys had a playful streak in him and came up with an idea. Unbeknownst to any of us, he snuck out the back of the hospital and ran back to his bed space. He took with him a sterile kidney basin, opened a can of spaghetti, took out the longest string of pasta he could find, and placed it in the basin. Returning to the hospital, he walked in where a few of the guys were standing and joking about the worms and who had the longest up to that point. He made an announcement to get their attention, telling them he thought he had the longest intestinal worm so far during the shift. Then with a clean glove on, he picked up the spaghetti, which everyone else thought was a worm, and held it up saying, "Check this one out, I think it's the longest." One of the other guys spoke up and said that it wasn't and held his parasite up to compare. So then, taking the string of spaghetti, the first guy tilted his head back and slurped the "worm" down, to everyone's disgust. It was a macabre but extremely funny moment, one of many we used in order to lighten the mood in a difficult situation.

> *Unfortunately, the intestinal parasite incident wouldn't be the only such misadventure during our time in Rwanda, but this was the way it seemed the tour was going. Often, decisions didn't make any sense, and even when you could logically show the most likely outcome, you were not listened to because the decision was made, and come hell or high water, they were going through with the plan. At times it felt like we were being made to watch a preventable car crash. The worm incident only lasted a couple of days and then it quietly stopped and went away. I'm not sure what made it stop, but it stopped very quickly and suddenly we weren't treating for worms anymore, crisis over.*

Other than the worms, the evening went well for all of us and it went by very quickly. All my patients were good and thankfully no one died. My only slightly hard case was a sick baby with a NG tube in. I had to give him 10cc of oral rehydration solution every thirty minutes. He was a lot of care but seemed ok as we ended our shift at 23:00 and then went back to the milk factory for a little sleep. We will see what tomorrow brings.

Saturday, 27 August

We got off at 23:00 hrs last night and went back to our bed spaces. I really needed some good solid sleep. This morning there was some mail; a few letters from my mom and aunt, but other than this mail today, it was slack. It gave me the time to finish writing up the letter for Cpl. Scott Clucas and MCpl. Rick Melanson, for their help a couple weeks back at the mass casualty accident. I got this done at around 12:00 and gave it to Tim to pass in through the chain of command. I'm hoping that these two guys get recognized, especially after what they did that night at the accident scene. After this, I had lunch and then went back to my sleeping area. I had an old American rations tin can that was used to hold cookies. It's a big tin box, so I went and made hinges for the top and found a way to lock it, got a can of red spray paint from the supply guys and painted it red, finally writing "MAIL" on it. I then put it in the eating area so there would be a place for people to put mail, which would be emptied at the end of each night by the administration people.

After this I didn't do too much else, just found things to do and keep busy. There's always something to do, unless you're lazy.

Sunday, 28 August

Woke up this morning and while sitting having breakfast could hear a low buzzing sound coming from outside. I got up from my bed and went out the back door of the milk factory to see what was going on. Walking to the front of the building, I heard what sounded like singing in the distance, along with whistles blowing and boots hitting the ground in rhythm; left, right, left, right. Then it got louder and coming up over the hill from the RPF camp just down the road from our camp, we could see six platoons or more of RPF soldiers running by our compound, doing their physical training, though it was more likely a show of force to intimidate us, I was thinking. Whatever it was for, it was impressive to see how fit these troops were, carrying heavy weapons and running so easily.

Today is the last of the eight-hour shifts for the next thirty-two hours. We were working from 07:00 hrs to15:00 hrs today and it was a busy day. I don't know why, but it seemed to get away from us all. A while later there was an emergency, which came to our front gates and it just seemed to be my tipping point. Morale was now at its lowest and although I held out hope it would go no lower, unfortunately, I would later see it would.

Overall it had been just a regular, normal day when in the late afternoon someone came to our treatment area with a small child in their arms. A mother had brought in her child, who was in distress. The child was very underweight and looked extremely ill and had apparently already been in cardiac arrest. Then, while in the screening room he went into cardiac arrest again. I think most in the room knew that this innocent child most likely didn't have much of a chance and that he was probably better off.

When I heard the commotion, I went up to see what was going on. I felt sad for what was happening, but I also felt a calmness within myself that the baby was out of his misery. Then suddenly, out of the blue, one of the MOs arrived and said something like, "Out of my way, I need to get this baby breathing again." he took the little guy, resuscitated him and worked on him for a while doing CPR, directing someone to bag him (ventilate). The doctor worked hard to revive the baby, getting a heartbeat and breathing back. As he did this, I looked around the room, and could feel no one was happy with this intervention. In normal circumstances we all should have been glad for this turn of events, but no one really said anything, there was no cheering or any hallelujah, just a sense of deflation as this child symbolized what was taking place at that time in Rwanda; children dying needlessly.

Although the child was unknown to the doctor, the doctor's heroic actions on this afternoon affected everyone who was working the hospital tent that day, and not just for that day. There were long-term repercussions that many would have years after this futile attempt, which only extended this child's life of misery for another two days.

We were not really a hospital, we were more of a walk-in clinic with a no surgical capability, having a few doctors, nurses, and medics. We didn't have full diagnostic abilities such as a full laboratory or imaging department. We didn't have all the equipment one would need to sustain this little guy such as pediatric ICU drugs, or ventilators, or other equipment. I wished for a better outcome, but this child lived only for a couple days more before finally succumbing to his fate and dying.

This death really bothered me. I was so pissed as were as many of the other medics I worked with. We all thought pretty much the same thing, that all that was done by resuscitating this child was to prolong his misery and that of his mother. His fate had been sealed no matter the intervention. I think this is where the conflicted feeling for many came from, in that there is always hope, so that's why we were sent here and that's why we try. I understood the desire to keep him alive, I understood we came here to give the best medicine possible, but on the other hand I also understood and thought that we couldn't just click our heels and be back in Canada with all the medical tools at our fingertips, we were in a third-world country without the ability to incubate or ventilate. The ability to sustain life was not at the same level as it would be in Canada. I understood the desire of everyone here to provide first-world medicine in a third-world country, because that's where we were only a few short weeks ago back in Canada at our hospitals and clinics with diagnostic tools and medicines at our fingertips. The transition in changing our view on when, and if, to intervene as we would back home in Canada and when to allow someone to die in Rwanda, was a difficult pill to swallow for all of us. So many ethical decisions were to be made throughout this deployment by those involved.

The doctors, nurses, and medics did no wrong; they all did what they were trained for and did an excellent job of it, but our lack of knowing what equipment we needed, or what injuries or illnesses we were going to see, and not fully understanding that we were only political dressing for the wounds of the world that had sat on its hands, as General Dallaire had screamed for help and the UN and world had turned their backs. We were but a visual representation of the token response that countries all over the world sent after the slaughter. Being placed in a desperate situation didn't help us either. In the death of any child there is no wrong with an attempt to save their life, there is only sadness, no matter how matter-of-fact it is for the daily lives of those we were caring for in this unwinnable situation we were in that day, and the days to follow within the walls of our hospital tent.

But this event also showed me something very powerful. It showed that in the doctor's actions, and in the actions of all of us deployed to help these people, that we were colour-blind. It made no difference the colour of the skin, the status of the person we were caring for, or if they were Tutsi or Hutu. This little boy was treated as well as we would treat any child back home in Canada, with the expectation that every attempt would be made to save his life no matter what. The message was clear, that every single life which came to our field hospital was valuable and worthy of saving. This alone was a testament to the care and compassion of the men and women I was sent to Rwanda with.

After the shift I went and spoke to Fr. Bosse about the baby and he said that we've now lost about twenty patients so far, most of them babies. There's not much we can do about this. All we can do is our best and when that's not enough then we should give them dignity in their dying, that's all. That's what I think anyway. I asked Fr. Bosse about him doing Mass after supper tonight, and he said he would be doing a Mass up towards the front of the building. After this I had lunch and took it easy. I spoke to Randy and asked him about helping me organize the Terry Fox run for the 11th of September. I think it would be good to do it for the guys and gals here to take their minds off this place, and it would look good back home if people see we are able to do this while caring for the people here in Rwanda. I think what we will do is whatever monies are raised, we will make two big receipts and pull names from a hat with the names of those who donated. I don't want the tax deduction as it's a group effort, so I think this would be the fairest way, so someone benefits tax-wise from the donation.

Just took it easy the rest of the day and kept myself occupied, as I was waiting for Mass tonight after supper. When I went after supper to the front of the building for the church service, Fr. Bosse was there and those in attendance were all French. Fr. Bosse asked me if I would mind if he did the prayers in French. I know the prayers off by heart anyway, so it's no matter to me French or English, I will understand and am able to follow along. It was a good Mass and seemed to pick up the spirits of the few of us in attendance. Afterwards, I spoke with the padre about going to a church located near Gisenyi next week and conducting a Mass there. I can't wait. It should be good.

Monday, 29 August

I slept in today, really needed that with the last shift. When I finally woke up at 10:00 hrs, I just got dressed and went for a coffee. Today was a quiet day so I just took it easy, wrote a few letters, talked for a while, and a few of the guys asked me to cut their hair. They wanted to buy me a pop or something for doing this, but I told them I am not a professional so I couldn't take anything for cutting their hair. I said what they could do was put a dollar in the pot for the Terry Fox Run we were planning. Most of them did and so now I'm raising a few extra dollars every time I cut hair.

I wanted to get some sleep this afternoon but there was a compulsory talk on tuberculosis or helminths or something like this by one of the doctors who had come up from the stadium in Kigali. I didn't understand why no one could understand why they should allow the twelve guys going on shift the ability to get some sleep prior to being up all night, instead of having to sit and listen to someone talk about worms or TB or whatever. This was fucking stupid. Any of our doctors could have done this task, we didn't need a guest speaker. We are picking worms out of the arses and mouths of the kids on the ward now, so I really don't care much else about the life cycle of a worm! All I care about is that we've got a shift from 23:00 hrs to 07:00 hrs and our section needs sleep. This is the stupidity of this organization; we are working eight-hour shifts since we got here, and now they want us to sit here with no sleep and listen to this doctor from Kigali talk about worms and parasites, stealing our downtime, so afterwards we can go back to the hospital dead tired and make some medical errors, maybe kill a few patients in our sleep-deprived state! I am unsure of where these decisions are being made but they are affecting me and the guys around me.

As soon as the lecture was over, the guys in my Det went immediately back to our sleeping area to grab a little sleep prior to our shift. It wouldn't be much, only a few hours, but better than nothing. I got up at 22:00 hours had a quick coffee, and then got ready for the shift at the hospital.

When we came on shift tonight, I found out that the baby who was resuscitated the other day had died. He had already been out of his misery but was brought back to enjoy a couple more days of misery. This is so crazy. We are trying to operate as if we are back in Canada without the same equipment or resources. I understand our desire to give the refugees the best possible care, but maybe we have to realistically look at what resources we have and what we can do with them.

We were also told that disposable gloves are now a hot commodity and that we were to only wear one pair for the entire shift and to make do. We are running out of gloves because we are chewing through them the same way we do back in Canada, changing them every time between patients, after a procedure, or changing a dressing. People are forgetting that we just can't walk down to the local pharmacy and pick up more when we run out and the supply chain isn't the fastest. So now we have resorted to wearing the same disposable gloves all shift. Maybe if one breaks, we change them, but for now, in between patients, we are washing the gloves in a wash basin of Chlorhexidine, while still wearing them on our hands. For now, this will have to do. I know it's no one fault, but I'm tired of it all. We might as well be wearing those thick industrial gloves my mom uses to clean the toilet back home. They're just as clean when doing dressing changes or feeding babies and they're easier to wash between patients.

I had another little boy die on me tonight. It really bothered me as he was only five or six years old, just like the last fellow who died on me a week ago. Sadly, I am becoming numb to these happenings and the routine in notifying the nurse and doctor to pronounce him dead; the going to the milk factory and getting Father Bosse; the process that goes with the preparation of the grave and body for burial before giving the child Last Rites; and the final, sad detail of burying him and filling in the grave. Sadly, I found the rest of the evening pretty easy as I carried on with my shift.

After my shift was over at 07:00 hrs, I went and grabbed a shower then sat on the grass out back of the milk factory. I was just sitting on there with my back leaning against the wall talking with my friend, Michelle. As we sat there talking, there were some of the off-duty guys and girls playing volleyball while others sat along the wall and watched. Local children, from the village, were along the wire fence watching and giggling and smiling at all this activity. Small birds were flying in and out of the bushes close to the building, and I could feel a nice warm breeze across my face.

While Michelle and I were sitting there, someone unexpectedly brought over a little bird and laid it down in front of us asking, "What do you think we should do with this little guy?" The bird was a little African chickadee and it had fallen into our wastewater, which was full of oil and human waste. As the bird sat in front of us you could tell it was weak. Its eyes were slow to open, and it bobbled back and forth with barely enough energy to stand and its beak was moving but not a sound was made. It was dying from the wastewater it had flown into.

I was frozen with what to do but knew what needed to be done. I thought to myself, *why did she bring this bird over and place it in front of us? Couldn't have she figured out what to do with it herself?* But as with everyone else here who had been working in the hospital, she was probably tired of death and the sadness we had been witnessing since out arrival.

I looked at Michelle, then back at this poor, dying creature, not doing anything. Walking past us and seeing what was unfolding with the little bird, another soldier I served with in Somalia saw what we were looking at in front of us this small bird who was slowly dying. Looking over at me he said, "What are you going to do about this, Derrick? Aren't you going to do the right thing?" Although I knew what should be done, what had to be done, I was tired from everything I had been seeing and doing in the hospital since our arrival in Rwanda. I couldn't seem to find it in myself to put this little guy out of his misery. Rob then looked at me and paused for a moment, shaking his head in disappointment for my inaction. Then, without warning, he swiftly lifted his foot and with his heel stomped on the bird, again, again, and again until finally it was dead. Then with the toe of his boot, he moved it back and forth, filling in the indent from his boot with some earth. The indent had now become the bird's grave, and he patted it down and walked away.

It would have seemed a cruel thing to do in any other situation, but it was a far crueller thing doing nothing here in this place, as I had been doing just sitting there, frozen with inaction. In the end this was more humane because the bird was going to die, and if we did nothing it would just suffer longer and die a slow and painful death. I had dealt with so much death and suffering the last couple of months since my arrival, this little bird was the last straw for me today.

Rob looked at me once more and left, once again shaking his head in disgust at my inability to do anything. I got up and looked at the freshly disturbed earth where the bird lay and unable to say anything, I looked at Michelle, sadly nodded to her, and then went back to my bed space where I sat with my head in my hands and sobbed. I had nothing left to give. The last six weeks here in Rwanda were finally catching up with me.

Tuesday, 30 August

I awoke at 13:00 hrs and got ready for 15:00 hrs. I hope tonight will not be another bad night. The other sections are now calling us "The Angels of Death," because it seems to everyone that whenever we come on shift the patients seemingly wait until we are there, and then they die. We are then left to do all the work around getting them ready to bury, getting the padre, digging the grave, wrapping the kid in a blanket and putting him in a plastic bag so the dogs won't dig him up, going to the graveside with the mother and padre, then filling in the grave and finally washing your hands and going back to work on the ward. It's all just too surreal and absurd but a regular day now in

Rwanda. It's downright depressing, but we are wearing it as a badge of honour that patients are waiting for us, so we can comfort them in their hour of death.

There was a man brought in today who had been attacked with a machete and as he was trying to defend himself, he put his left arm in the air in front of him as the assailant was coming down with the machete and cut off his hand clean at the wrist, continuing with the blade and cutting into his cheekbone. He is in the hospital now and stable. I think they are sending him off tomorrow to the hospital in Kigali. Every time I see these types of wounds, I am still shocked back to reality by what took place here over the last few months.

Our shift was from 15:00 hrs to 23:00 hrs tonight and there wasn't a heavy workload with the inpatients on the ward. At 20:00 hrs Tim let Ron and me go back to the sleeping area. I went to sleep at around 23:00 hrs.

Wednesday, 31 August

I awoke at 06:00 hrs got washed and just putted around. Holy shit, I am beginning to feel drained. I hope I'm not getting sick, but I'm feeling like maybe I am or maybe things are just catching up with me? It was quiet as all the guys were still sleeping, so I slid my pants and shoes on and went out for a coffee to see who was around. It was nice, there was no one, not a soul around. Anyway, we are working in the screening tent today, so I guess the guys will get up soon, we are pretty used to getting up, dressing, eating, and getting to work on short notice, making the most of the little time we have to sleep.

When Tim Ralph awoke at 07:00 hrs he told me that they had lost two more last night. One was Chris's patient, a four or five-year-old little boy. The other was Kelley's, a man in his forties. Death never stops here. I think this is getting hard on all of us at this point, everyone has had multiple patients to bury since we got here, and it never gets any easier. I find that some of us are getting more protective about doing the whole burial thing, especially with kids, that's ok for now considering where we are.

With these two deaths during these first weeks of operation, we quickly learned that hypothermia was going to be an issue in our hospital tent, so much so it was affecting the patients' well being and outcomes. Who would ever have thought that in the middle of Africa patients would die due to the cold? However, with being four thousand feet above sea level in the Virunga Mountain range at night, the temperature can go down to zero, resulting in the hospital being extremely cold and difficult on the patients who are having issues with temperature regulation due to their injuries or illness. We lost a few babies and it was becoming more and more difficult on all of us as the days passed. The unit sent an urgent message back to Canada for an immediate operational requirement, requesting a Yukon heater for the hospital, but this would take a week or so to arrive from Canada. In the meantime, one of our electricians, MCpl Mark Tracey, had an idea from when he was a kid and he had helped his father or grandfather during the spring hatching of chickens. He and a couple of the other engineers thought of how to build an incubator for the orphans we had, using wood and parts from around the milk factory.

With this knowledge from Mark's childhood in mind, they got to work with using some scrap plywood to make a simple wooden box, and installed a light source for heat, and a humidifier, socket, and cord. Finally, to complete the incubator, they needed a door we could open to have access to the babies inside. Mark remembered that he'd seen a door on a piece of machinery inside the milk factory, which was on the bottling machine. The door was a perfect fit and had a window so we could observe the babies through it.

Every time we opened that big orange door for the remainder of the tour, we would think of the ingenuity and dedication that MCpl Tracey and the other electricians had shown on making this for our most vulnerable of patients.

However, with the cold at night there was still an issue with the older children and adults trying to keep warm, so the electricians weren't finished. They took one of our fridges and somehow reversed the polarity to make it into a blanket warmer, an ingenious idea, and at the time very much needed. Thanks to the actions of the electricians and engineers, many lives in our care were saved because of their resourcefulness, and for this we were grateful.

There are times, and I don't know how or why, but it seems I've once again lost a couple of days. Everything is so busy with working on the ward, and then trying to eat, wash, and sleep before it's back on the ward. The days seem to run into one another with the eight-hour shift schedule again the last week, so that every day is a Monday. I can't see the end of it. There's not much really going on that's ever changing, but really there is so much going on for the guys with our Det and all the work here in the hospital with non-stop patients, running, feeding, medications, and the cycle of this every day.

For today, we are in the screening tent. This should be good; we will see what happens in the screening tent today. The lineup was crazy outside the main gate and it's like that every day, so I guess we will be busy today. There was this man who showed up with one of his feet that was gigantic, it looked painful. Chris took him as a patient and did the screening with the interpreter and then spoke to Dr. Keeler, the doctor that was with us on screening, and WO Tardiff. Dr. Keeler told Chris that the guy had an infection, or a parasite and it was causing elephantiasis and he would eventually lose the foot. The patient was put on antibiotics and Chris was given the task of scrubbing and dressing the wounds on his feet. It was funny, but not, because when Chris began to wash the man's feet, he looked up and said something like "Holy shit guys, look, his toes are falling off!" As he was scrubbing the dirt and corruption off the foot, a couple more of the toes popped off. Anyway, Chris has a great attitude and ability to see the lighter side of things. It helps us all, I think, to get through each shift, joking around with each other.

I had a patient with pneumonia and took care of that with the doctor, then there was a little baby that needed to be admitted. I started a butterfly IV on him and a naso-gastric feeding tube and got him and his mom to the ward. There was another young guy who came in with his throat cut from ear to ear and later another guy with a deep machete wound to his face. Both of these were old wounds which needed to be debrided, cleansed, then given antibiotics for the infection. The doctor started the antibiotics and told us what to do for the care and treatment of these two patients. It was nasty, but this is only a little taste of the craziness that went on here for a couple of months. We were still seeing injuries on the ward and now here in screening from the results of the war.

All in all, it was a busy day, but in a different way from being in the ward with the fact that once we were done, we knew that we could close up the screening area and go back to the milk factory for the evening. Unlike the ward at the hospital, here it's was a more realistic eight hours on and then sixteen off schedule.

After we finished work, we went back to our bed spaces, got our shave kits, and washed before supper. We all sat together and ate, and then it was shower time. Today I washed with Kwellada, a shampoo to kill nits and scabies, as do many of the guys once in awhile. Most of the patients have scabies or some type of nit, and although we try to have them washed and scrubbed with anti-scabies shampoo before they come into the screening tent or hospital, we still have patient contact and each of us has possibly had scabies at least once during the tour.

After washing up, we all went to the kitchen. Tim had told us to meet him there, he wanted to get all the guys a bottle of Pepsi from Sgt. McInnis as a treat. So here we all were, all six of us having a drink tonight, talking, laughing, and enjoying a Pepsi. Just then when Tim took a big swig of his Pepsi, he suddenly goes and spits the drink in his mouth out across the room and there was this black thing going across the floor. We went over to inspect what he has spit out and here he had drunk a dead mouse and spit it out. It must have somehow found its way into the bottling factory. The Preventative Medicine Tech had told us that carbonated drinks were the safest, but after this incident with the mouse, we all lost our taste for pop. Instead of finishing my pop, I poured it out and went and had a coffee instead. The guys and gals laughed a lot and made a big deal out of this for a few minutes, but then it was time for bed. Went to bed, still not feeling good, hope it passes.

They wait patiently lined up on stretchers - Photo Chris Cormier

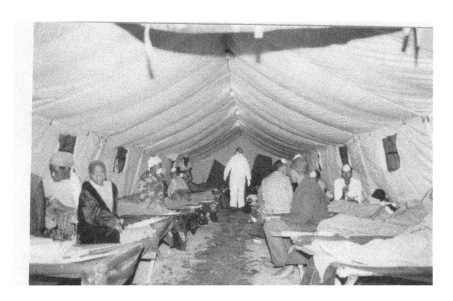

Patients admitted to ward – Photo Chris Cormier

The day the floods came -Source unknown

Local water point Field Engineers repaired – Source unknown

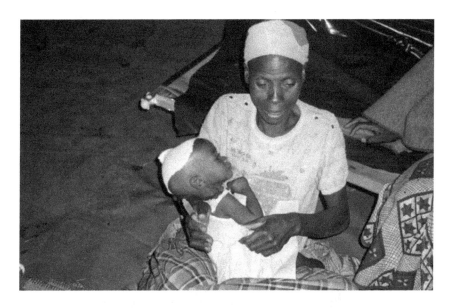

Rwandan mother with child – Source unknown

Childs grave marker – Source unknown

Hospital cemetery – Source unknown

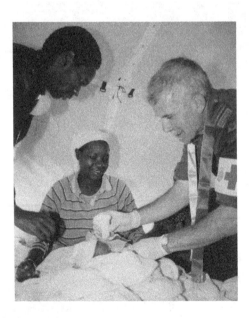

Father Whelan Bosse baptising newborn – Photo Chris Cormier

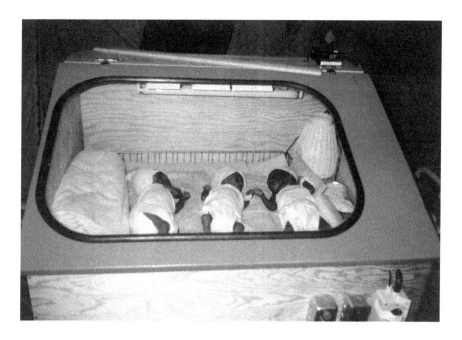

Improvised incubator designed by engineer section – Source unknown

Nyundo Cathedral– Source unknown

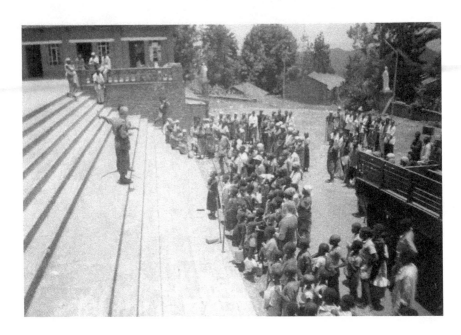

Nyundo Cathedral clean up day - Source unknown

Outreach clinic set up in Kora – Photo Chris Cormier

Author cutting interpreters' hair – Source unknown

Local craft market near the city of Gisenyi – Photo Chris Cormier

The Moth

I am but a moth, tattered and torn,
my flight meanders once airborne,
I am up, down, sideways to the ground.

I once knew a better way to fly,
but this is what's left and woe am I,
I go here and there fluttering around.

Though the flight's no longer true,
forward, towards the light, still I move,
my destination, in time, I will come to.

Derrick Nearing, MMM, CD

September 1994

Thursday - Saturday, 1-3 September

All these days run together now. It was a terrible experience I just had over the last three days. On the first of September, our Det was in the screening bay during the day, treating patients. I felt somewhat sick, but not too bad, so I kept on going. It was the regular stuff on the screening and as usual we were seeing so much dehydration and so many sick babies. Nothing hard came in as far as trauma, though, and this was a good thing, kind of a break.

We finished around 16:00 and packed it up and went back to the milk factory. Right after this I began to feel unwell. I was lying in my bed and shivering, and I could feel a sweat on. Then, for some reason I suddenly felt extreme pain and spasms in my lungs, and I began crying with the pain.

MCpl. Ralph came over to my bed space and asked me if I was ok. I looked at him and said no, that my chest and stomach were hurting badly. He told me to get dressed and took me down to the MIR we had for the staff, and I was seen by one of our doctors, Dr. Campbell. He did the usual and listened to my chest and heart, I had a low-grade fever at the time. He got me some Tylenol 3's but the pain was incredible in my chest and stomach and I was fully out bawling in pain. Dr. Campbell, along with the medics working there, got some Buscopan ready and gave this to me IV. He asked me if this had ever happened before with the chest pain and crying. I said no, not sure what that question was about, as he alluded to mental health and Somalia during his questioning. However, with the Buscopan and Tylenol, things settled down about a half hour later.

I went back to the milk factory and got a shower, then off to bed right away. I still felt so unwell that I couldn't even eat, I was just wanting to lie down and be left alone. This was about 16:30.

Then at 20:00 I couldn't breathe, it felt like cramping started in my lungs and my lungs were on fire. Every breath was painful. I was lying in my cot and began to cry, with tears running down my face. It hurt so much. Tim was in his cot and rolled over and said, "Derrick? You ok?"

I said, "No Tim, I really don't feel well."

He said, "Ok then, pal, let's go." He was going to take me back down to see Dr. Campbell again. I tried to stand up but couldn't, because it hurt too much when I tried to stand straight.

As Tim assisted me down to the MIR to be seen again, boy oh boy it hurt. Dr. Campbell saw me again and took some blood for the lab tech to run a WBC. My WBC was up to 22 and temperature was now 39.9C. Dr. Campbell looked worried, and then he started to ask Tim again about my time in Somalia. Tim confirmed that I had been there, but that was all he could offer on the question. Then Dr. Campbell asked me if this current situation with the crying and my seeming over-reaction to the chest pain had anything to do with my tour from Somalia. I told him no. I wasn't sure why he was asking me stuff like this. Obviously, I was sick, I was crying and in so much pain. I told him no, I didn't think this had anything to do with Somalia and it wasn't stress-related, it just hurt in my lungs when I took a breath in.

Although I only found out later it was serious enough, because this time I got IV morphine and more Buscopan, but it still hurt, it wasn't touching the pain. An ECG was taken and an IV started with injectable antibiotics (Abx) given. I'm not sure what they gave me, but now I had a saline lock or what is commonly called a "hep-lock" in place. I went back to my bed space and then to ground around 22:30 or so. It was a long restless night.

Friday, 2 September

The next day as I awoke, I still felt like crap from last night and all day yesterday. I am so tired with no energy, still somewhat feverish, and my lungs still feel as though they are burning. It hurts to breath. I can't eat right now, just had some water. Tim said that he was told to get me packed up with my overnight bag and that they were going to send me down to the field hospital in Kigali, so the doctors there can have a good look at me and do more complete lab and X-rays to see what's going on. I told him I was starting to feel better and after just a couple days on Abx and rest I would be ok. But they wanted me to get a good checkup with the field hospital.

I was packed up and sent down to Kigali for an X-Ray, but before I left a got another dose of IV Abx and was taken down with one of the truckers and Sgt. McInnis the kitchen officer (KO). It was the same madness on the roads all the way down to Kigali, as I watched the avalanche of humanity walking along the sides of the roads back into the country from Zaire. As we headed to Kigali, the old dead body about two km away from the milk factory was still there on the hairpin turn. He'd been there so long people had started to use him as a reference point, "You make a sharp left after the dead guy on the right." Anyway, you'd think someone would have attended to this by now. He was there when I first got here some five weeks ago.

It took about an hour and a half or so to get to Kigali and by the time we arrived I felt better already, must be the antibiotics. I went into the stadium and to the field hospital tent, which was located in the middle of the stadium. Dr. Boucher was waiting for me and took me right away. He checked everything and he saw something on the X-ray. With the lab and X-ray, he said that I had bilateral pneumococcal pneumonia and he told me he would call back to the milk factory to tell them what was on the go with me and ask what they wanted to do.

I was kept on observation for the night and given a place to sleep within the field hospital. I took advantage of the fresh rations. Too bad I had to get sick to get down to Kigali to eat fresh food, but now that I am here, I am going to get it into me. I also took this as an opportunity to grab as many apples, oranges, and bananas as I could for the troops back at the milk factory. These UN guys are living like kings here at the stadium with fresh food and twenty-four-hour access to food and drinks. It's shameful that we are only a couple hours up the road and the Op Lance leadership can't see their way to shuffle a few fresh rations to us occasionally, sad.

I ate my fill and took what my pockets could hold without being conspicuous, then after I ate lunch, I went back to the field hospital and spent some time shooting the breeze with PO1 Gary Cue, Cpl. Greg MacDonald, and some of the other guys from Kingston. Then Capt. Sherry Butt, a nurse I knew who was working at the hospital, dropped by to say hello. She told me the engineers I had asked six weeks ago to build her some shelves and a clothes rack had taken care of that for her. I knew they would because they were from 4 Engineer Support Regiment in Gagetown, some of the best troops I ever worked with.

I went back to the hospital and slept a bit and later, a medic with the Airborne Regiment, I had served with back at 2 Field Ambulance, stopped by and we went to supper together. After supper we just talked for a while and then I was asked to return to the hospital where Dr. Boucher wanted to speak to me about the plan for me. Initially he said they were talking about repatriating me back to Canada due to the seriousness of the pneumonia. I said emphatically "No!" I couldn't see being sent back, and I pleaded with him to let me return to Mareru with a hep-lock in my arm so I could finish my antibiotic therapy back with my Det and get on with the task at hand caring for the sick and injured people coming back in from Zaire. He told me he could promise nothing, but that later he would speak with Lieutenant Colonel (LCol) Scott about my case and what was the best way ahead.

As I lay in my bed, I could see Capt. Boucher walking towards LCol Scott and they began speaking, occasionally looking back towards where I was lying. There was some nodding back and forth and shaking of heads, and then it stopped. I knew a decision had been made and I was hoping I wasn't being sent home.

Dr. Boucher came back to my bedside after speaking with LCol Scott and the plan was spelled out for me. He told me I was going to be sent back to recover with my Det at the milk factory and was to be given a few more days of IV antibiotics and light duties. He said I should stay away from patients and the hospital until the antibiotic takes hold and told me that I was going back tomorrow.

I breathed a sigh of relief on hearing the news and was glad about going back to my section. I didn't like to be away from them for too long, and I certainly didn't like the idea of being repatriated to Canada. Later in the evening I went for a cup of tea and liberated a few more pieces of fruit and a couple packages of cookies from the kitchen. I walked around the tables where cookies and goodies were kept and took as much as I could for the guys and gals back at the milk factory. I was happy to be heading back tomorrow and getting out of here, because I didn't get a welcoming vibe here towards those of us who were from Operation Passage.

Saturday, 3 September

Woke up around 07:00 this morning and am beginning to feel somewhat better now. I'm still a bit weak from the pneumonia but overall much better. I went and had some toast with tea and spoke to Gary Cue and the guys while waiting to get picked up. I can't wait to be out of here and get back to the guys up in Mareru.

I felt a lot better and I was happy to be getting out of the stadium in Kigali and back to my Det at the milk factory. Sure, this place is a lot nicer and there's more room with fresh rations, but I don't really feel welcomed here by a couple of the Senior NCOs within the UN tour. Not sure what their problem is but they aren't acting very Canadian at all. As soon as they see I am new in town and ask me where I am from and I tell them, right away there's hostility. It's not from the troops, but more so from a couple of the senior NCOs and officers.

I was picked up about 10:00 by a couple of our supply and mechanic guys and we headed back to the milk factory. The long and winding ride back to Mareru was dangerous with the high mountains and twisting roads, many with no guardrails along the way, not to mention the crazy drivers passing on blind turns and the continuous stream of humanity heading back toward Kigali from Zaire. I cannot believe how many people are walking on the roadside back into Rwanda. Millions left during the war and are now returning from Zaire, Uganda, and Burundi. Wow, it's amazing how many people must have left the country. I can't even imagine what went on here for the three months prior to our arrival.

When I got back, I checked in with the administration section at the front of the milk factory offices, so they knew I had returned. I then headed back to my section, and when I got there the room was empty except for the guys sleeping that were probably on shift last night. Tim and the guys were in screening yesterday and today, so I didn't miss too much and my not being here wouldn't have affected them as much in screening as it would have on the ward, anyway. I'm glad to be back and hope I can just get right back into it right away. I am still tired though, so I went to bed, lay down for the afternoon, and slept.

I got up around supper time and spoke to Tim and the rest of the guys. It was good to see them. I guess I didn't miss too much while I was gone.

I emptied my backpack and gave out some of the goodies and cookies to the guys in my section, then put the rest of them out in the common area where we ate. Later in the evening I had to run over to the building where the doctors lived, which also doubled as our clinic, to get another dose of IV antibiotics. After this, they took out the hep-lock, I was then put on an oral antibiotic for another week. It was nice to lose that IV port in my arm.

Later in the evening, Tim spoke to me and said that they were reviewing the memo I sent up about Cpl. Clucas and MCpl. Melanson's nomination for recognition with their assistance at the mass casualty incident on August 10th. I was told that it's not getting much support from my superiors or their field troop commander, their own boss. I asked why? I can't believe that after what happened that night there's no support for some type of commendation. What the hell is going on? Later, in the eating area, I spoke to an officer and told him what I was trying to do, and he looked at me and said, "Well I was there, and you never mentioned me in the memo!"

I said to him, "Well that's because when I saw you there on the roadside, you were an onlooker, for the most part. Why would I mention your name when it was the two engineers who I witnessed helping?" I wondered to myself why there are always complications for something that appears to be so easy, such as assistance at an accident site. First aiders assist and then first aiders get recognized. No brainer, right? Wrong!

I grabbed a shower and went to bed pissed off. It's now about 21:30 and time for my Antibiotics and some sleep.

Sunday, 4 September

After getting the IV hep-lock out of my arm the night before, I still felt a bit sore in my chest from the infection when I was breathing. However, things were slowly getting better, and it was time to get ready for the day ahead. After breakfast, Tim approached me and asked if I wanted to volunteer as Fr. Bosse's driver down to a local village, between Gisenyi and our location in Mareru, and to help him at the local church. Francois and Daniel are telling me that the French guys are calling me Fr. Bosse's b'de l'autel, I think it means Keeper of the Altar or helper, I just laugh and take this as a compliment since I help out the padre occasionally. When I am not at work, I talk with him a lot and I assist with Mass on Sundays. When he was sick last week, no one knew because I took care of him with Cipro and Imodium and some Gravol until he recovered. He didn't want anyone to know he was sick and couldn't be called upon to care for the spiritual needs of the sick and dying.

He and I left for the village to conduct a Mass. It was a little village off the highway approximately fifteen km before Gisenyi. I took a jeep with the padre and a couple of the supply and trucker guys followed us in their truck.

The parishioners hadn't had a Mass at their church since the civil war began back in early April. I jumped at the opportunity and was excited to go and help with the church. We met the local Rwandan priest and he and Father Bosse sat and spoke with one another about the needs of the church and what we could possibly do in the short time we were to be deployed here. Afterwards Fr. Bosse asked me if I would mind attending the Mass since I was here, and if the opportunity presented, take some pictures as he conducted Mass.

It was a beautiful Mass and the children's choir was great, with their angelic voices so happy. They certainly have so much hope for people that have come through so much. I wish I could have understood more of what was spoken, as the Mass was conducted in French, but no matter, it was a very moving ceremony regardless. What I found amazing was that when it came time to pass around the collection plate, they passed it back and forth along the rows from the front to the back of the church and then it was brought forward to the priest. Compared to what I was used to witnessing back home in Canada it didn't seem like very much as they had only collected a paltry $1.35. But with much excitement and praise, the Rwandan priest told them how much had been collected and how amazing it was to collect this much money in one Mass. His voice was excited, and the people were smiling. He told them how proud he was of their work and that the money collected was the beginning of a new church. It was a lesson in humility for me to witness this, because I came to an understanding in that moment that I have more than they could ever imagine but I don't really appreciate it, not really. I will remember this moment for a very long time.

After Mass, we went down to give some cookies out to the kids, and this began as an innocent-enough venture. I had secured a couple of large cans of American ration cookies, about 500 in each of the tin cans, more than enough for the entire village. Fr. Bosse, along with the local priest, asked everyone to line up at the back of our truck as we had some cookies to give out. He said that everyone would get two each. Initially, everyone lined up and prepared to receive the cookies, but as soon as I opened the can up there was panic and everyone went on a rampage; pushing, shoving, punching, and crushing each other for the cookies. I was amazed at what was taking place before my eyes.

There were some small kids at the back of the truck, and as the crowd began surging towards the truck, I saw that one little girl was about to get crushed against the back bumper. I bent down and grabbed her under her arms, picking her up and pulling her onto the back gate of the truck with us. Then I hopped out to the side of the truck, passed her down, and asked the other soldiers with us to close the back of the vehicle.

It was surreal, I couldn't believe the turn of events from calmness when we had told them there was enough for everyone, to this feeding frenzy. Fr. Bosse and the other priest began screaming out to the crowd, "Arrêtez! Arrêtez! Il y a assez de cookies pour tout le monde. "or "Stop! Stop! There are enough cookies for everyone!" But it was getting more frenzied, like sharks feeding, and even though they had been told we had enough cookies before we began, this had suddenly happened. I didn't understand it. I did, but I didn't.

We immediately stopped giving the cookies out and after five minutes or so the crowd began to dissipate. Fr. Bosse spoke with his Rwandan colleague and it was decided to give the cookies to him so he could allocate them to the members of the community in a more controlled manner. For myself, it was a lesson in doing the right thing but perhaps in the wrong way. Sometimes we have good intentions in things we want to do while deployed, but not being from Rwanda and unfamiliar with the culture or how things worked there, we could do more harm than good, so it was a good lesson learned that day.

After Fr. Bosse sorted things out with his colleague at the church, the others who had come with us in the truck went back to camp as they had other tasks, while the padre and I went down to the Meridian Hotel in the village of Gisenyi, on Lake Kivu. He decided to treat me to lunch. After the morning we had just been through, he thought it might be nice just to relax away from the hospital, and it was an opportune time. The menu wasn't overly populated, only a few items, so I decided to have pommes frites, samosas and a Pepsi for lunch.

It was nice just to relax away from everyone and everything back at the milk factory. After my illness the last week I needed this, perhaps as a little boost for my personal morale. It was nice to sit on the patio and overlook the beach. When the food came, it smelled wonderful as I had been eating hard rations now for almost a month as I had done for my entire tour in Somalia, so I couldn't wait to dig into this treat.

I am unsure why, but as we began eating the samosas there was an uneasiness in me. They were filled with a stringy meat with an almost pork-like consistency. I began thinking about last year in Somalia and the time I was sent to exhume a body during my tour there. Everything was right there in front of me once again as I sat there at the Meridian Hotel in Rwanda. I began to imagine the smell of the rotten bodies in the meat I was eating. With every bite I was eating flesh, and all I could smell was the body which I had exhumed. Suddenly I felt this clutch of butterflies grab my stomach. I was overcome with an immense sadness and didn't want to continue eating the samosas. I was in the throes of a flashback and could only see the rotting body of the Somali whom I had exhumed a year earlier. With every bite of food, I thought of this guy I dug up. Then my mind switched as I remembered where I was in Rwanda and I began thinking of the hundreds of thousands who were killed here. I began to wonder where they got the potatoes for the French fries we were eating, thinking of the bloody dead bodies that had once been in the farmers fields, probably lying on top of these same potatoes I was presently eating. I couldn't get the picture out of my head of local fields full of bloody bodies everywhere with dogs eating human flesh.

I was unable to say or do anything for those moments. All of this was taking place inside my head as Father Bosse was sitting and eating in front of me, occasionally looking over and smiling. My thoughts were racing, and I could feel my pulse increasing, my throat drying up, and as if everything was closing in around me. I wanted to run away from the restaurant as quickly as possible. I kept telling myself to relax, calm down, and act normal, but it wasn't working.

At the time I didn't know what was taking place, I never for a moment thought about PTSD or why this was happening, and so I didn't say too much to Fr. Bosse and I let it pass. I knew it would pass if I could somehow calm myself. I'd had this happen many times before, it was just memories from Somalia, mixed in with the new Rwandan experiences. As I sat there eating, I was sure this tour to Rwanda hadn't helped with this, but I thought it would settle.

After lunch we headed outside. I was still sickened by my memories and would later come to understand that what had taken place was a dissociative moment. But right then, I needed to get up and move around to change my thoughts and move on.

As we walked around the hotel lobby, you could tell it had been a beautiful place at one time. We continued walking towards the front doors, and outside as we left, we saw a few tourist stores. The venders were smiling and talking to us in French, trying to get us to buy their wares, but we politely told them no thanks and moved on. From afar we could see Lake Kivu in front of the hotel and the beautiful sandy beaches along the water's edge. We decided to go down to the beach to enjoy the simple beauty. As we approached, that all too familiar smell of rotten corpses began to invade my nostrils, and I saw that on the beach and along the water there were at least twenty or more bodies in differing states of decay. There was a hand here and a foot there sticking out of the sand; some half-decayed bodies and skeletons along the water; and in the distance, like buoys, others were bloated and floating on top of the water moving up and down as the small waves pushed them closer to shore. My mind was once again assaulted, and I went numb. I recall thinking that I couldn't take much more of this, I was so tired of seeing all this madness and the grotesque killing which went on here in Rwanda.

When I came back around supper, I spoke to the pharmacy officer, Roxanne Kerns and told her about eating the local food. I asked her if I could get a dose of Combantrin, because I was worried about getting worms from eating the local food and taking care of patients during the last month. She told me to speak with Corporal Mike Hackett and he would have some for me.

After supper, around 18:30, I was asked to do some haircuts. Tonight, I think I gave haircuts to about seventeen of the guys and made a few more dollars for the Terry Fox run next week. With the other twenty-two haircuts last night, the money for Terry Fox is adding up. At the end of the day, when I was back with my Det, I told the guys in my section what had happened at the church. I still couldn't believe it but one of them said, "Imagine if it was you getting the cookies and had nothing, and you didn't know if you would ever have this chance again for food."

I could see his point. Hunger has a way of changing the way we see things and our ability to be rational. The whole country probably has PTSD from what went on here for those three months of the civil war and genocide, the craziness of it all.

Monday, 5 September

When I got up today, I got dressed and ready for the day, prepared to head out with my Det to run a clinic about forty-five minutes or so east of the milk factory. Tim told us yesterday at the briefing that we were going to a village called Ruhengeri to do some outpatient work. We found out that this was the village where tourists would begin their trips to the Virunga Volcanoes Mountain Range to see Dian Fossey's Karisoke Research Station and the mountain gorillas. Only one section was going to the Ruhengeri clinic today, and our section was chosen. We left around 07:00 to arrive and set up early before we began seeing patients.

The MSF (Medicine Sans Frontier) doesn't want the army to be here in uniforms with guns, and I understand this as they want to be neutral and not bring on any shit once we leave. Oh well, we came to help, and we came in uniforms and we have guns. The last time soldiers were told to lay down their guns here a couple months ago, ten Belgian soldiers with the UN were killed. With the MSF, I do admire them, though, for what they do. They really put themselves out there and are very vulnerable. Unlike most other NGO agencies, these guys put themselves out there on the pointy end of this crisis. I'm not sure I could do it.

It was a so-so day. Tim and Chris had some crying babies that wouldn't stop; cry, cry was all they did. They were probably scared of the big brutes. It was a lot of volume but not a lot of real bad stuff that came in today that I saw. None of the guys mentioned anything too dramatic, but that's a good thing. We closed the clinic at around 16:00.

I am glad that it was only for one day that we were sent here to Ruhengeri, because I am already tired of this. I really think the tour from Somalia is finally catching up on me, and it seems that in this Rwandan tour there is no slowing down with the number of sick people just pouring in—no end in sight. I don't mind helping and doing my part, I just find it overwhelming right now and I wish, if only for a moment, that I could have every Canadian come here and experience this shit and open their eyes. We spend more on our dog's food and toys than we give to charities in Canada. We spent more on our pets than we can ever imagine giving or doing for the kids we buried here in Rwanda. The stupidity of it all. Drives me crazy and I'm losing faith in humanity more and more every day.

Once we returned and unloaded all the kit, the rest of the afternoon and into the evening was just sitting around talking and taking it easy. After supper early in the evening, I called my roommate back in Petawawa just to check in on him and to see how all was going. He will be leaving for Croatia soon, probably will be gone before I get back, or I'll get back just in time to get the keys to the apartment from him. Around 23:00 I went to bed.

Tuesday, 6 September

I got up at 06:00 for my phone call home, and I called Mom and talked for a few minutes. She's happy I called, she is always worried about me, I can hear it in her voice. I think everyone's mom is like this when we are overseas, and they watch the news seeing and hearing all the craziness that goes on. It makes them all worry. It's easier on this end because I know what's in front of me every day and see what the reality is. I think Mom is proud of me and what I've done so far in my career. I know this from when I was home from Somalia last summer and she kept telling all the neighbours about me and what I did. It gets somewhat embarrassing, but I guess moms want to have something to be proud of in their children. I guess our parents deserve this, at least, after all the shit we put them through growing up.

After my phone call, I went right back to bed for another half-hour sleep, but then got up at 08:00 to go to Gisenyi for the morning with Fr. Bosse. He was going to talk with the local priests at the seminary to see what he could offer and do for them while he is here. We got ready and left about

09:00. I had the morning off and wasn't working until the afternoon, so I enjoyed the break away from the milk factory and this opportunity to work again with Padre Bosse. When we got to the site where the old seminary was, I was amazed at how beautiful it was. It had beautiful brick buildings used as dormitories with flowers and vines growing all over them, and there were long, bricked walkways through once beautiful gardens. With the serenity and simple beauty, I was witnessing, it must have been a wonderful place prior to the war with the hundreds of nuns, priests, missionaries, and lay people here. We met the local priest, who had survived the war by blending in with the local population and pretending to be just an illiterate local.

He told his story to Padre Bosse saying that he was a highly educated priest and teacher, but as the civil war worsened, the Interahamwe began killing anyone who was educated. They wanted to exterminate anyone around who could lead dissent or educate the population, including children and women who could repopulate and educate the country after the war. Because they were held in high esteem in the community, doctors, teachers, and priests were protected and kept hidden by the population, while the Interahamwe were killing anyone educated or who may have witnessed the genocide and might live to testify about what had taken place. Even the books, birth, and baptismal records or anything else which could be of use in the future rebuilding of the country was destroyed. As the priest spoke, I was thinking the insanity of what had happened.

He showed us the beautiful Cathedral Nyundo, in Rubavu; it had these wide, narrow steps the entire width of the cathedral's front, leading up to the heavy double doors. On entering the cathedral, the first thing that struck me was that all the pews were gone, and it was totally empty, while the stained glass was intact and there were church papers and debris strewn all over the floor everywhere. As we walked toward the altar, we saw it had been destroyed and all that remained was a large white cross on the back wall. At the base of the cross there were blood stains and splatters of blood all around. The priest told us that they had executed the bishop and some of the priests and seminarians there when they found them hidden within the church and the grounds. We then went to the back of the altar, where there was a narrow passageway leading to all the rooms of the sanctuary and sacristy where the priests' garments and church records and books were kept.

The floor was littered with so much paper and books, it was like walking in high grass where every step needed effort. All the records had been defecated and urinated upon, ripped up, and made to be unusable or recoverable, or at least very difficult to do so. It was easy to see that the Interahamwe carried out a burnt-earth policy of destruction as they moved through the country.

We then went to see some other buildings and sleeping quarters at the back of the cathedral and everywhere we looked was destruction.

After we had been shown around, Fr. Bosse and his fellow priest wanted to speak for a while, while they spoke, I sat outside the dormitory area on a rock. I stayed away to give them some privacy and then walked around the seminary grounds. I think they needed time to be alone to talk, and I think Fr. Bosse needed to talk to speak with another man of faith. After about an hour, he came and told me it was time to head back, so we said goodbye to the priest and were on our way. On the drive back, Fr. Bosse mentioned that he wanted me to see if I could get some volunteers together to go back later in the week to help clean up the church. That's all he said, we drove quietly back to the milk factory.

When I got back it was around a little after noon or so, so I grabbed a quick ration pack, ate, got dressed, and went off to screening with the rest of the Det. I worked at screening but for the first hour I worked in ORS (Oral Rehydration Section), anyway it was not much of an eventful day. I think we've reached our peak and now numbers are slowing down as the bulk of the refugees coming in from Goma are mostly back. It seems we are treating mostly locals now. We closed early at 15:00 and went back to our sleeping area.

Tim told us that we are getting another talk tonight from one of the doctors out of Kigali. Why do they come here? We are in the middle of a deployment, working crazy hours. Do they invite themselves or do our people invite them up to bore us to death? This week it's a lecture on tuberculosis. I really don't care and after today couldn't care less. We had supper and relaxed, waiting for the lecture tonight. At 19:00, the doctor gave us a talk about TB, and this lasted almost two hours to 21:00.

After the lecture, Tim came and told me to get another memo written up for MCpl Rick Melanson and Cpl. Scott Clucas. It had to be changed again because it would not be accepted as it was. I went black, I wanted to scream. I didn't care anymore. I tore up my original memo in front of Tim and threw it in the garbage. I told Tim I didn't care anymore, and then he freaked on me and told me to get a grip. I know he understood my frustration with this because he was there with me, but he was right, I need to get a hold of myself before I say or do something stupid. I am so frustrated with something that on its face seems so obvious to do. These two guys deserve to be recognized for what they did at the mass casualty incident, but I know they never will be. Because of what or why I don't know. But it's over. No matter what I write, those in charge have already made their decision, so why write anything? Fuck! I hate stupidity...I'm going to bed.

I had just gotten to bed when a bug-out drill was called, getting us all up with the need to get fully dressed in the middle of the night, when most of us were either in bed or getting ready for bed. Some were asleep, and some were just getting off shift in the hospital. What in the fuck is this about, really? What a bunch of shit heads we've got gathered here. I think that if anything were to happen such as us being attacked, I would just go over with the infantry guys and see if I could be of help, or head out into the jungle, jumping the fence and heading north to Uganda to take my chances. In the event of anything taking place, I believe that there's a plan to send all the nurses and doctors in MLVWs down towards the border with Zaire. Some of us would be left behind to see what our fate would be and what would happen. There aren't enough vehicles for everyone to drive out of here if we ever get attacked, so it would be a fight for survival once everyone was gone. If I stayed here with the medical people, I would most likely die with their level of situational awareness. I would feel better with the airborne and engineer troops.

Wednesday, 7 September

This is the first time I had a chance to sit down and write for a few days. It seems that not too much really happened over the last three days, but much has, and it has been very busy. Weird how everything catches up on you. Lately I've been frustrated many times and been sad, depressed, and happy, but life is all these emotions, isn't it? This is one place which will bring them all out, I'm finding. I also decided in the last day or so to go UTPNCM[3] if

---

3   University Training Plan Non-Commissioned Members

possible. I joined with my Bachelor of Arts and am educated, so I should be able to become an officer if I apply, if not in the medical field, maybe infantry.

After I got up, we had a day off, basically. Speaking to Tim I asked if I could go down the highway a few miles to a local tourist-type store that did their own carvings and paintings and take my Det and some of the others. Tim went and asked up front for permission and they said no problem. We rounded up everyone who was off and wanted to go. While they were getting this organized, I went and signed out a MLVW, did my driver's inspection on it, and got ready. There were about fifteen or so people wanting to go, so they grabbed their weapons and off we went at around 10:00. It was a short drive towards Gisenyi to a small shack on the right-hand side of the road. The roads were not all that wide, and so as we arrived, I tried to pull over to the side and the MLVW began to lean sharply to the right. I got everyone off and towards the building and then I nervously drove the vehicle straight ahead until it seemed to grab back onto the road and straightened out. Then I turned it around, pointing it back towards our camp. I was slightly embarrassed because I'd almost rolled a MLVW. If this had happened, I wouldn't have lived that one down. More importantly, no one got hurt and the vehicle didn't roll, thank God.

When we went in, I immediately saw two carvings that I wanted to buy. The first was an ebony cross and I could see that at my mom's. The second was an ebony nativity scene for a very good friend of mine from Cape Breton, Fr. Bedford Doucette. I know he will like it and when I drive home at Christmas and stop in New Glasgow at St. John's Church, I can give it to him for Christmas.

Everyone was enjoying the shopping trip and bought a lot of stuff. It was good for everyone to take their minds off the things we were seeing and doing in the hospital at the milk factory these last few weeks.

We drove back afterwards, and everyone hopped off and I fuelled and put the vehicle away, still thinking about how close I'd come to messing up earlier in the morning. Afterwards we just had lunch and took it easy and everyone started to wrap up their carvings, preparing them to mail home to Canada.

In the afternoon I talked to Randy Murphy about the route for the Terry Fox run on the 11th. It's a simple run; left at the main gate then down the highway for five km, where there will be a turnaround point, and then five km back, simple. There should be someone at the turnaround point to give everyone their time, and it should be a good go. Randy and I were excited about doing this and we got a few posters made up by Rejean Michel and put them out around the milk factory.

Thursday, 8 September

Up today at 06:30, dressed, washed, and had a coffee. Today we were on general duties with cleaning around the camp, washing and cleaning the floors in the common area, and cleaning off the tables after each meal. Otherwise it was a relaxed day, not as much stress washing floors as working on the hospital ward. I had time today to speak with Scotty Clucas out by the ROWPU after lunch. Scott's a good guy, I enjoyed working with him when we were in the militia.

I just took the time to read and write a few letters for my friends and family back home. I packed a couple of parcels and mailed them back as well. I'm trying to keep my personal backpack and equipment light, so I don't have too much weight with me when this tour is over. Later, I cut some hair in the afternoon and went and spoke to Fr. Bosse about when was the next time, he wanted to go to Gisenyi for Mass. Other than this, the day was uneventful. Went to bed early.

Friday, 9 September

Up early as usual and got ready for the day ahead. Today I went for a run with WO Martell to see how the ten km course would be for the upcoming Terry Fox Run. I enjoy a good run and especially if I get into a groove and today WO Martell and I had a good one; about ten km in forty minutes or so. Got back and got washed and ready for the day, it was another quiet day of doing general duties, cleaning the milk factory and taking out garbage. This is the first time our Det has had this much time off the ward since we got here. It's a good thing to have a break from the hospital.

After lunch, Randy and I worked together on the route and some forms for those participating in the Terry Fox Run. I think that we will make two separate donations to the Terry Fox run. In this way, we'll get two larger tax receipts and draw for them out of all the names of those who entered the run, for a better tax break. With everyone donating a dollar here and there, there will not be much in the way of a tax receipt for anyone, so I thought just taking the total amount and dividing it in two would be the fairest way for everyone who had made some type of donation.

The rest of the day I just washed my clothes, cleaned my bed space area, and spent time talking to everyone and joking around. I wrote a few letters to people back home and had supper. It's been a nice few days with it being so quiet, but now it's time to get back to the business of taking care of patients. Tomorrow we are in back in the hospital on the ward at 07:00. Time for bed, morning comes early.

Saturday, 10 September

Got up this morning at 05:30, just woke up, got washed, and got ready for the day ahead. It was nice, hardly anyone around yet, so I had a couple cups of coffee and time to myself. Today our Det is on the ward. I am kind of looking forward to getting back to the ward and the patients. I know its kind of weird, but we have been there most of our time since we first arrived and now it seems strange being on general duties. We are taking a shift from the guys out of Calgary today. I hear they are going to be going home soon, not sure when but soon. Then we are back to either screening or on general camp duties for another day or so.

We all went down to the hospital before 07:00 and took over from the others. We were on the ward from 07:00 to 15:00. I had a few smaller kids with NG tubes for feedings and a couple of dressing changes. Other than this there's not much really to say for this day, nothing exciting went on during our shift. After work, I met up with Randy and we were very busy all night with the planning and organizing for the Terry Fox run, making sure we had enough people along the route, and everyone was ready. Things seem to be going well, I just hope it works out without a hitch. There's about ninety of the people here with us on tour going to run, should be a good time.

After supper I went and spoke to Fr. Bosse and asked about what time he was doing Mass tomorrow. He said that it will be in the afternoon after the run and asked me if I would help him during the Mass by doing a reading. I told him no problem. I mentioned to him that there was another parcel coming from my mom's workplace for him. It was another bunch of hand-made rosaries for him to give out, and it should be here in the next week or two. The rest of the evening I just sat around and talked and made sure all was good to go for tomorrow. Went to bed early so I could get up early tomorrow and check for any last-minute problems that may come up.

Sunday, 11 September - Terry Fox Run

Well, I got up at 07:00, showered, ate, and got ready for church with Fr. Bosse. He held Mass at 09:00 this morning, but only seven of us were there in attendance. Although a small group it was still a good Mass. He is such a nice gentleman and has a good way about him, I hope that I can continue to go to church with him down at the seminary and in the local villages, it's probably one of the things I enjoy doing the most here.

After mass we prepared for the Terry Fox Run. Randy Murphy and I have been working together the last couple weeks in preparation for this event. We had asked a few weeks ago if we could do one here in Africa. We thought it would be good for morale as well as a distraction from the day to day goings on here for everyone.

By now, I have been in theatre for seven weeks and I think things are catching up on me faster than I realized. I'm not sure if it is with the things I saw and did on my last deployment to Somalia, now added with already so many shitty things we've witnessed here in Rwanda, but whatever is going on I can feel a shift in my soul.

For today's run we would be running down the highway towards the RPF camp. Then at the five km mark there would be a couple of our guys in a truck indicating the turnaround point, and then everyone would head back towards the milk factory. We had been at 4000 feet above sea level for a while and gotten used to the thin air so the altitude wouldn't be an issue. In total we had eighty-eight of the soldiers with us available for the run. Between what the troops donated in money and the monies the guys donated every time I did a haircut ($1.00 a haircut), we raised $1400.00 US in total, so all in all a pretty good day. After the race, I did the draw for the two $700-dollar receipts, and the CO said a few words as well as the RSM. It was a good break and a few laughs after everything we have been through over the last month and a half. Afterwards everyone got on with the rest of the day.

I went back and got showered and changed, read awhile, and wrote a few letters. Rejean is writing an article about us doing the run in Rwanda for the *Petawawa Post*. He told me once it's done, he will show it to me before he sends it off. Just had supper and took it easy the rest of the evening. It's now 20:30 and I'll be heading to bed soon.

Monday, 12 September

I don't know how or why but I've again lost the last couple of days, everything here melts together. It seems so busy with working on the ward, trying to eat, wash, and sleep before it's back on the ward and days seem to run into one another with working sixteen out of every twenty-four hours. It's driving me into the ground. Today a member of our section, Ron Andersen, must leave back to Canada for compassionate reasons. I'm unsure as to why, but I think someone may be ill at home. He is being replaced by another medic who was recently posted into the unit prior to the deployment. He seems to like joking a lot and very witty, he will be a good fit in replacing Ron. Other than that, not much really going on that's ever changing but so much going on with our Det and work and running.

Tuesday, 13 September

We have only been in operation for a month or so now since we set up our facility, and we have consistently been having a hundred or more in-patients since opening. We could keep 100-150 patients at a time with one empty ward to use for roving patients and cleaning up the ward as they were taken out. There had been a rumour that in two days General Dallaire and General Tousignant would be coming for a visit to see the facility, do a walk through, and see just how busy we were. The talk on the street was that the UNHQ wanted us to move down to the south west corner of the country next to Burundi to the south, where there was still some fighting going on and we could be better utilized for our capabilities. I thought this was great, nothing better than doing what you trained for. This is what I did in Somalia last year before and was ready to do again.

The day before the two generals were to arrive something so weird began that even as I write this in my journal, I still shake my head. The cargo trucks were sent out and were picking up sick people along the road from Goma and bringing them back to our location. I thought what, this new nonsense is. I didn't know what to think, I just did as I was told. It wasn't more than a couple of hours when we went to full capacity. I wasn't sure why we were doing this or if it was even necessary, but it was bizarre going out and taking people back to admit to our facility.

Unknown to most of us, the next day Generals Dallaire and Tousignant arrived via a UN helicopter and were taken to see our commanding officer and his staff at the milk factory where they were given a briefing. After this meeting, we were told to take our stations and be polite and short with the answers to any questions the generals might ask us. A typical "dog and pony show," which is a very controlled, almost scripted, presentation where the two generals and their entourage would be corralled around the hospital in order to give the best light to what we were doing. After their meeting with the CO and RSM, the two generals were taken around and shown just how busy we were, not knowing that only eighteen hours earlier this facility wasn't being fully utilized, even though we now had four wards full.

As this was taking place, I finally got it; my lightbulb moment came to me and I realized why we were stocking the hospital like a fishing pond! All this was for the benefit of the two generals to give the visual impression that we were so busy and needed here that to move us down to the Burundi border would take away from the need here with this many sick people. A bit of smoke and mirror work being done here, which I thought was a bit backhanded by those in charge of our mission. I didn't understand why they didn't want to move, we had medical stock and equipment, we had about eight doctors and fourteen nurses and around six physician assistants and a hundred or so medics, so why not move? I didn't know why and wasn't privy to the decision tree and the whys and how's of this, but it still felt like a little fainthearted act in my opinion.

After the meeting, the generals boarded the helicopter and left. I under-stood what had happened and my place on the food chain and I felt a little empty. I always wanted to be in motion and doing the most while we were here with what resources we had, and this just seemed a disingenuous way out of doing the right thing. It was not going to the worst areas of fighting and of need because of our personal desire to be comfortable and safe.

Surgeon General Morrisett came yesterday, visited the hospital, and just basically checked out our operation here, I think this is his last hurrah as the rumour is that he is retiring very soon. Col. Manning and the FSM from CFB Petawawa also made appearances. I find when these upper ranks come into the hospital it's almost not real. People around me act and speak differently when they come around. They give the answers that they think are wanted by the visiting dignitaries instead of the answers which should be given. Kind of crazy, but I guess that just the way it works. I wish I would get asked once in a while what I think, but that's probably why I don't get asked.

That's why we're staying here in Mareru instead of moving down to the Burundi border as General Tousignant and General Dallaire were told what we wanted them to hear, not what they should have heard. Oh well.

After the shift, back to eat and wash and I found out that I am going with Fr. Bosse tomorrow to the church we were at last week. I don't mind doing this at all.

Just talked with Michelle Tremblay and Christine Pissinger. They look tired. We're all tired but I've only been here since 25 July so I really shouldn't be that tired. Only thing I can figure out is that Somalia and the work schedule here is catching up on me. Went to bed early tonight so I'd be ready for tomorrow.

Wednesday, 14 September

I got up, washed, dressed, and went to speak with the padre. Today I am going to Gisenyi with him to check out some stuff and to do another Mass at the little church in the village near there. I feel like I am doing a good job helping out the padre. If I wasn't in the army, I think I would like to be an NGO and live here in Africa and work for a charitable organization.

Fr. Bosse met the local priest and they talked in front of the church. There were lots of kids around giggling and laughing, nice to see healthy and happy kids. I didn't have anything to give them, so I just smiled at them and waited to see what was going on with Fr. Bosse. I think he is arranging to do another Mass and I think the Rwandan priest is asking about us maybe coming to help at the seminary to clean it up from the killing and destruction that went on there not that long ago.

The local priest walked around with Fr. Bosse as they both spoke in quiet conversation. I could understand here and there that the Rwandan priest was showing our padre some of the things that were destroyed when the war was taking place and Interahamwe were coming through as they retreated to Zaire. Father Bosse was asking if there was any way he could offer help or supplies to get the church back to a workable condition. They spoke for a little while, and then it was time to leave. We only stayed for an hour or so before we headed back.

When I returned, I quickly ate and went to get some sleep and get rested up for work at 23:00.

Thursday, 15 September

The guys from 1 Fd Amb Calgary, left yesterday for Kigali and won't be back. They are flying out in two days back to Calgary. I heard they were leaving last week, and we knew it was coming, but it seems like this is really fast. Wow. But I'm glad they are gone home to their families; there is no real need for them, especially with the way we were worked over the last two months. I think we could have gone it alone as a unit and done this whole deployment on our backs, especially the way we have been employed since our arrival. Sure, it was nice to have the guys from 1 and 5 Field Ambulance here, but they weren't used as much as they could have been or in the right way, in my opinion, at least from what I saw the last seven weeks since I arrived. I know it's not their fault and they are great troops, but I think with having the leadership from our unit as the lead element and then a platoon of medics from all three of the Field Ambulance units, the CSM and OC throughout the tour defaulted to us for most of the shitty taskings just because they were familiar with us and didn't want to pass off some of this work to the others and appear unfair. They probably don't even realize it, but it's hard on the guys and gals who are here with the work routine they expect us to maintain.

We worked a couple of shifts on the ward over the last few days and then ended with a general duty shift. Today was just cleaning up around the milk factory and small jobs, nothing really; clean, sweep, and wash the floors; clean up eating area and around the building. Afterwards, I sat and talked to Scotty Clucas and I told him I had put Rick Melanson's name forward for some type of recognition for the vehicle accident a few weeks ago. I also told him that it wasn't getting much support and that I didn't understand why but would try to keep moving it forward. I'm only a worker bee, so not much drag here to reward people.

Tonight, at the Orders Group, we found out that the Critical Incident Stress Debriefing team has finally landed. I wish we could avoid them. I never want to talk, and the way things are, if you admit there is a problem then you will be put in a medical category and eventually released. So, not much for me to say and I suspect the others won't either. We were also told tonight that a ton of mail has arrived in Kigali. That's a good thing, the mail is slow to arrive, and I suspect that as with most things we are competing for space on the aircraft with the UN mission.

Finished the day and nothing else really went on. Went to bed early, very tired lately.

Friday - Monday, 16-19 September

Most of this week was just a blur for me, as has happened a few times now in the last two months. It seemed like we were just on the ward for the rotating eight hours on, eight hours off crazy shift schedule they continue to maintain, even though it is quickly wearing us out. There is barely just enough time to eat, grab a shower, get back up, dress and go back to the hospital. There's no time to sit and think, no time to have a mindless moment! No time. But wait!! All the troops from 1 Field Ambulance were sent home two days ago because there was not enough work here for them, even though we are having to maintain this shift schedule. I just don't understand how the leadership works here in regard to management of us. With using us guys from Petawawa so often, we probably didn't need the other two Field Ambulance's medics. Mostly they were underused the two months they were here, so they sent them home a month early. Maybe while we are at it let's get ready to send the guys from Valcartier back to their base as well.

I don't know who's running this place, but it feels that they are disconnected from what we are doing in the hospital or at the clinics we are sent to and from the work schedule. It feels as if those in charge don't have a clue about how to work people, organize a simple shift schedule, or manage even the simplest of tasks.

I enjoy the work at the hospital, working and taking care of the people here in Rwanda, but it's the way we are being utilized that I am having the problem with. The funny thing is we who are caught in the middle of this senseless schedule can easily see how dysfunctional it is, but it's lost on those in charge of us. I can't figure this out. When I spoke to some of the guys from Calgary, even they thought the schedule could have been planned differently. Anyway, this last stint was only a five-day run on the ward and now we are off to general duties for a couple days.

Tuesday, 20 September

Finally finished on the hospital last night and today when we woke, it was onto the screening bays. This is not too bad. It doesn't matter how many sick or injured come in, because we only work the eight hours and then we are finished. It will be nice to be off the eight hours shifts for a while.

Tonight, while eating, I lost the filling in my right molar, shitty dental. I am always embarrassed about the dental shit. When I grew up all we had was one dentist in town during the 1960s and 70's, for almost 14,000 people. Coal miners had no dental plan back then and pulling teeth was the norm, so now I've got a mouth full of caps, fillings, and bridges. I went down to our MIR and saw Dr. Campbell, and he said I have to go down to Kigali tomorrow to see the dentist at the field hospital to get this fixed.

At the O Group tonight it was mentioned that we would be going to Dian Fossey's Karisoke Research Station located in the hollow area between two dormant volcanoes, the Visoke and Karisimbi Mountains to see the gorillas in the next week or so. This will be exciting for sure and after all the time we have spent in the hospital working, I think it will be good for all the guys to change it up and see something other than the inside of the hospital.

Wednesday, 21 September

Off to Kigali today, for my dental filling. It was smooth actually; I got there and was taken in almost immediately and had it done before noon. Nice to get that fixed. Said hi to Gary Cue, Greg MacDonald, and the others I knew, and then had a liquid lunch, my mouth was still frozen after getting that filling. Still don't like coming to Amahoro Stadium, always feel unwelcome and unwanted when here but that's more likely because of my earlier experiences while on the recce.

After lunch I helped to load the MLVW with our camp's mail, pop, and ration packs, and then we left for the milk factory. On the way back, I just sat there and didn't talk very much, kind of in a daze. I was watching all the people, still thousands of them like ants, walking along both sides of the road as we drove back. I wonder where so many people are heading all at once.

I know that I am still amazed at the beauty of this country; the green forests, the hills and volcanoes, the wild animals, the people. I saw a little boy up ahead in front of us as we drove. From a distance he looked like he had on only one red shoe. I wasn't sure why he had only one red shoe but there it was. However, as we got closer, he was the boy with one red sock on. Poor guy, no shoes, but most people are barefoot here anyway. Still, I found this peculiar as we passed by him.

My mind has been going wild lately with these people's lives here in Rwanda; with their country, with the wild animals, the gorillas. I'm sick and tired of being this way. I'm stuck in a rut and it's time to fish or cut bait. I don't have a lot invested in the army, so leaving and starting over won't be a big thing. I want to get something going with my life. Maybe when this is all over, I should look at what NGOs do; where they work, how much they make. Maybe it's time to switch it up and leave the army and try something different? I'm not sure right now but I know I need to do something to mix it up.

We got back to the milk factory close to supper, drove to the loading dock, and unloaded the rations, pop, and mail. The troops will be happy for the mail. Then I went back to my area and told Tim I was back and got up to speed with what's going on for tomorrow.

Tonight, it was our turn with the stress debrief team. To send over a stress debrief team, I believe, was a new concept at this point, but I wasn't sure that it was the right place to have this debrief right now. Sent over as part of the team were a couple of social workers, a mental health nurse and a psychologist, looking all clean and fresh faced, ready to save us from ourselves and what horrors they think we saw here in Rwanda.

Not wanting to waste time and wanting to get a debrief in with the troops almost right away after arriving, to save our minds and make sense of the horror we've seen, almost as soon as they arrived, they drew a schedule up for all our sections. At tonight's Order's Group, the schedule was given out for all the sections in our camp. We were told the time when our section would see them and that attendance was compulsory but talking wasn't. There was no doubt in my mind that no one wanted to talk about what we had just done and been through; many of the medics were skeptical at best. This was a new thing to be tried, a debrief team parachuted into this shitty situation, briefed by our headquarters who hadn't stepped into the hospital and didn't know the reality of its inner goings on during our time here on tour. To have this team suddenly show up and proceed to tell us how and what we should feel at this point...

We knew we had no choice but to attend and listen even if we didn't want to add anything to the conversation. We were a captive audience.

I had been to Kigali for dental work this morning, while the rest worked on the ward all day. I really wasn't ready for this debrief; it was more like I really didn't have anything to say. The awkwardness of this debrief felt like in high school when you meet a girl for that first date and don't have anything in common to talk about yet, so you sit there looking around awkward. So here we were, all sitting around, listening and being told by the CISD team what we had just seen and been through, how it would affect us, and the possible difficulties in processing this deployment we would have when returning back home to Canada from tour.

Their monotone voices began to drone out on me, and I really didn't care at that point. I just had a shitty tour a year earlier in Somalia and since had seen some of the guys back home in Petawawa from the Airborne Regiment come forward with mental health issues, only to be released quicker than a puff of smoke in a windstorm. I didn't think anything was wrong with me anyway. I felt somehow inoculated from the last tour and I spoke to the other four medics from the Somalia tour who were with me and they felt similar. Maybe we were lying to ourselves...most likely, but then again maybe it just wasn't time to let it out?

We were told of the signs and symptoms of PTSD we should look out for when we got home. Shit, as I listened, I realized that I had experienced over half of them since Somalia but thought nothing of it. We were then advised that on our return to Canada we were going to be given a mental-health questionnaire on our arrival to Petawawa or the other bases we came from, and that we would have other follow-up questionnaires over the coming years.

One of the members on the CISD team said something that shut me down about ten minutes into the debrief. Whenever someone is trying to help but says something like, "I know how you feel," or "We've all been there before, it will be all back to normal once you get home," he lost me. Who is someone who has not been here during the tour doing the hours in the hospital we had done, to tell me how and what I will feel? They don't know what we did or went through, so I shut down and started to think of the work I still had in the ward next shift, thinking of my bed space and how tired I was, thinking of anything but this debrief and just wanting out of here.

Within a day or so of arriving, it seemed, the CISD Team had seen all the different sections and with this task completed, wanted to go to the local craft market, eat at the restaurant in Gisenyi like the tourists they were. As predicted, we found out tonight that the entire CISD team would be travelling with us to Dian Fossey's Karisoke Research Centre, to see the mountain gorillas in a couple days. This was crazy, I thought, screw the gorillas. Aren't they here to work? I was having an intense internal dialogue and upset, but didn't really know why. I thought I had worked the whole tour, through pneumonia, the emotions with dying and with burying children, and seeing mass graves with my Det members. Others during the tour were sent to a Catholic convent for a mental health break or given large amounts of time off from the ward, but our section wasn't given that opportunity. Myself, I worked no matter what and never stopped for the whole time in theatre unless sick or ordered to do another task. But now for someone to just show up from Canada, then to tell me what I need to do and how I should feel after being here caring for these people, then two days later go on a mountain safari . . . I thought to myself *What the fuck!?*

I know how I feel and what I've spoken, and I knew what to expect when I get home, I didn't want to talk to anyone about my time here. It's now 21:00 and I'll go to bed soon. We are in screening tomorrow.

Thursday, 22 September

Got up around 06:30, washed, and had a coffee. Today we are in the screening bays so shouldn't be too bad of a day. The thing I like about screening is that once you're done for the day, you're done.

It was a steady day in screening but nothing too outstanding struck me today as far as patients for me; some malaria, gastro, dehydration, and skin infections. We seemed to be slowing down and the traffic out on the main road in front of our facility doesn't seem as busy with people walking by. They probably know we will be leaving soon. Today, we saw 228 patients. Most of them fortunately weren't too sick, just a little dehydrated on their walk back to their villages as they return from Zaire.

After our shift I washed, ate, and sat around watching the guys play volleyball out back while having a quick cup of tea and writing a few letters before going to bed.

Friday, 23 September

Well, getting up today was the start of what I thought was a good day ahead. I was up at 05:00 grabbed a shower, ate, then at 07:00 our section, the CISD team and a section of infantry left for Mount Visoke to see the mountain gorillas. We were going to go and sit amongst them and then afterwards go to Dian Fossy's Karisoke Research Centre and see a piece of history.

We drove to Ruhengeri, then made a left turn off the highway and drove a little while longer to the base of the Visoke Mountain on the Rwanda side. It was a one and a half hour climb up the mountain, so hard to breathe with the altitude, but no one was going to pass this up. Our guides (they are nicknamed cowboys) took us right to the mountain gorillas and they were beautiful. There was a big male silverback and about ten to twelve females and three babies. They were beautiful and so gentle. One rubbed up against me and checked me out by licking my ear and sniffing me. I loved the experience, but at the same time I was thinking about all the deforestation around the base of their mountain and how little space was being left for them.

We spent an hour or so there with these beautiful creatures. After we left the gorillas, we walked uphill another hour and a half to see Dian Fossy's research facility. Dian Fossey's research centre is in Rwanda's Virunga volcanic mountain range, between Mount Karisimbi and Mount Visoke. She combined the two names of these mountains to come up with Karisoke, using this combination to name her Camp. It was a real neat experience, but some of the buildings were pretty beat up from the war. You could see that people had been using it as recently as February or March this year from some of the rubble and letters scattered all over on the ground.

As the guys took pictures, walked around the site, and visited the graves of Dian Fossey, Digit and the other gorillas, I walked around by myself picking up all the letters off the ground around the research station. As I was picking them up, there were two main names on the mail; one was a large collection of handwritten mail addressed to a Ms. Amy Beavis, one of the Karisoke Research Center staff, for the Diane Fossey Gorilla Fund. The other collection of letters was from the Dian Fossey Gorilla Fund. I gathered up as many as I could take and stuffed them into my cargo pockets on my pant-legs pockets. My thought was that I would put them in a plastic bag when I return to the milk factory, and when I return home to Canada, I will then send these letters to the two main groups named on the envelopes. I read one of the letters and it was about six months old. As I was reading, I could feel the family of Amy Beavis was worrying about their daughter and warning her that they'd heard on the news it was getting more volatile in Rwanda. Hopefully she listened. I wasn't sure when I would, but knew I had to mail the letters back to the owners for sure after reading this letter, I believe she will appreciate getting these personal letters back. The other group of mail to the Dian Fossey Gorilla Fund, I will send back to them as well on my return back to Canada. While I was in the mountains, I got the grids of where the gorillas were from the Airborne sergeant with us, how many we saw and the makeup of these groups. The Gorilla Fund people will probably appreciate hearing this news.

We stayed for about hour, taking pictures of Dian Fosse's grave as well as the grave of her favorite gorilla, Digit. I then took pictures of Tim, Luciano, Mike, and a few others as I had a couple of disposable cameras, so it wasn't a big deal. I'll give them their pictures when we get back to Canada. Once we had our fill and with time getting late, we left to come back, and it took about another two hours to walk back to our vehicles. After walking up and back down the side of the mountain, I have a new-found respect for the research people who walked up there every day. But it was an experience that I will remember the rest of my life. It was amazing to sit amongst the great apes and make that connection with them.

When I got back to the milk factory, I had to check the two big blisters on my heels, and clean and put dressings on them. I was beat from the day's events. We had a meeting later in the evening and it was passed onto us that the redeployment message came in today from Canada. We will be closing the clinic on the 15th of October and everyone will be back home no later than the 22nd of October.

After the meeting, I had a few pops and went to bed early, very happy with the day's experiences.

Saturday, 24 September

Woke up early, muscles are a bit sore from the long walk up the mountains yesterday. I'm still amazed at the beauty of this country and what I just experienced sitting amongst the great apes. After breakfast we got together and headed down to the hospital, today we were in the screening tent. It was another busy day, pretty steady. We saw about 198 patients coming through today, but I'm getting somewhat suspicious with some of the patients lately showing up with shoes on and watches. When you see these things, you have to be suspicious that they have a little more money than most Rwandans and aren't the run of the mill regular patients we have been seeing the whole time here. With us getting long in the tooth and maybe leaving soon, some people are now coming to see what they can get and then selling it on the black market, got to keep ahead of this. Just give those types some magic water and a goodbye.

At supper we heard of one of the guys from the D&S platoon had a bad fall earlier today while mountain climbing. Apparently, he had to be stabilized and flown by helicopter to Kigali where he had surgery for what may have been a broken pelvis, but no one was sure. I sure hope he is ok; the guys have been phenomenal in doing their job in protecting us throughout the entire time we have been here and helped in more ways than just D&S, with the occasional shift in the hospital with us on their off days. Not much else happened today so I went to sleep early tonight after supper, still tired from yesterday's climbing up the Visoke mountain and the walk to the Karisoke research buildings.

Sunday, 25 September

Today we were GD (General Duties) for the camp. We cleaned the eating area and around the building. A couple of us took garbage to the dump down the road, while a couple others showed one of the locals, acting as interpreter, and his fellow Rwandan workers how to set up our tents. We also had a couple of the workers mix up some more Gatorade for the screening area ORS (Oral Rehydration Station).

After this, I attended Mass with Father Bosse, who held two masses for us today, one in English and the other French. Afterwards I went with him to the Nyundo Cathedral where he held a healing Mass for the local diocese. I wish I could live here in Rwanda; they have such an enthusiasm for life, you can hear it in their singing at church today and in the beautiful music during the Mass. Our padre has done a lot to help while he has been here and during the many services he's held since our arrival. The Rwandan minister conducting the Mass with him acknowledged his contributions to the diocese and all the local churches in the area. I was glad to see this, I have accompanied him on most of his trips here and feel, in a small way, as if I were a part of all the good, he has done here.

After we returned, not much else happened the rest of the afternoon, it was very quiet, and I went back with my section to our sleeping area and talked for a while before supper. I wrote a few letters and went to speak with Fr. Bosse about another upcoming trip he wanted to take down to the seminary near Gisenyi.

Monday, 26 September

Well, today we were back to screening patients. It was a light day with only 159 persons showing up. There is no doubt that we are winding down. The last couple of weeks we have delivered some babies and taken care of some chronic illnesses, but in reality, we are not really doing the urgent-type of medicine I thought we were sent to do, or the refugee care for those travelling back from the refugee camps in Goma. With the low number of patients, we finished our day at approximately 14:30 and then went back to our sleeping area. Later in the afternoon, I cut hair for an hour or so. Even with the number of haircuts I've done since my arrival here, I am not getting any better at cutting hair, but at least it's short and easy to clean.

The Critical Incident Stress Debrief team who arrived a week ago to help us or prepare us to go home after our tour, are leaving today, I hope they enjoyed their vacation and the sightseeing of the gorillas and local craft stores, I think they were more successful at this than in debriefing us. One of the social workers I had met on RV92. He is a good fellow was talking to me for a while, I asked if he could take some mail back for me so it could be mailed from there, and I gave a few letters to him to drop off for me back in Canada. Anyway, the rest of the day was mundane and nothing exciting or new went on. It's now 21:00 so now it's off to bed.

Tuesday, 27 September

Today I got up early and was excited for the day in front of me. I had arranged with Tim for our Det to go up to the cathedral at the seminary that was close to Gisenyi. I have been there a couple times before with Father Bosse and there is a lot of work to be done, too much for today but at least it will be a beginning. The whole Det went, and when we got there, the local priest had arranged for some locals to be there to help too. The cathedral is beautiful. It is one that you have to look up to and there are about twenty-five long, narrow steps leading up to the gigantic main doors. It was dirty outside with a lot of garbage around the building.

When we went it in was a huge space, and there was nothing inside, not one thing was there. We were told that all the pews had been used for fuel wood during the war and the altar as well. Up on the altar there is a giant cross on the wall and at the base of it you could see splatters of blood on the wall and at the base of the cross from when the bishop, other priests, and some seminarians had been lined up and executed there.

I went to the back and down the backstairs, where the rectory was with the papers all over the floor and all the church records full of human waste and destroyed. It was a terrible sight. Sizing up the building, we figured out the work that needed to be done and we were paired into teams and went to work.

Chris, and I went outside to the back of the church, we didn't know how it had happened, but there were a couple of cars up on the roof and in the middle of the stairs. The stairs zigzagged up and there they were…cars in the middle of the staircase. It was a strange sight. We went about with ropes and old-fashioned hard work and pushed the cars over the stairs and into the main courtyard below. From here they were dragged out towards the front to be taken away.

Tim, Kenny, and Kelley cleaned inside the Cathedral, once we finished with the vehicles and other work outside around the back of the building, we went to the front and began to clean the front of the cathedral. I noticed Tim was walking around talking to the guys as he was looking around. When he got to me, he said to begin moving slowly towards the vehicles, we were going to leave! I said, what's up? He told me that the locals had been told by someone that for the day's work helping us, that *we* would be giving them food. I had been here with Father Bosse earlier in the week and that had not been discussed or mentioned at all.

We slowly swept and slowly made our way back to the trucks and made out that we had to leave for a while but would be back later.

After we left, Father Bosse wanted to take us to the Meridian Hotel in Gisenyi for some pommes frites. We drove down to eat, but when we got there, we didn't get any food because the local merchants are getting greedy, they have hiked the exchange rate way too high. We didn't eat and instead went back to the milk factory and would eat on our return. After supper, we just shot the shit for a while, then I went to bed at around 21:00. Overall, I thought it was a good day. We all had done a great job cleaning up the cathedral.

Wednesday, 28 September

Up at my usual 06:00 or so. Soon as I got up, I had a coffee right away so I could have some time for myself before everyone got up. It's a rare thing to get time alone when you live with two hundred or so of your best friends in an open area, but I like sometimes just sitting to myself.

I was pleased with yesterday as were all the guys. It was enjoyable to help and be a part of something bigger than ourselves. Father Bosse was appreciative of our work volunteering at the seminary.

Today we worked on the ward from 07:00 to 15:00. I oversaw the six babies on the ward on this shift. We had a new, healthy baby born a couple days ago and there were beautiful twins born today, so I had my hands full with babies.

The three orphans are leaving for an orphanage just down the street. It's being run by an American lady named Mrs. Rosamond Carr, a long-time resident in Rwanda, who has decided to help Rwanda heal by opening an orphanage. Not sure when the babies are leaving us but it's soon. I feel the one we named Chip has AIDS and is not doing well, he may die soon. It's been very difficult watching him these last few weeks. When he tries to cry you can barely hear him, it's a silent crying. You can see he is sick and wants us to comfort him but in his weak state, no real sound comes out of his mouth. So shitty to watch this. Chip's weight was down again today when we weighed him, he's not improving.

The other little guy, Angus, most likely has some type of brain damage, I think, due to the way he rests; he is always sort of in a fetal position. He's a trooper, though, he was the little guy left at the front gate one night and the Airborne guys found him and brought him to the hospital. He has probably the best chance of survival at the orphanage. The only problem with him is that we have him so spoiled that his transition to Mrs. Carr's orphanage might prove a little difficult.

After work our Det went up to our bed space area and relaxed. I went and had a shower, ate, and talked for a while to the guys. Today was BBQ day again. Once a week they try to do a BBQ day, but I usually don't partake in these. Last year in Somalia we were on hard rations all tour and I just found eating the same was easier than eating one fresh meal a week, and then getting the shits. Throwing off the whole digestive system with eating fresh food once weekly is not worth it for me, so I'll stay with eating ration packs. So as usual, tonight I didn't eat BBQ again.

We had the MO in charge of the field hospital down in Kigali, along with the UNAMIR contingent, arrive and talk to us again last night about malaria in Sub-Saharan Africa. But at this point in our tour, who really cares? He talks about this while we have had to treat patients with malaria since our arrival, and I am so tired of the way we have been managed since we began. It's all too much at times; the shift schedule, these lectures in the middle of our sleep cycles, and the way all the medics have been managed. I'm afraid I am going to say something soon and get in trouble, it's not worth it. We are all tired here and our focus is only two things; working at the hospital and trying to sleep the hours in between the shifts. But once again, now we must attend a lecture for an hour and a half. Once he finished, I didn't stick around and went right to bed at 20:30. We'll see what tomorrow brings.

Thursday, 29 September

Up at 06:00 today and went for a run with the entire Det. Tim likes to do a lot of things together as a Det to keep us intact and cohesive. I think at this point it is serving us well and with all the shit we are doing and seeing here, it's good for all of us to depend on one another. After we finished our little run down towards the RPF compound and back we had a shave and shower and then breakfast.

We were sent again with Father Bosse to the seminary to help him and the local clergy continue to restore the seminary and cathedral there. We concentrated on the seminary today, but it was a good day's work. We picked up from where we were last time and cleaned out the rest of the cathedral, rectory, and glebe house. A very productive day and after this it was about 13:00 when we finally finished the tasks we had for today. Afterwards, we went to Gisenyi for some pomme frites and today we weren't going to get ripped off as we had brought Rwandan money with us.

We sat for about an hour and half at the Meridian Hotel and had a nice meal of samosas and pomme frites. Afterwards, we decided to go down to the beach to explore. It looked good from where we were eating, and when we got there, we only saw one old dead body, mostly buried in the sand, so we dubbed him Bernie at the Beach! But as we walked along the beach in the washed-up grass and vegetation, we still saw many body parts and bones along the shore. They are probably washing in from Goma where they had more than 100,000 die from cholera only two months ago as we were just arriving.

After we walked back to the Meridian Hotel, we left for camp and once we got back had a quick meeting and ate supper. We found out that again tonight, at 19:00, we have been blessed with yet another lecture tonight with the doctor visiting us from Kigali who arrived yesterday. He gave a lecture then, but now another tonight. Holy shit! Why are we such an attraction?

Doesn't anyone in charge of us understand that when we are made to sit here for two hours, that means two hours less sleep in an eight-hour timeframe before our next shift at the hospital?

After the lecture, it was about 21:00. All I really want is to go to bed, but we've probably got another O group before we sleep. I am not looking forward to the next few days with us back on the ward in the rumoured winding-down of the facility in the next couple of weeks. Oh well, go to bed afterwards.

Friday, 30 September

The last couple of days have been busy on the ward. Lots of patients on our first day back, but now, slowly the hospital is emptying. We were still doing our regular eight hours on and eight off shift schedule for the last two days. Even though there aren't many patients any longer in the hospital, the wards are still busy with those having IV meds, dressing changes, and the regular ebb and flow of the shifts and patients we have. I'm not really sure at this point but I think that our doctors are getting ready to close the hospital. I think they want out of here and back to Canada. Right now, I think all we are actually doing here, and all we actually did this whole time for the most part was chronic care with the exception of some traumas, live births, and MVAs[4].

---

4   Motor Vehicle Accident: when a vehicle hits a person, object or another vehicle, causing injury or damage.

The Other Side of the Fence

I look at him, he looks back at me
I see him smile as I smile at he
He nods his head and I to him
He has nothing, I everything,

I look at a child, he sees a man
I see poverty and he wealth
He has the tribe, I my brothers
He has hunger, I a full stomach

I look at results of this war, he looks at my peace
I see sadness across the wire, he sees happiness
He has his lot in life, mine is not here
He waves good-bye as I nod and bid adieu

Derrick Nearing MMM, CD

October 1994

Saturday, 1 October

I am losing my mind I think; I am so tired with this last few days and nights of shifts on the ward. With the end in sight there isn't much left in the tank. I can't concentrate and just want out of here. Today the RPF were running up the highway again, singing and pumping their weapons into the air. We were told that it was a national celebration or something like this. Overall it is quieting down, and the flow of patients seems to be dropping as each day passes.

Sunday, 2 October

We had a briefing tonight after our last shift on the ward. Tim informed us that we will close screening down and see our last patient on the 8th of October and then by the 11th of October we will close down the entire hospital. Those patients we will have remaining here will need to be transferred to another hospital in the area. Then, once we have the hospital emptied, we will be able to take down the facility on the 12th and pack it all up, I will be glad to have it done with. I know it wasn't exactly a waste, but I did feel that the last two weeks were a waste of time as we were just looking for work. There was no real reason to stay here as we were under-employed. We did some good overall during our couple months here, but our job is done now and it's time to go.

Monday, 3 October

Well, up early today, we were on the ward again. Only one shift after this and then we are on GD for a day or so. When I got to the ward I wanted to go right away and see the little boy I had last night as a patient. He was pretty sick when I left, and I was worried about him.

I guess the little fellow was having seizures after we finished our shift and he died around 23:00 late last night.

Anyway, off to work we went for 07:00 and the day was very quiet. We only had fourteen patients left in the entire hospital. It was decided to consolidate them all into one ward and we started to do terminal cleaning on the beds and equipment in the other three wards, since they were being unused. The hospital's beginning to gear down fast now, you can see it. All the troops really want out of here now. I think we've done our best work and it's time to leave. In the last couple of months since the conclusion of the war, there have been so many agencies and NGOs arriving and filling the healthcare and refugee gap that our presence is no longer needed here. Give it a week and they won't even remember who was at the milk factory.

Once work was done for the day, the entire detachment went for a run. It felt pretty good with the six of us on a run. I think that I'll be getting back into running quickly once we return home. Being up here in the mountains the last three months in this high altitude, we have adapted and breathe so much easier now. We were joking about how in the first few weeks on returning home to the thicker air at sea level in Canada, that we will be running so fast no one will keep up with us. Can't wait.

After the run I had a shower and pop and I talked a little with the guys. Then after the O group at 21:00 I went to bed.

Tuesday, 4 October

Up early today, 06:00. Got washed, shaved, and had a coffee. I am up early because I am excited that we are going again to the seminary today again with Fr. Bosse. It should be good. I can really begin to see the difference we are making getting it cleaned out and preparing to start Mass there again.

Today was a GD day, so I was sent with Fr. Bosse to go to the seminary to help them clean up the place. My Det didn't go this time, they are staying back to do some work around the milk factory, but Tim didn't mind letting me go when Fr. Bosse requested me. Today it was MCpl. Joanne Leadbeater's Det with Shane Williamson and some new girl in the unit, Christine Pissinger,

Dave Follett, plus a few others that went. Anyway, it was a good day as far as the cleaning goes. I think the inside of the cathedral is ready for painting and then I guess they will have to see about getting new pews. The ones that were here originally were used as firewood during the war when this place was packed with those trying to stay alive and not be killed. Sad state really.

Fr. Bosse and I were walking around the compound, it was so beautiful with green everywhere and the most beautiful flowers. As we walked, we came upon an opening in the ground and to our disgust found at least twenty-seven bloated bodies in the septic system in different states of decay. It was sickening with the smell of rotten bodies. I can't imagine what evil would cause this to happen. After three months here now, I am still amazed at the hate that must have fuelled this war.

Not sure but these people in the septic system were most likely priests, nuns, and seminarians. It was an upsetting thing and I am sure something that will be with me for years to come. Father Bosse reported our findings to the local bishop, for them to follow up and investigate before proper burial of the bodies.

After we finished our time cleaning, we went to the local school close by and gave some blankets and food. Not sure why but it reminded me of when I was a kid in school back in the '60s, where as kids would all sit up nice and straight at our desks, hands folded in front of us, and we would all say, "Good Morning" whenever an adult came into the class and was introduced to us. The discipline and manner of the kids today just seemed to remind me of this for some reason.

We also visited the local orphanage between Gisenyi and our location. It was the one run by Mrs. Rosamond Carr. I had been there a couple times before and she was such a nice person. I am still amazed that she stayed and lived in her home during the war, but this has been her home for most of her life. After the war she saw a need for the children whose parents were killed during the war, so she began an orphanage for them.

Mrs. Carr would later call her orphanage "Imbabazi" which translated means "forgiveness" and she went onto care for hundreds of orphaned children from the genocide and lived in Rwanda for more than 50 years until her passing on September 29, 2006.

She told Father Bosse her plan to begin an orphanage and that she needed a little help to get her home back into shape after the war. This was important for our troops on many levels. With parents who now had nothing so were dropping babies off at our gates, we would be unable to handle all of them and that was not what we were there for. We also knew that time for us was short and we would be in Rwanda only be a couple months at the most, so the orphans we had would need a place. With the knowledge of Mrs. Carr's orphanage, this provided us comfort in knowing there was a place where our orphans would be cared for.

Father Bosse had asked us if we would mind helping at the orphanage, with a little cleaning and fixing up around the building. One of the most pressing issues for Mrs. Carr's orphanage was electricity. With her generator not working and many doors and windows now broken, this would need the mechanics and engineers' help.

> When we got back later in the day, the need would be sent to the command team, and the mechanics, electricians, and engineers would later be sent to fix the generator and handle carpentry needs for the orphanage. The engineers with us were an amazing group of soldiers with an equally amazing skill set. Once they were asked if they could assist, they quickly volunteered and went to work helping Mrs. Carr get the home back into shape for her and her children. They went about fixing windows and doors, getting the water running, and repairing the electricity, for all of which she was extremely grateful.

> As this was taking place, many of us sent letters back home to our families in Canada telling them of the situation at the orphanage and asking them that instead of sending us packages of goodies for ourselves, to send infant and children's clothes, shoes, diapers, powdered baby formula, and other essentials to be donated to the orphanage.

> We would visit the orphanage a few more times in the two weeks to come before our departure, and we brought the children's clothes, diapers, and food that our families back in Canada had sent over.

As Father Bosse said goodbye to Mrs. Carr, looking around I really think we accomplished a lot today, cleaning up in such a short time, a lot of good was done today. After our little visits to the school and orphanage, around 13:00, we went to the Meridian Hotel in Gisenyi for some pommes frites and a pop with the padre. I really enjoy it when I come here. For only a half hour or so it's a little piece of normal and takes you away from what we are doing back at the milk factory. Unfortunately, it didn't last long before we had to come back to Mareru, and that was basically all the day's work done.

The rest of the day I just took it easy, cut a few heads of hair in the afternoon, had supper, and into the evening we all just took it easy. I went to bed about 21:00.

Wednesday, 5 October

Well, awoke early as usual, and said a Happy Birthday to me. Today I'm thirty-three but who really cares?!! Just another day and another birthday passing. Today we were on the ward at 06:30, and when we got there during the hand-over, we were told that there was a pregnant lady at the front gate, we should go up to see what was going on. Tim and I went out to the main gate to see her problem. The Airborne guys were there and were the ones who had notified us about her.

When we arrived up at the front gate, it was obvious that she had lost her mucous plug and her water had broken and she was having difficulty with her unborn baby's delivery. We had her taken up to the hospital to our delivery-room area when Dr. Jacques came to examine her, and after he finished, he said she was about seven cm dilated. Tim told me to stay with the doctor and help with the birth this morning.

It was a long morning, or at least it seemed long to me, and I wasn't even the one giving birth. The lady was in labour for hours until finally at 10:56, she delivered the baby and I was there to assist in the delivery. It was amazing as I had never seen or participated in a birth before. I assisted by clamping, then cutting the umbilical cord, and then I was asked to weigh the newborn and give a Vitamin K injection and eye drops to the baby. For me this was an amazing experience. I had never been involved in a birth before and enjoyed the experience. I know if this ever happens in future not to be afraid and that

I'll have some skills in how to handle it. It gave me something to be happy about unlike the many gruesome things I have seen over the last few months. I was so happy with how this turned out.

After I finished my duties assisting with the newborn's birth, I returned to the milk factory for a quick lunch before heading back to the hospital. Before lunch I went to my bed space to get my eating utensils, and as I walked into our sleeping area, I saw someone working on medical bags. There were six of them laid out in a row and on closer inspection it looked as though one of them was mine. I thought to myself, *What the hell is he doing with my med bag?* This was the med bag I've had since deploying on the recce, and it was packed for the way I like to do my business as a medic, not packed for him.

I went over and asked what he was doing, the way he answered it sounded like he already had all six bags stripped and repacked to be the same, mine included, I was getting pissed off quickly. I went over, looked at my bag, and noticed that he had screwed around with the entire way it was packed. I told him that no one should ever mess around with another's equipment, and that he had no right to have repacked my medical bag. There was no reason for it to be touched; it's a personal piece of kit and never was his responsibility to touch. He was only doing what was ordered, but those in charge should have known better than do this during a tour!

What made me upset was that I had personally signed it out months ago when I came over on the recce and had organized for my preferences being lefthanded. Now it's all screwed up and most of the medications I once had have been removed. I told him that I treat people well and with respect and I think it should be the same back to me. I said I really didn't need this shit, and there was no reason to touch my equipment.

The rest of the afternoon I was upset with this bullshit going on, having someone in my kit. It's these things on tour that piss people off. Space is limited and what little privacy and the few personal items you have, should be left alone...not having people in your kit without permission. I was so upset the rest of the shift. I understood that he had been directed to organize the med bags, but the one under my bed I had signed for and had configured for my use since I had been on the recce. He had no business in my kit and now he thinks it's funny to see me so pissed off about it. But the trouble comes when there is a mass casualty or vehicle accident like the one Tim and

I attended to on our arrival here at Mareru. It's during times such as this you can see why it's important not to change someone's personal equipment. If I were to get a call right now to a site, it would cause delays with treatment. I would have to check all the pockets for dressings and bandages that have been moved from where I was familiar with. No need for this!

We finished 15:00 at the hospital and I was still pissed with the exchange I'd had earlier in the afternoon, so before I said anything in anger, I went out for a forty-minute run with WO Martell. I really needed to run and forget the day. We ran a good ten km and I think the endorphins kicked in and changed my mood. After the run I had a shower and ate a ration pack and a cup of tea. Then at 18:30 our O group was held, and Tim told us a few more details as to the hospital closing and tear down within the next five to seven days. There was a BBQ tonight with some beers, which I skipped, not my thing. Later in the evening I ate some soup with crackers and was in bed by 21:00. . . Some birthday!

Thursday, 6 October

Today we were in the screening bay and it was a very busy day. We saw around 306 patients coming through. The locals now know that we are leaving soon, so they are trying to get all that they can from us. We can tell that some have nothing wrong with them, so they get vitamins and are told to take one a day. Others get electrolyte water. I still think that we should have been using indelible ink the whole time here to decrease unnecessary repeat customers. But I guess I can't really blame them for trying to get all they can from us while we are here. If the roles were reversed, I would certainly be trying to get everything I could and more!

At the end of the day before supper I went for an eight km run with WO Martell again and we did it in thirty-eight minutes. I forgot to mention that this morning my Det went for a five km run with the Airborne platoon and then did a bit of upper body work with some of the guys from the regiment about an hour before work. It was a great start and end to the day.

After the run we got washed and then had supper and sat for a while and just talked. Later I was going to sit and write in my journal and a few letters home, and I was looking forward to being on GD tomorrow. But then the day ended on a sour note. Instead of us being on GD, Tim told us that we are now taking 5 Fd Amb's place on the ward tomorrow. This pissed me off a bit. I went to bed at 21:30.

Friday, 7 October

Just got up and snuck out of my bed space area. I wanted to be up and alone because I needed time to think. I slept very badly last night, all night tossing and turning, so finally at 04:00, I got out of bed. There's too much going on in my mind with this deployment and the shit going on back home with the Airborne Regiment in the news, our tour in Somalia and all the shit that took place there, losing Mike Abel, exhuming a body, the attacks on us at the end of that tour in Mogadishu, and so much more that happened there.

I've been thinking about our time here…and just what we have done over the last few months. I'm not sure of what I've done sometimes, or even if it was worth it. Funny how I get knocked off my horse so easily now. I've been in a bad mood for the last two days now, ever since I walked in on my medical bag being reorganized without anyone asking me. It's silly to be stuck like this, but I feel sort of violated with my personal equipment being taken and changed by someone else. No sleep is not good for me—then I'm all tired and get cranky and stop talking to everyone. I close down. Don't mean to be cranky but it happens.

Saturday, 8 October

On the 8th we closed out screening, it was an easy day overall. I worked in the treatment area with a MCpl Cormier from 5 Fd Amb. Very nice guy and seems to know a lot about medicine, he was a great instructor who made things easy to understand as we worked together through the day.

At the end of the day, I was a bit frustrated as we were not allowed to go for a run. I'm not sure why we weren't allowed to go because we've been doing runs most of our time here. I thought that it might be that we are so close to leaving they didn't want anything to happen at this point, or it might be that something might be up at the RPF base down the highway. We've had some issues with them a couple of times throughout our time here. This place is frustrating. I don't mind orders, but I do like to know why sometimes as well. I know it's not my business, though.

The rest of the day was pretty good. Patients weren't that ill or injured so it was a good day to close out screening.

After supper we got mail at 19:00. I received six boxes of children's clothes from my friend Lisa back in Petawawa. What a sweetheart, doing this for me. I also got mail from my friend Bill, Lisa's husband, and my roommate J.C. as well as Mom and Sister Catherine MacKinnon from The Holy Redeemer Convent. It made my whole day just to get all that mail, especially the clothes and parcel from the convent. I will take these clothes down to the orphanage later in the week before we leave. I know they will appreciate them as they are overrun with children after the war and any help is welcomed there, every little bit helps.

The parcel from Sr. Catherine contained another four hundred hand-made rosaries as well as some home-made fudge this time. Once again there is a letter on top of the rosaries. I opened the letter and read:

September 23, 1994

Dear Derrick,

Thank you for your beautiful letter. I shared it with your dear mother and with the president of the C.W.L., who has not returned it as yet. Hopefully on Sunday, when we have Holy Hour (Last Sunday of every month) she will bring it back, as I want to send a copy of it when we are giving our report for the third quarter of 1994.

The accompanying fudge was made on the evening of September 21 and 22, I hope it arrives in good or even excellent condition. (I did my best to seal it against the "perils of transport.") Hopefully it will not be opened by anyone before you get it, so that no chance of contamination occurs.

Take care of yourself by the usually prudent precautions. I am enclosing a medal of St. Michael the Archangel and of Our Lady of the Olives (Peace) obtained from Christ, the Prince of Peace. Blessings and protection upon all you "Keepers of the Peace."

It will be great to have a cup of tea with you on your return. Your mom will be so proud to accompany you when you come to visit us. Our hearts will probably be torn by some of the pictures you may have to show.

I want to get this into the next mail so that Father Bosse may have more rosaries to distribute at Sunday Mass. God love and protect you and all the guys and girls whose presence there makes such a difference, God bless you all.

Your mom will be coming in at 3 p.m. This goes out at 1:30, so I had her sample the fudge both evenings as soon as it was cold enough to eat.

Love and Prayers

Sister Catherine

Sister Catherine tells me in her letter that mom is worried about me, but also so proud and knows that I am doing good work here. She wants me to come to the convent for a visit when I get back and have lunch and tea when I return and tell all the sisters about my adventures here in Rwanda, I guess I can do this but there's really not much joy in what I've seen and done over here. There's not much to talk about here in the hospital except death, sickness and the occasional birth, however my trips out by myself with Fr. Bosse, and those times with the others from our mission, are the most enjoyable for me so I can certainly talk about this. She says the fudge was made on the 21st and 22nd of September, I am not worried about getting sick from it, it will be eaten.

I took the whole parcel and gave it entirely to Fr. Bosse, I think he is tired from everything he has been through here and needs this to help him through the next few weeks. There has been so much shit here and things that cannot be explained by God. It certainly tests your beliefs and I know he has been tested many times over the last few months, like myself too many times. This parcel will hopefully lift him up a little.

I went to Fr. Bosse's room and gave him the parcel. He seemed surprised that I would give him all the fudge, but I told him that it is homemade from Cape Breton and I would rather he would give to those who would benefit from a little kindness. He insisted that he and I have a piece of fudge together, and he was amazed at all the rosaries that the nuns from Cape Breton made for the people here in Rwanda. He said we will give them out next time we go to church and that he will ask the CO to allow me to come with him as his driver. I feel content and happy that I am of some use to Fr. Bosse in helping others out in the community as well as in the hospital.

Later, I went out to the front of the milk factory with Fr. Bosse and we just sat there on the front covered-porch area and had a pop and some of the fudge that Sr. MacKinnon sent to me. We talked awhile, then some of the other troops showed up as well and sat with us, and he gave out some more of the fudge. It was a small taste of home. Afterward I was tired and just went to bed.

Sunday, 9 October

Today we were on general duties all day and it would end up being a pretty dull day. We began taking down some of the canvas wards that made up the hospital and packing them away along with some hospital equipment. Not much else noteworthy happened.

After work I went for a run with Mike Holmes and it was six km in twenty-nine minutes. I think that is very good. This running and exercise helps to keep me calm, I think. I don't know what I would do if I couldn't run every day. After I got back from the run there were letters on the pillow again tonight from my roommate and another from Sr. Margaret.

I got a briefing from Tim and it looks like we are out of here in about a week or so. With the closing down of the screening, we will finish up with the patients in the hospital.

They are also going to do the 3.2 km Battle Fitness Test a day or so before we leave. Wow, I would have thought that we could have waited until we got home to do this, we all passed it within the last year, but why do this now? Afterwards, I got washed and then off to bed. We'll see what tomorrow brings.

Monday, 10 October

Up and at it early this morning, just a quick wash and teeth brush before a coffee and a run with the guys from the Det. This morning we started off with a forty-minute fartlek[5] training run. Felt good just to get out and it's always fun joking around afterwards with the horseplay. After this we got washed, had a quick bite, and down to the hospital continuing the teardown, as much as we could. I think we could have got the whole thing down and packed up today, but we still have a few more days here, so I think they want a slow and controlled teardown.

The rest of the day was easy. In the afternoon I was sent up to the milk factory while Tim and the others stayed down packing up some equipment inside the hospital. I helped WO Tardif until 16:00 with Randy Murphy and Christine Pissinger, just getting packing lists done and preparing equipment to go home. After work, I got changed, had supper, and shot the shit for awhile with the guys. Around 21:00, I just got a shower and went to bed.

Tuesday, 11 October

This morning I woke up at 04:30, not sure why, but thinking a lot about my tour in Somalia and this one here in Rwanda. I really want to continue from this tour and join the UNAMIR tour afterwards. There has been a lot going on in my mind, I just can't get back to sleep. My phone call today was at 05:15, but when I went to the MRSAT phone to wait my turn, there was no one ahead of me so I called early. I spoke my roommate to see how he was and to wish him well during his tour in Yugoslavia. He is leaving tomorrow and will be returning by the end of November for his UN leave and we can reconnect then. I wished him safe travels and a safe tour over there.

At 06:15 we went for an upper body workout and then to the showers. I got dressed and had breakfast and afterwards just sat in my bed space to myself and wrote and thought about things I wanted to do! I am hoping they will allow me to stay after my unit goes back to Canada. I was off until 11:00, and then Chris Shadbolt and I had to go work the front gate. This was only

---

5   Periods of fast running intermixed with periods of slower running

until 13:00. After this I ate dinner and then went out for a run with Capt. Linford. After returning, I went and had a shower and relaxed.

After supper, Tim approached me and asked what's going on, what did I do? He said at first when the list came out for the Battle Fitness Test, I was with those leaving first, and now I am suddenly at the very back. He started to give me shit for wanting to go last on the 3.2 run on the 14th. Although it was already roughly decided what positions we would all run in, I had gone and spoken to the training officer and asked if he could move me to the very last position. I saw what I did was wrong and that I should have spoken to Tim about this. But all I wanted to do was be the last guy at the back of the Det and support the slower guys from the rear and encourage them, so we would all pass the 3.2 run. Tim was pissed at me, and I can't blame him for this, he just wanted me to do as I was told and do the run from wherever I was placed.

I went and spoke to the training officer and told him I'd screwed up and to please put it back to the way it was. I don't care anymore, I just wanted to help. Shit, I've done the 3.2km run for years now and always passed. I'll just go to the front and whoever passes, passes. It's now around 19:30 or so and I'm just waiting for the O group and then off to bed.

Wednesday, 12 October

Today was just a relaxing day. We had to do a few things to help set up the party taking place tonight, and after this, it was a very easy day. I went for a run with my weapon and web gear. It was a good run, I needed this to relieve pressure. At the party I sat with the field engineers during the meal. I'm not sure why but we had been eating ration packs the entire tour and tonight we were given lobster tails and salad with our beer. I think we all ate too much and drank a little more than we should have. There were performances with a group of tribal drummers and singers as well as dancers who sang traditional Rwandan songs while they danced. The show lasted about an hour or so until the sun went down.

Then, as we drank a little more, there were a few funny skits, and everyone was having a great time. I was having an enjoyable time, up until I messed up and split a glow stick in half, accidentally spraying some into a guy's face as I flicked it at the ceiling. I didn't mean it, but I really felt bad about this, I messed up. I apologized to him, but like myself, he'd had a few drinks and with the glow stick fluid in his eye, was in too much pain and pissed off at me to care about an apology. I don't blame him, but with him getting angrier and wanting at me, I felt it was better to leave right then before it escalated, which was probably a good idea. The guys took him down to the clinic and they flushed his eye out and put some drops in it. We would talk the next day. I went to bed at 24:00.

Thursday, 13 October

As soon as I awoke today, I had this terrible, empty feeling in the pit of my stomach, and then I felt nauseated, like I was going to be sick. Quickly, I ran out to the toilet area at the back of the milk factory and there was a lineup of soldiers already there, with the exact same symptoms. It seemed that every single one of us got ill from the fresh lobster and salad last night. We had been eating basically sterile food the entire tour and with the bacteria in the shellfish, our stomachs weren't used to it, so now everyone has nausea, vomiting, and diarrhea. It would be a long shitty day ahead for sure. I self-medicated with some Imodium, Pepto-Bismol, and Cipro, drank lots of fluid, and stayed close to the toilet area.

There was another pressing issue to take care of early in the morning. I had to find the Field Engineer guy from last night who I accidently sprayed in the eye with a glowstick. I felt so bad about what I had done, getting the glow stick fluid in the guy's eye. Not the way I wanted to end my tour with this taking place. I went over to the engineers' building and spoke to a couple guys from Cape Breton I knew. They went to get the fellow who I had gotten in the eye with the glowstick fluid. For sure he was really pissed off at me and I don't blame him. I awkwardly apologized to him as best I could and was very remorseful. He told me he was really pissed at me and would like to punch me in the face. I understood his anger at what took place and would have deserved a good punch in the head. But he was the bigger man and said he understood with all of us drinking and being stupid, that it got a little out of control and that he would let it go. He was actually very good about it and although still pissed at me, gave me a reserved smile and said, "Let's get on with tearing this place down and forget what happened last night," as we shook hands. I nodded appreciatively for his accepting my apology.

Friday, 14 October

I took a predawn walk out behind where the hospital once stood, in the northwest corner of the compound, where we had begun our hospital grave-yard only a few short months ago. There was the mass grave in the corner with the bodies our troops had moved initially from their shallow grave site to a more permanent and proper burial site in the corner of the compound. Then there were the little white crosses lined up in a couple of rows, some with names and others with the word "Innocent" written on them, reserved for the many babies we had buried. It had grown from that initial mass grave, to another forty or more individual graves from the patients we cared for during our time in Rwanda. Many of the people buried here died while our section was working, but we had done our best for them when they entered our facility. There were many we could help in a small way by healing their physical injuries, but for those who lay in our hospital graveyard their fate was probably sealed even before they had come to us. I wanted these few moments alone just to walk amongst the mounds of earth, so I wouldn't forget why we had been sent here.

Later in the afternoon there was to be a closing-out parade at noon, and some would be leaving for Kigali this afternoon. The rest of us will go tomor-row, driving the vehicles and equipment back to the 3 CSG compound. On the hand-over, Cpl. Rejean Michel and I went out on the top of the overhang in front of the milk factory where we had set up a flagpole at the beginning of the tour, to fly a Canadian and Medical Branch Flag. As the parade was taking place, we stood at ease waiting to be directed to lower the flags. When the time arrived, we both saluted and began to lower the flags, one at a time. Rejean held the first flag as I unhooked it from the rope. Then together we folded it properly, and we did the second flag in the same manner. Then we brought them downstairs to hand off to the Commanding Office, Jim Anderson and Regimental Sergeant Major, Patrick Doyle.

Saturday, 15 – 17 October

We went to Kigali today in preparation for our flight home. It was sort of anti-climatic with many of the troops from Calgary and Quebec already having left earlier. That night most people sat on the stadium seats and talked all night. The excitement of going home and the pressure of the tour now melting away, made conversations easier. I laid there looking up at the African sky, just wanting this to be over.

The next day we finally were taken to the airport and loaded on the commercial airplane. With this, our tour was over and we were heading back to Canada.

It was a long, two-day travel time with the time-zone changes from Kigali to Ottawa with several stops along the way. I really didn't care, I just wanted to get home and I had nothing left to give. It was beginning to settle in on me again just as it had a year earlier on my return from Somalia.

My return home to Petawawa was no different than my return a year earlier from Somalia, we arrived around midnight back in Petawawa and unloaded from the bus. There were a few of the married guys' families waiting for them, but it was subdued just as it was last year getting off the bus on arrival from Somalia. There was no big fanfare, no marching band or reception, no one waiting for me as I got off the bus. I grabbed my backpack and barracks box and made my way over to the 2 Field Ambulance parking lot where I had parked my car back on the 27th of July, when I first left for Rwanda.

> My return was treated no differently than any other tasking I had ever been on before, and I went home to an empty apartment as my roommate had left for Croatia, two weeks earlier. But I could feel that things had changed inside me . . . I could feel it, and over time, over the next days, weeks, months, and in the years to come, there would be many storms in my life that came and went with the ebb and flow of more and more military deployments. There would be mental health issues which would arise, until eventually the accumulation of all these tours and experiences would prematurely end my career... but that's another story.

PART TWO
REFLECTIONS

The Loss

I found it in a book of old,
Tossed in a box a while ago.

I lost it over many years,
Given up in youthful glee.

I missed it then for years and years,
Thought it had died so shed some tears.

I mourned it for too long a time,
Memories buried far behind.

I found it most recently,
all of what's was lost ...
...was me

Derrick Nearing, MMM, CD

The Way We Think

One of the biggest things I encountered during my time in the military were the many times those who I worked for were unable, or unwilling, to change course or seek advice once they had made a decision, even if those decisions may have led to outcomes of unnecessary hardship or additional work. I had seen this theme of black and white versus grey thinking, repeatedly within the pages of this book as I was typing my journals. It can be seen from the pointless order for all inpatients at our hospital in Rwanda being prescribed medications for intestinal parasites, to hospital staff being kept up in the middle of a sleep cycle to listen to a lecture, or the shift schedule we had to endure on the ward. There are so many other examples of these decisions and when looking back, I believe they can be reduced to the two types of thinkers: black and white versus grey, of which there are more of the black and white type in most walks of life. I believe we can and do switch back and forth during our decision-making processes and this is good, often though as we learn what an organization wants and expects, we also learn to conform towards black and white thinking. It's the easiest in the decision-making process and creates the least conflict with superiors, which quickly leads to promotion within the organization. During my career, I often found myself most often as a grey thinker, attempts were often made to whip me back into black and white camp, as many of my supervisors were uncomfortable due to the unpredictability and the risks inherent in a grey thinker. It's just not safe or good for one's career to have subordinates who take risks where very often the outcomes are unknown. Myself, I liked the "Better to ask forgiveness than ask permission" on those occasions where a decision had to be made in the spur of a moment and time wasn't available to ask superiors.

Throughout my career, I believe I often thought outside the box and improvised ways to get a task done and this was especially true whenever deployed overseas. I was often the "go-to-guy" when things needed doing when we first arrived in country and resources were scarce. I would busily go about scrounging, liberating, and acquiring whatever was needed to get the mission done. However, once my task was completed, then when the bulk of other soldiers and supplies began to arrive, life got a little more comfortable for everyone and I found myself quickly restrained and put back into the box, with the reins on me because of the perceived risks to my supervisors of me being a loose cannon.

There are soldiers preordained to rise through the ranks, to achieve success because they are within the acceptable stream of thinkers the military finds comfort in. Ultimately, they are a sure thing; safe and within the black and white thinking model which the military desires. It is what I have come to call "institutional or intellectual incest". What I mean by this is a system where those higher in rank seek out younger troops similar to themselves, in thought and mannerism, then they mentor and push forward these like-minded subordinates who eventually get promoted and move into leadership positions who eventually replace the mentors. This ensures the gene pool is continually well stocked with like minded thinkers, thus making it difficult for grey thinkers to ascend the ranks.

Black and white thinkers are great; they are reliable, make decisions easily, follow the book and rules that are prescribed and safe to make decisions from. There is little chance of getting into trouble or making errors because the algorithms of leadership are there before them with the mantra, "I was only following the rules." This type of thinking is often seen as leadership or strength. However, often it takes more strength to make a grey decision and live with it, not knowing the exact outcome or the possible consequences in making these decisions, than to follow a leadership algorithm. Taking that leap of faith instead, and at times doing what is right, not what is correct according to a manual. The world is more nuanced than black and white, and often the thought process of black and white can lead to positions which become rigid. Take, for example the ward in our Rwandan hospital, specifically the shift schedule we followed working on the ward in Rwanda, why hadn't any of the senior leaders working with us speak up and address this? We were quickly fatigued during the first weeks of the hospital's operation; with the demanding schedule we never caught up on the sleep deficit during the rest of our time there, which contributed to our physical and mental health during and after the deployment. I often wonder the damage caused due to this rigid approach to managing us as we worked sleep deprived in our facility, why couldn't our fatigue and the demanding work schedule be seen or understood?

The struggle I had over my career was that black and white thinking competes in a world which leaves lots of room for grey. Often, we are deployed to unstable and hostile areas, where decisions are required to be made on the run, there is a need for decisions that are not anticipated. For example, when we needed vehicles in Rwanda on the recce, black and white thinking would have dictated that we go to the UN Headquarters, get permission, do the paperwork, follow the procedures set in place and send messages back to our National Defence Headquarters in Canada, all of which would have taken time, time we didn't have. In this situation, grey thinking led me to liberate an abandoned vehicle to get the job done. If we had done the black and white thinking, followed the protocols at the time, waiting for a vehicle I believe may have cost us another week or more to get the recce done, time we simply did not have. The paperwork would have been proper and all those in charge happy and feeling secure with the chain of approvals. How many more returning Rwandan refugees would have died from illness or their injuries, while hundreds of our soldiers sat at an airport hanger in Uganda or Kenya, waiting on us to finish the recce?

During the time in Rwanda, I had immense pressure put on me, threats of being charged or disciplined by some of the UN staff for things I did during our recce, but, once our hospital facility was established, I was quickly made compliant. In the black and white thinking model, I was in the wrong no matter what the operational need or urgency was, unless of course it was required and, in these cases, "look the other way" was employed, suddenly it was ok to act this way. An example from Afghanistan occurred when rules were in place not to treat locals in the Forward Operating Bases. However, when a child arrives at your doorstep with his heel hanging off and Achilles tendon exposed, you do what is right, not what is policy. If this situation took place again, I would not change my decision of being faced with the threat of being charged or punished. These conflicts of opposing mindsets left me to feel as if I was wrong, not because I necessarily was, but rather by default because they could not understand my grey thinking approach as they stayed in the safe zone with the rules to work from. This is the type of moral conflict I dealt with very often, I have come to believe these situations cause moral injury to soldiers, who are split between obeying the rules which are seen are legitimate and right or doing what is ethically and morally right.

I watched leaders making decisions based on policy, in favour of the institution, instead of erring on the side of a soldier where it would have been warranted for them to "ask for forgiveness, rather than ask for permission." The fear of breaking the black and white policy, possibly sacrificing a promotion or receiving a reprimand, was often too high a price for many where freethought was not encouraged. I believe it takes more courage on these occasions for those who were grey thinkers, than their black and white counterparts, because the latter have rules to go by, and in most cases grey thinkers only have their beliefs of what was right, wrong, and necessary to do. The black and white versus grey thinking is perhaps the way it is meant to be? I have come to understand that there are times in any profession or walk of life, where one or the other way of thinking is needed and valued, the trick is with the understanding when to employ one or the other.

I Awoke to PTSD

I had returned to CFB Petawawa after my Physician Assistant (PA) course in November 2004. A few months had gone by and it was now February 2005, we were up early on a sunny Sunday morning. I fed the baby as my wife was getting ready for morning church service. Maureen was now five months pregnant with our second child. Things had seemed to settle down since my PA course concluded in November and after our posting from CFB Borden to Petawawa. Life seemed a little more stable.

Once we arrived at church, we took our place sitting in the front row and listening to the Priest's Homily. Afterwards, the choir began to sing the hymn "The Summons" while I sat there holding Hannah, who was a little over a year old and sleeping contently in my arms, enjoying this moment with my wife and child.

The priest concluded his homily and sat. It was beautiful that moment, quiet with the soft sounds of the music and choir singing, the light coming through the stained glass and peacefulness of that time. As I looked down once again at my little baby girl in my arms, unexpectedly, thoughts of Rwanda flashed into my mind. I was having, *what I learned later*, what is called a dissociative moment and it felt it was no longer Hannah I was holding, as I looked down in my arms it was a little boy who had died in my arms ten years earlier, while on shift in our hospital one night while deployed to Rwanda. My surroundings that day in church became darker as everything closed in on me and suddenly, I was alone, everything from that time was there in front of me from ten years earlier during my time at the hospital ward in Rwanda. It was just me, the little boy in my arms and the unmistakable stench of sickness and death all around me. Once again, I could hear in the background fellow medics working hard, busily caring for people in our hospital after the terrible war the country of Rwanda had just come through.

I don't know how long this experience was, nor did I realize that I had tears running down my face with these memories. In the distance I once again heard the music and song from the Mass in the background and slowly was brought back to the present; "You satisfy a hungry heart, with gifts of finest wheat." As this hymn wafted through the air, Maureen touched my shoulder. I heard her voice speaking to me and then I was back in Our Lady of Lourdes Church. As I wiped tears away from my eyes, I looked over at Maureen and she asked, "What's wrong Derrick, why are you crying?" I replied, "Nothing is wrong, Maureen, I'm just thinking of how happy I am with you and Hannah in my life." However, inside me I knew I couldn't hold this off any longer as it was happening more and more frequently. I needed to see someone, to come out of my mental-health closet where I had resided for far too many years.

Monday morning, I went to work at the clinic and saw Dr. Brady, telling her I needed to talk, and she asked me what was wrong. As I was telling her the details of my experience at church the day prior, she looked at me and said, "I think you need help." She was going to send me for a mental health assessment in Ottawa. I was scared, scared of this moment which I had avoided for many years, the moment that would be the beginning of the end of my career, I thought. I had a wife, a small child, and one on the way. What if they kick me out? How will I live, make money? All these thoughts were racing through my mind.

Once I was diagnosed with PTSD in May of 2005, it then became only a matter of time before I would burn out and be medically released. I had no sense of how bad it really was because I was too preoccupied with salvaging my career and getting on with the job at hand of being a soldier. None of my supervisors knew what I was going through, my silent torment. I didn't tell anyone exactly how it felt, but it was like being on the inside of a packed room with everyone, but alone, not enjoying the moment.

I went back to work, seeing patients and doing rounds with the doctors, nurses and PAs I worked with, and we would discuss patients, treatment plans, and courses of action. Through it all I sat there with this little voice in my head, *"If they only knew. I shouldn't be here. I am one of those they are talking about."* These voices of inner doubt, of not belonging, peppered my entire time at Petawawa as a PA for the next ten years until my release due to PTSD, depression and an assortment of physical injuries from my career. But throughout it all was an inner shame and desire to please my supervisors and bury my problems, which I did and deployed twice more in my career to Afghanistan, which would ultimately end in my medical release.

Sanctuary Trauma

I believe that the concept of sanctuary trauma goes hand in hand with institutional betrayal. They deepened the difficulties I encountered at the end of my career, and, like the effect of institutional betrayal, sanctuary prolongs recovery for the injured member. Together this can be devastating.

Sanctuary trauma was first described by Dr. Steven Silver in a paper about the inpatient treatment of Vietnam War veterans. He defined "sanctuary trauma" as that which "occurs when an individual who suffered a severe stressor next encounters what was expected to be a supportive and protective environment and discovers only more trauma"[6] I became aware of this concept while trying to move forward with my own issues and reading about it in a psychology article. As I read, I began to think of my treatment on returning from my final tour to Afghanistan and wondered if this had occurred in some form to me. I have a simple example of this concept which took place at the end of my last tour.

---

6   Silver, S., An inpatient program for post-traumatic stress disorder: "Context as treatment in Trauma and Its Wake" Volume II: "Post-Traumatic Stress Disorder: Theory, Research and Treatment" C. Figley, Editor. 1986, Brunner/Mazel: New York

I was asked to return to Afghanistan a year after having just come off a year of working with a psychologist, when I was placed on a Temporary Category or TCAT[7] after my first tour to Afghanistan. Shortly after having the TCAT lifted, I received a call from the Medical Headquarters asking if I could return once more to Afghanistan, followed by my Commanding Officer and Regimental Sergeant Major requesting I meet with them. I met with them and we spoke about going back overseas, I was told it was a courageous thing to do, it would make 2 Field Ambulance and the solders of the unit look good, and finally, it would make me look good.

I was tired after only returning eleven months earlier, nevertheless I needed to know if the outcome on this second tour would be any different. Unfortunately for me, I had probably not recovered from my experiences the year prior, was still depressed and having issues with PTSD. I wasn't myself and something just didn't feel right. I was still occasionally tearful with thoughts of things I had seen and done. I couldn't shake my self-doubt over my performance as an independent Physician Assistant throughout the last tour.

Going back to Afghanistan would be the worst thing I was about to do. While deployed there, there would be feelings of betrayal by the chain of command, with everything from all the past tours bubbling up and coming together to overwhelm me, which eventually ended my career. Once deployed, I struggled with my superiors, how they treated their subordinates and myself. I had made an error and was informed they were looking into charging me for sending messages over the internet to them, unsecured. This was investigated and I was cleared. However, my chain of command back in Kandahar Airfield kept this decision from me for the entire tour and instead used it to control my voice with the threat of being charged or disciplined. From December until we left in May, I was socially isolated for an honest error I made. It ended up being a very difficult tour when there was no need and I returned extremely disillusioned. As well, there were things I was unaware of about to greet me on my return, more silence.

---

7   TCAT: A medical measure where a soldier is suspended from deployment, or courses, in order to allow a period of time to be in one location and treated for their illness(s).

When I returned from tour, the promises of letting me slow down for a while to rest used to get me to go on tour, never took place. There was no time to complete my master's degree, the promise of staying at my unit 2 Fd Amb, turned out to be wishful thinking. I wasn't ready for the level of careerism I was thrown into; I felt like fodder for those careerists, at home and while on tour in Afghanistan. On my return, what I found was anything but supportive. My first day back to work, I went to 3 Royal Canadian Regiment with whom I had served prior to tour, as well as whom I was deployed overseas with. I was reporting for duty, expecting to be employed once again in their clinic. However, when I arrived, the doctor there asked me what I was doing, he didn't think I was working in his clinic any longer and redirected me to the base medical clinic. At the base medical clinic, I spoke with another doctor to ask about where I was to work.

I was upset and angry with not knowing what was taking place, my first day back to work and it began with being denied returning to the unit I had served with prior to deployment and whom I had been with the past two years. I asked the doctor what was going on? He told me he couldn't tell me why this was happening, but confided in me that those in charge wanted to have me close so they could keep an eye on me, there had been calls received from my supervisors in Afghanistan and while he didn't know what I had done, it didn't look good for me. On hearing this, I quickly realized what was taking place, the fix was in and my career was as good as over. There was an air of silence and dismissal towards me from that point on. I was given what was called an "office" in the hallway. They had basically taken a utility room and made it into an office, with a small desk and exam bench, to make me feel as if I had some purpose, which was only an illusion.

Hidden and left to my own devices, not having a real job or a patient load it felt so isolating, like a second-class citizen. I didn't deserve to be treated like this, yet no one wanted to deal with me since my return and I didn't know why. I was not spoken to once about what the issues were. There was no me, no plan, direction or expectations for my return to duty. This entire situation only served to isolate me further, having no one to speak to about why this was taking place.

This silence continued for the next month until one day while sitting in my utility room closet office, I got an unexpected phone call from the career manager in Ottawa who wanted to speak with me. He had called to tell me that I was being posted to a new unit, 1 Canadian Field Hospital. I couldn't believe this, it was unexpected. First, I was isolated, then placed on a Permanent Category (PCat) and awaiting a decision from Ottawa to be released medically or retained, still seeing a psychologist for issues which took place overseas and now with little explanation. I was being sent to another unit; I was extremely angry with the betrayal. Prior to going on tour, I was made to believe that it was a good thing to deploy again, I was made think this would make the unit and myself look good in caring for the troops overseas. In reality all I did was make my leaders look good, further their careers and for me it meant the end of my career.

The promises made to me on my return, to be protected for a time to recover, to complete my master's degree, to get grounded again with my family, and to recover from the last two tours were not based in truth or spoken with integrity. Once I completed my tour and returned home injured, the promises made somehow now hadn't taken place, I must have misunderstood I was told. My mental health had taken a beating the last two and a half years with spending seventeen months in Afghanistan, and now it felt as if I was back in Afghanistan, out by myself in a Forward Operating Base, isolated with having to make important medical decisions on my own. I quickly found out that I was going to be given a Permanent Category (PCat) and eventually be medically released. During this time, I had thoughts of suicide and self harm as I did not know what was taking place. No one communicated with me within my chain of command. Thankfully, I had a moment of clarity and realized that those I worked for most likely wouldn't be affected by my passing, it would only alleviate a thorn in their sides. I was expendable and their posting me to another unit, to be rid of me, only served to solidify this belief.

Upon my return, being immediately removed from the soldiers at the unit I once served, being placed in an empty hallway utility room office, given minimal or no information, all served to isolate me, just as I was isolated while in Afghanistan. This was a recipe for a deeper descent into PTSD and depression. The place I should have expected the most help from, became the place which did the most harm. I was a Physician Assistant, working within a hospital, full of medical professionals, but the respect and attention I needed and deserved was not there.

I use this story to show how when we sometimes seek help, it turns out to be the replication of the trauma that drives you deeper into depression and PTSD. The silence and isolation I received on tour in Afghanistan was now being replicated in a place where I expected to be cared for, this is sanctuary trauma. The institutional betrayal lies in the unfulfilled promises of care on my return from tour, promises which were made to me to get me to deploy again and to make the unit and my supervisors look good.

Institutional Betrayal

Many years after retiring from the military and seeing a psychologist, I learned of a concept called institutional betrayal. The more we discussed what I had seen and done overseas; the more I began to understand what took place not only on deployments, perhaps more importantly upon my return to Canada. I began to understand that in my last few years while I was waiting to retire, that the treatment I received from my superiors had done as much, or more, damage as anything I had experienced on all my tours. It was then I began to realize this treatment, in the dwindling years of my career, was one of the main ingredients impeding my recovery from PTSD and depression.

Psychologist Dr. Jennifer J. Freyd, coined this term in 2008. It was used to refer to "wrongdoings perpetrated by an institution upon individuals dependent on that institution, including failure to prevent or respond supportively to wrongdoings by individuals (e.g. sexual assault) committed within the context of the institution." [8]

An example of this occurred during the last year I served. I was only a few months from retiring when I became seriously ill. It began while I was on annual leave (vacation) and began coughing up blood. I didn't know what was going on, but I was scared and immediately went to see my doctor,

---

[8]   Freyd, J.J. (March, 2008). "The Psychology of Betrayal Trauma: Memory, Health, and Gender" Lecture, Thompson Hall Science and Mathematics Seminar, University of Puget Sound, Tacoma, Washington, 6 March 2008.

bringing a sample bottle full of blood from my coughing to show. He ordered blood tests and a CT scan and eventually I was diagnosed with a cavitation pneumonia, an illness where a bacterium eats the lung tissue. The treatment was triple antibiotic therapy and rest and frequent follow up to ensure it was under control.

At work, my Company Sergeant Major (CSM) was also on leave and had not returned, I sent an email informing him as to what was taking place with me and my current illness. I was also having difficulty with PTSD, depression and various physical injuries, I didn't want the younger soldiers in my platoon seeing me this way. In the email I also requested to discuss my place in the unit over the last few months before my retirement, perhaps allowing me to be put into a less demanding position away from the troops.

After treatment for the infection for two weeks, I went back to work. That same day I was taken by my CSM to have an appointment with the unit Regimental Sergeant Major (RSM). Walking into the office, I was directed have a seat and as the conversation began, was asked, "PO Nearing, do you know why you are here?" I smiled back saying, "I'm guessing it may be something to do with my upcoming retirement and request to go to another job as I prepare to retire?" Then as quick as things seemed friendly, the smile was gone, the tone changed, looking directly at me, the RSM then spoke words to the effect, "Well let me tell you PO Nearing, when you signed on to be accommodated in this unit, it was for three years and at that time said you would work until the end of that contract. Now, if you cannot fulfill your end of the deal and work as a platoon warrant within the unit, please tell us right now so we can contact Ottawa and cancel your contract, assisting you in getting out of the military sooner. It's not your job to be deciding who goes where in the Company or unit, or to decide who should replace you in the platoon, that's not going to happen."

I sat there in shock, I didn't know what to say or how to respond, my mind was blank. I was thinking, why were they not understanding how sick I was. I was trying to figure out why I deserved to be treated like this, put on the spot for such a simple request? It was obvious this had been planned in advance by the CSM and RSM, to tell me a call would be made to Ottawa as soon as I said I could do it no more and have my contract cancelled. There was so much in those moments going through my mind, I was overwhelmed, then suddenly I felt tears running down my face and began sobbing out loud, I tried to restrain it but I couldn't stop it and began crying uncontrollably. I felt so embarrassed, here I was 52 years old and crying in front of my two supervisors, it felt like I was a kid in kindergarten being scolded. I felt immense shame, felt so small, so insignificant as if my entire career was a failure because, even though I was sick, it was I who was letting the organization down and even as ill as I was, I did not deserve compassion. I felt as though I didn't give enough of myself to this organization over my career and now everything, I had done for all those years meant nothing. I felt this overwhelming sense of emptiness in the pit of my stomach and wanted to die, I wanted to send all my medals back to Ottawa and tell them I didn't deserve them, that I was a failure, my career was a failure.

My supervisors both sat there looking at me as I cried, then asked what was wrong, but I couldn't speak, my throat was too dry and I was still in shock, not knowing or understand at what just took place. There was an awkward moment of silence, then I was offered some tissue and without missing a beat, the conversation continued, "So, tell me your answer PO Nearing, can you still do the platoon warrant position, or should we have your accommodation cancelled? Think about it for the rest of the week and next week tell me your decision." The following days as I thought more about this encounter, I could not understand was how I was in a medical unit, sitting in a room with two qualified physician assistants and even with me breaking down during the meeting, they couldn't see I was unwell? There was no understanding or compassion from them as to where I was at that time. I was made to feel like just another meaningless number, who would be replaced at the snap of a finger, felt I could not, or should not, care for myself until fully out of the military. In the end, what else could I do? I went back to work in the platoon and worked there until my retirement.

I use this personal story to illustrate how for soldiers seeking help, it is often not there when needed the most, institutional betrayal is one of the main catalysts which drives soldiers deeper into shame and depression, even suicide as I thought about on this day, despite any other injuries they may have had prior to requesting a position change a few months prior to retirement. I began to understand that, for me, this institutional betrayal took place so many places along the way in those last couple of years, once I could no longer fully perform my duties. I thought back to the promises made in order to get me to deploy on another tour, to continue pushing on and to put the unit, supervisors and the military above my own welfare. I was duty-bound to continue giving even when multiple levels of leadership should have known better and given me an opportunity to recover, in reality it was the abuse of my blind loyalty in getting me to go on that last tour. It was never about me, rather for the good of the institution, good of individual supervisors careers, which in fact ended my career as I came to understand that it was never about doing what was right (or caring) for me and in the end I became expendable once injured.

From the day we join and go to recruit school, the lifelong indoctrination begins. Throughout the years we adopt a collective group identity and mentality, which feeds into black and white thinking and adopting the institutional or policy point of view. Institutional betrayal tends to put blame on the individual and allows the institution to go faultless. There is a high value placed on a soldier's physical and mental prowess, and once one or the other is compromised and not quickly remedied, the descent begins, and superiors want to have you removed and replaced. Reflecting on my time in the military, I found it odd that after thirty-five years of service, both Reserves and Regular Forces, at the end of my career when I needed support, it simply was not offered by many of those in charge of me, those whom I had thought so highly of when I was able to do my job. Those who sought me out on so many tours for my abilities, were those same ones quick to dismiss me when the roles were reversed and it was I who need them and the institution.

Should one expect to have more dignified treatment by superiors when preparing to depart from an organization such as the military, an organization in which you have invested the greater part of your youth and adult life into? Yet, in the middle of one's personal chaos and illness, the institution we proudly and loyally served lets us down, we are often treated as if we had done something wrong in getting physically or mentally ill. The feeling amongst many members being released medically is that they have let down the organization. However, nothing could be farther from the truth; in fact, the member is sick and needs the institution's support more than any other time in their career. Often those closest do the most damage, pushing away or dismissing a soldier's injuries and demanding we continue to work at a level that is no longer sustainable. I believe this concept of institutional betrayal needs to be investigated further and to understand its role in delaying recovery from PTSD and other injuries in the military.

What is needed is a paradigm shift through institutional and leadership changes in order to address these concerns. When I initially joined, we were taught about military ethos and code of ethics, Principles of Leadership, so many powerful words and concepts. Throughout my time in the military I came to understand that these ideals are more than words on a piece paper. Ethical behaviour is found in the actions of how you treat others when you are in a position to lead soldiers, especially when they are at their most vulnerable. Looking back at my treatment during my final years in the military, when I needed support the most, often these ideals and values were not afforded me.

Sense of Understanding

My life was forever altered from the time of my return from Somalia. In the years which followed, I walked around feeling unwell, my perception of day to day living was altered, my brain felt fuzzy and I would swing from talking to a friend to being angry or depressed. Throughout this time, I did not know or understand why. I thought that this was just me. Thinking back on the twenty years I served in this mental health abyss, I wonder why others around me had never noticed the changes in me? A year after my retirement, a friend said that he did in fact notice my personality changes but was frozen with inaction not knowing how to approach me when I was angry and passive aggressive or silent and depressed. At the time I wasn't aware of it being anything to do with my tours. I am saddened by the fact that I worked 22 years in the medical profession, around medical people, yet they felt they couldn't approach me or know how to broach the subject. In the light of this, I wondered about the care of the regular soldier who is struggling with PTSD or depression. If this is a deficit within the Canadian Forces, it needs to be addressed.

Psychologists Richard Tedeschi and Lawrence Calhoun coined the term "Post Traumatic Growth," or PTG. Posttraumatic growth is: "positive psychological change experienced as a result of adversity and other challenges in order to rise to a higher level of functioning" and, "life-changing psychological shifts in thinking and relating to the world, that contribute to a personal process of change, that is deeply meaningful."[9] For me, the evolution of Post Traumatic Growth would take place, but it would be many years after retirement. While still in uniform, still serving, I was stuck trying to sort out what was taking place with me in those last few years of my career. Once it was known I was to be released, a shift took place and no longer was I allowed to attend certain courses, even if they were at no cost to the unit but might benefit me after release. I was no longer treated as the whole and functional soldier I had once been. My own feelings of inadequacy with not being able to deploy due to medical restrictions we amplified because of this treatment and contributed to my anger and depression as well.

During the years since retirement I have read much about moral injury, trauma and the circumstances which affect a person healing and moving forward in life. My psychologist introduced me to the concept of the "primacy and recency effect." Early memory research by German Psychologist, Hermann Ebbinghaus came up with the theory of Serial-position effect, where "the tendency of a person to recall the first and last items in a series best, and the middle items worst."[10] In his experiment it was demonstrated that when subjects were given a list to memorize, the majority of people tend to be able to recall what was at the beginning and end of the list, or the more recent information. The middle items on the list often get forgotten about or are sent to long-term memory storage. For myself, the recency of how I was treated at the end of my career overrode everything. It was during the last three years of my career when I began seeing a psychologist, but we never spoke about my tours. On arrival for appointments, I would be so upset and distracted by how I had been treated at my work since my last appointment, that we actually spent more time diffusing the recent events which angered or saddened me. These overpowering memories from what had taken place the week since the previous appointment, were so strong, that any past trauma

---

9   Tedeshi, R.G., & Calhoun, L.G. (2004). Posttraumatic Growth: Conceptual Foundation and Empirical Evidence. Philadelphia, PA: Lawrence Erlbaum Associates.

10   Coleman, Andrew (2006). Dictionary of Psychology (Second Edition). Oxford University Press. p. 688.

from my tours, were set aside. This continued until I was finally released from the military. Long after my release, I was still preoccupied by how I was treated at the end of my career, much like the recency effect would suggest as this was my most proximate experience. With the benefit of 20/20 hindsight, I have come to understand these things could have been avoided with more understanding by my supervisors. My distress at the end of my career could have been bettered by recognition of my service, care and understanding. Most of these things are leadership issues: leadership that knows when a soldier needs time to heal and an understanding that the demands made of a soldier who is ill and his treatment will affect healing. Sadly, while I did see a psychologist for many years prior to release, it would not be until I was fully retired and clear of the military that I could begin the process to heal and work on the events from my tours.

It should not be underestimated how the demand to continue to perform at a pre-PTSD level, while I was sick, and the additional sanctuary trauma on top of pre-existing trauma had prolonged and interfered with my recovery. The institutional betrayal and sanctuary trauma are separate from those things I had witnessed and done while overseas and made healing much more complicated because the focus then becomes the most recent events which end up taking precedence over the core of the actual injury, past traumas of deployments.

During the dwindling years of serving in the military, I was treated by many supervisors as if I was not giving my all. What they didn't understand was that I was actually compensating, so well in fact that I did not look ill and always pushed through, as we were trained to do. Subsequently, when I sought help or asked for a break, I was viewed as weak, perhaps even a malingerer. My stoicism allowed me to continue giving to the military organization I had grown up in and loved, when in fact my personal torment was covered up too well, and I compensated for the pain by working harder and harder until it was no longer sustainable. Alongside everything I had been though overseas which was not dealt with, unknowingly or uncaring, there was a new layer of trauma from the treatment of my superiors being added on here at home. Kind of ironic that I was a Physician Assistant in a medical unit, and therein received some of the most disrespectful and poor treatment one would not expect.

I am glad to say that things have moved forward since this time. With ongoing care from a psychologist and the guiding wisdom of art therapy, I have begun to understand so much of what took place. Much of the anguish at the end of my career wasn't necessary and this is the part the military has to re-evaluate and fix. Looking back and dealing with the deaths, mass graves and disturbing situations overseas all seem easier now, now that I have worked through the institutional betrayal and sanctuary trauma. The road to healing is not straight, nor does it happen overnight, it is a few small steps forward then the falling backwards at times, but always leading to small gains in a positive direction.

Changing Personality

From the late 1990s until I retired, I was often seen as a problem soldier. I was deemed undisciplined and that I offered opinions when not asked. In short, I was what is often called "a problem child". That time during my career now colours so much of my career. It wouldn't be until I returned from that last tour and finally was released from the military, that the dust settled and I could begin to take apart my time in the military and look at where it went wrong, and why I didn't see it coming.

When I looked back at my time in the military, I saw it in two parts. The first was transferring from the Reserves in 1991, full of optimism and bringing a healthy work ethic inherited from my parents. The early part of my career was wonderful. On joining, I did well on the first course. Then I was sent on multiple smaller courses and was eventually picked up to be deployed with the Canadian Airborne Regiment to Somalia in 1992/93, where I showed my worth in being able to turn my hand to most anything. On my return I was accelerated to the rank of corporal. Shortly after my return, I was once again sent away on a medical course at Borden, where I would be presented with the top candidate award and then head off in the summer of 1994 to Rwanda on the reconnaissance party. Here too I would prove my value with acquiring the tools and equipment we needed in getting the recce done. The next year I was presented with the Special Service Force Soldier of the Year Award for CFB Petawawa, promoted to master corporal and then posted to 1 Canadian Field Hospital. Then I was sent over to Bosnia in 1997 and it would be here where I would begin to slip, not in a big way, but slip I would, and cracks began to show.

The cracks were beginning to show after Somalia, but my supervisors and peers thought I was adjusting to coming home and it would settle. It did, but I had changed and didn't smile or laugh as often and didn't like crowds or going to unit parties as much. But I compensated and it was my new baseline, no one noticed, no one knew. The same was repeated after Rwanda, then Bosnia and suddenly I was very combative with my supervisors, difficult to say the least and I would say insubordinate. I began to get into trouble and get spoken to until the unit decided I should be posted.

I was promoted and posted to Trenton in 1998, which was terrible. I could not adjust and had no one on whom I could lean or confide in after leaving everything and everyone I knew behind in Petawawa. Now isolated, I fell into a depression which I hid from everyone at work and then I was sent away for another six-month medical course. On the course, I struggled. I failed the first three tests and was on the verge of being sent back to my unit, but somehow got it together. My reward for passing the course was to be promoted and posted once again, less than a year after arriving in Trenton. Posted to Thunder Bay, where I really began to falter and could barely keep it together. I lived in the tallest building in the city, on the 18th floor, where one night I tested the waters and crawled over the railing on the balcony. I felt I had nothing to lose as I put my arms behind me and leaned forward, but I was dating Maureen, who would become my wife two years later, and so I came back onto the balcony. There would be other times that it just felt so lonely and there were so many things I couldn't understand from my deployments as to how my attitude and personality had changed so much. It had to be me; I wasn't a good soldier.

In 2000, I was posted once again to CFB Borden as an instructor. It was here I would begin self-harming, cutting, and hitting my head so hard off a wall that I split the eyebrow wide open only a week before our wedding. I cut my wrist and hand but bandaged it up and carried on. I would eventually be placed on my physician assistant's course, very messed up and struggling with undeclared mental health issues. I completed this course, barely passed, yet completing it and was promoted to Petty Officer 1st Class and posted to CFB Petawawa, back to the base where I had begun my career and called home.

It wouldn't be until 2005 when I had the dissociative episode in church and it was this incident which sent me to seek help, which I received. But I was fortunate, or perhaps not, to be deemed still employable and deployable as I carried on doing the two tours in Afghanistan and was eaten up by the green machine and spit out when there was nothing left to give.

This is the *Reader's Digest* version of a twenty-two-year career as a Medic and Physician Assistant, all of it is to say that along the way I received verbal warnings several times, was disciplined with extra duties and weekend duties, and received formal warnings and threats of being released. Meanwhile, unknown to myself or my superiors I was very ill, and my behaviour was the outward cry for help. My subconscious and body knew something was wrong, but my brain couldn't relay this. For all the years until finally diagnosed in 2005, I struggled and was getting warnings and disciplinary measures to control my behaviour. I know no one ever looked at my past, at the early successes of my career, and apart from an offer from a supervisor to call a help line, no one ever out and out asked me, "Are you ok, Derrick?"

There are different methods available in the military to sort out soldiers when they need correction or guidance to put them back on the right track. When dealing with soldiers who are acting up, I would say that instead of considering soldiers' mental health, far and away the most oft-chosen way to deal with them is either the administrative or disciplinary, or a combination of both.

The soldier who is acting out may not realize he is ill or has mental health problems. Admittedly, it can be a difficult thing to sort out whether it is a medical issue versus administrative or disciplinary. To be honest, amid the business of being a soldier or a supervisor, there very often isn't the time for a front-line supervisor to get into the forest to decide which it is. In most cases, though, the medical option is the last to be looked at or it doesn't get looked at all. Rather, the choice is to be swift and exacting and to dish out the discipline in the form of fines or extra duties or ceasing career progression. This is followed by administrative sanctions such as verbal, written, formal warnings, counselling and probation, and finally, in most cases, dishonorable discharge from the military.

When I began my career, I was perceived to be what one might be called a "streamer," ascending the ranks swiftly because of perceived skill and aptitude for being a soldier. Then something happened and I fell off the good-soldier applecart. When soldiers are suddenly not worthy, there is an abrupt urgency to get rid of them quickly or to send these problem children over to the medical system and let it sort them out. To the uninitiated this seems terrible, but if you are a company sergeant major or a company commander in charge of a hundred troops or more, you don't have the time to get into the weeds. You need to sort this guy out quickly and get on with the business of soldiering.

We had a saying when I was a supervisor, which went like this, "Ten percent of your troops take up ninety percent of your time." That is a fact that I can attest to, and in a busy operational unit, time is precious, and one has to get on with the task at hand. If the administrative or disciplinary route wasn't working, I tried the medical route to see if it was something I was missing.

To be fair, what is said in a couple of sentences on paper, in real time can often take over two or three years, there is time for soldiers to get help, to right their ships and get on with their careers. Fortunately, I kept it together long enough to complete my career, but I unnecessarily created some bad blood along the way with peers and supervisors, still there were also those times I was also kicked when I was down by those whom I worked for. This is another reason many soldiers don't come forward to seek help. When they see someone such as their platoon warrant who is higher on the rank structure, such as me, receiving poor treatment from superiors, they wonder to themselves, "how am I going to be treated if Petty Officer Nearing is being treated this way?" I believe over the last few years, since my release, there have been many positive changes made within the organization. It has gotten better and there have been educational components added to leadership courses, with more mental health awareness and advocacy, which will lead to a stronger and healthier military in the end, but this too will take time to implement.

The Value of Journaling

Looking back at my journals like the Rwanda one shared here in this book, I can see the rollercoaster of emotions: the highs and lows I was going through during these months away from home. I didn't begin keeping my journal because I knew it would eventually be there to help me understand what I went through. Looking back, I can't remember why I began one, but I am glad I did. I remember so many of the days in Rwanda when I was having a bad day, or was overwhelmed, those times when I was sitting in my bed space writing, there was a calming process taking place for me, a meditation and resetting of the emotions. That time alone to my journal was somehow restful and a slowing down of my thoughts. It was as if an old friend and I were having a conversation, just me, the pen and my journal.

I do recall both in Somalia and Rwanda, that it became something I worked into my routine, trying to write a line or two every night before bed or after a hectic day. I certainly couldn't write everything that took place each day, just the high points and the low ones as well. I never understood why I was doing it, but what it became was a way to vent. When we are deployed, there are lots of stressors going on for everyone there on tour. When I was writing in my book, I believe now that it was a way to express myself, to get things from the day off my chest, which is probably a much healthier way to manage my anger, sadness, or disappointment.

Reading the journal now I can see those times when I started out writing and was so angry, but then as I continued writing I would calm down and perhaps come to understand why someone had told me to do something which I didn't agree with. I believe the journaling helped with my emotional and mental health and calmed me. It was just a few moments out of those days on tour I had to myself, a chance to write down what was bothering me, or what went well, then clean the plate so to speak so I could begin the next day with a clean slate. I imagine how I would have been perceived, if I had of spoken everything at the time which I was going through, instead of writing it my journal. The looks I would have gotten from my section and the others I worked and lived with on tour, they may have thought me trivial, depressed, self doubting or mad, but the act of writing down the highs and lows was sedative, calming and allowed me to download these emotions and begin the next day with a fresh start

As I retired and was moving to a new house, I accidentally came upon these notebooks and initially I threw them with other scribblers and magazines into the blue box for recycling. For some reason, later that morning I went and looked for them and took them out. As I began reading, I realized that these books were in my handwriting and these were my journals. I had forgotten about them and blocked out any memory of having written them. What a serendipitous thing to find. I was having difficulty recovering after my last tour and on the eve of releasing from the military, I happened upon these.

There are conversations I have had with others who had been in Rwanda with me, where terrible sights and happenings have taken place, but I have noticed with the passage of time, there is a tendency to whitewash out the bad and keep only the good, focusing on these moments. I think this is only human, perhaps a way of our brains trying to reset those difficulties we encountered earlier in life. But like that old friend, my journal takes me back to the truth of those times. It is an honest broker to the realities of war when the years have passed, and our minds want to soften those experiences.

Reading my journal. I began to understand that much of my anger and other issues were not isolated to the most recent tour but were an accumulation of those tours before and after Rwanda. My journals became an instrument in healing, to see and pinpoint times, places, and people where things took place and how they affected me in that time and place. I also think that in the quiet of my bed space, writing in a journal provided me a chance to unload privately and unwind while on tour. If there is any one thing I would offer as advice, it would be to teach this as a course for new recruits to the military, encourage them to keep a journal throughout their entire careers. Journals are for the writer only, unless they decide to share, but perhaps once it has been reexperienced by the writer, shared or its time has passed, journals might eventually serve us years later once we have read and digested them, by letting the contents and those things holding us back eventually go.

My Eureka!

For years I understood very little of what I was going through. While initially suffering from PTSD after my first tour in Somalia, was I not even aware of anything wrong with me? I thought I was readjusting upon my return. Later, after my personality and mental state never went back to my baseline of what they were pre-tour, I always thought it was my fault and that

I was the cause of all the emotional upheaval and difficulties I would find myself going through the rest of my career.

I still find it difficult to shake this thing called PTSD and depression. After dealing with it for the last twenty-five years it feels normal to me, a part of my personality, to have the thoughts and memories from past tours and experiences so vivid and ever present. But the downside of this is that I know it is not good for me; the constant, intense memories and always being made aware of the past by my senses being suddenly fired up; the lack of sleep, only four to five hours a night for the last twenty-five years; getting startled and wired with adrenaline at the drop of a dime, it's no good really.

As medical people in the military, like the combat soldier, not only have we have been personally touched by one of our own comrades getting injured or killed, but mixed in with this is the fact that most often we are the ones giving the care. That dying baby in our arms, witnessing terrible sexual violations, witnessing injuries that display the inhumanity of our fellow humans, unimaginable pain and suffering many soldiers will never know. We work through it. We also have worked with that fellow soldier of theirs who was killed, we are gravely affected by these losses, we have walked a mile in another's footsteps, with and besides them. While we never speak of it and those whom we care for may never know it, we do understand intimately.

In the army, medics and physician assistants perform their duties alongside combat arms soldiers out in the field, in the same circumstances often the same venues; we are going through all these things as well. When shit hits the fan and there are mass casualties, you will not see the medic or physician assistant panic. Like the combat soldier, we are taught to suppress our natural instincts and soldier through it, which is to fight through to the objective no matter what. It is the medic's calmness which is counted upon; this helps to control the situation and give hope to those around them. It is very often the medic who becomes the anchor in the storm. Medics and Physician Assistants attached to combat units are often not afforded the privilege of expressing emotions such as sadness when someone gets terribly injured or dies. While as a medic and in the middle of a fire fight or situation, we are also experiencing these appalling things in real time as they unfold, but somehow, we are viewed differently, as if we are not supposed to allow it to affect us. We are somehow supposed to be unemotional. We are not given the same freedom to be sad, remorseful, or depressed we are expected to be detached. I can tell you that after eight months in a forward operating base, the strain, hidden from the other soldiers, begins to affect us as medical people, at least it did me. It's the strain of being the one everyone expects not to show emotion; of being on high readiness 24/7, as we wait for casualties, injured or sick troops for the entire tour, sleeping always with one eye open, waiting for the call.

Instead of us openly showing our grief and sadness or being overwhelmed, we meet soldiers with a smile, a slap on the back, an understanding ear or a moment to talk about home. However, medical people are also experiencing the loss of a comrade as the combat soldier does, but we do so as we go about our business of helping others, our own need for help or the opportunity for emotional release is suppressed. This becomes a lifestyle for most while serving, and afterward we continue to bury it by staying extremely busy, thus keeping that adrenaline load on and all the bad events and emotions in.

These expectations are true of all the helping trades, padres, social workers and medical personnel. I believe that there are times when those in charge of us don't see our vulnerabilities and mental health injuries in the same way as they see a non-medical person's injuries. There is a cavalier attitude within the helping trade that thinks "Well, this is what you signed up for." For me personally, I believe this was the reason I just sucked it up for my entire career, put my head down and kept moving forward. We medical personnel are viewed differently and assumed (or expected) to be more resilient when we see and experience these terrible things, but the reality could be no farther from the truth. Over my career I had many skeletons in my closet; suffering terribly from PTSD, depression, physical injuries and going through this while still trying to serve and care for others. Meanwhile my superiors' expectations were for me to continue caring for people above myself. This needs to change.

It was only with time and distance from these events, with the slowing down of the continuous adrenaline and stimulation after my release from the military, that I could begin to understand and heal. Just as Archimedes shouted "Eureka" while in the bathtub on accidentally discovering a solution to his problem, my "Eureka" moment came to me by accident as well. One day while I was looking at some old aerial photos of our hospital in Rwanda, when for some reason, I then decided to Google current satellite images of the site, to see what it looked like twenty-five years later. On our arrival in Mareru, the original site contained only the milk factory and five smaller buildings and within the surrounding community only a few homes, to my amazement, the most recent satellite images of the site showed there were now hundreds of buildings in the same community. With these pictures in front of me, I began to understand how these two images, of the past and present location in Rwanda, with its amazing growth over these past twenty-five years, represented me metaphorically. I finally understood that in my memories, I still was processing events of my tour as if time stood still the last twenty-five years, those initial buildings I recalled were my reference point, my mind-set of where I was still residing all these years later. In reality, Rwanda and its people have moved on, not forgotten the war or genocide, but had accepted the past and begun the healing process many years earlier. They had continued living life while moving forward, while I had not, I had stagnated. The current satellite picture of the community with its amazing growth, showed me the people of Rwanda's ability to move forward since that terrible time. Like so many of my fellow colleagues who deployed with me in 1994, I had been stuck, it was I who was still amongst those memories from all those years ago, my growth had ceased, and I was still residing in the past. It was this moment of seeing the current satellite picture when I had my "Eureka!" moment and understood it was time for me to move on. I had to let go of those times, events and things which had been holding me back for far too many years, in order to begin my healing, it was time to move forward.

EPILOGUE

My time in Rwanda was a mere seventy-nine days in total, from the initial landing as part of the reconnaissance group on the 28th of July, until my departure on the 15th of October 1994. Every single one of those days were intense, packed full of highs and lows, laughs and sadness, boredom and pure adrenaline. My hope is that the reader has seen from these journals how my time in Rwanda had affected me, and how these events had such life-changing impacts on all of us who deployed.

Walking Them Home: A Soldier's Journey in Postwar Rwanda, was written largely from my personal journal, which I kept throughout the tour, from the first day I was given notice of my deployment to Rwanda, until my return. This journal, along with letters from family and friends, conversations with those who deployed with me and insights twenty-five years later, together have given me much to reflect on as I write about this time in my life. As I retired and began to gradually move forward from these times, having had the opportunity to slow things down, take care of myself. It is only now with the benefit of 20/20 hindsight that the fog has begun to be lifted, I am beginning to understand just how incredible this mission was, both for the highs and lows we all went through during this time.

Op Passage was a rapidly assembled and deployed mission of 247 Canadian soldiers, sent to a country which had descended into the madness of a genocide, taking place over a four-month period from April to July. With the passage of time and benefit of my new perspective all these years later, I have a better understanding of what took place and deep admiration and respect for all those soldiers who I was fortunate to have deployed with. As I sat reading my journals and letters twenty-five years later, it is with awe I now view and understand what we had accomplished in such a short span of time, under austere and under-resourced conditions.

There were many times as I was writing this book where I felt like an outsider to my once thirty-three-year-old self, looking at the younger me, but with the benefit time and of understanding what took place and how I reacted to these events back then. It was as if this was not my story and I was but a voyeur, a time traveler looking back, trying to better grasp what the soldiers and refugees were going through in a country abandoned by the world. Then there are those times, when I have a visceral knot in the pit of my stomach as I read about some of the events I experienced and once again am brought back to those times, in the middle of the madness, recalling the terrible task of burying babies, the scene of the mass vehicle accident, or the bodies Father Bosse and I found in the septic system at the Nyundo Cathedral. I believe these two ends of one's memories demonstrate what time does to our understanding and beliefs; an ever-changing and developing perspective on those distant events which our minds initially shielded us from all those years ago, only to be processed later in life.

When deployed to Rwanda, little did I understand how this experience would forever change my life and view of the world. Chronicling my experiences through journaling every day throughout this time served as a time capsule, to be packed away on my return from Rwanda and promptly forgotten about. Perhaps the putting it away and forgetting about, was my mind's way of protecting me from my memories of these events, until those events were ready to be processed. It was at the moment of discovering these journals many years later, the seed was planted to one day attempt turning my journal into a book. As the years passed and I set about researching our mission there was nothing to be found, had we not deployed and been there I wondered? Of course, we did deploy and some amazing things were done while there, but then I began to wonder why more wasn't known by regular Canadians about what was done for the returning refugees of Rwanda. I felt after twenty-five years had passed, something needed to be written on the Rwandan Mission, to capture and perhaps to give voice to this little-known chapter of our Canadian Military history before it is forever lost, as those of us who were there grow old and memories begin to fade.

I have tried to write a simple story on many levels. First, it is about Canada offering help in the form of a hospital with a water purification capability, to a country torn apart during a violent civil war and a genocide. Rwanda was a country abandoned by the entire world, with only a few willing to follow Gen Dallaire's lead, to stand up and call out the madness by staying there for the duration and attempting to protect the innocent, in the madness of what would become known as the Rwandan Genocide. Secondly, it is a story about sending a diverse group of soldiers from across Canada, rapidly assembled and deployed to deal with the worst of circumstances the world had seen in 50 years, with little preparation, and yet to succeed and care for so many displaced people and refugees. It is testimony to how soldiers, from bases across Canada were quickly assembled and sent into an extremely difficult situation, developing into a cohesive team caring for returning refugees from the camps in neighboring Zaire. Finally, this book is my attempt to honour that time in Canadian military history, which saw the seeds of the modern-day Disaster Assistance Response Team (DART) being sown, while also paying respect to those whose lives were lost or altered due to mental health issues in the aftermath of this mission.

As I sat writing this book, I reflected on so many things from my time in Rwanda and asked myself, "Was it worth it?" I thought about this, reflected on this time in my life and how it affected me, wondering what exactly did we accomplish? I came to the conclusion the answer could only be, that of course it was worth it! It is always worth it to help others who are caught in the middle of madness and devastation not of their making, we have a responsibility to do this. I recall speaking with my mother the night before being sent to Rwanda and I had doubts as to what I was being sent to do, she told me to just do my best in whatever I was given to do, no matter what. Then she told me a quote by Mother Teresa, "We know only too well that what we are doing is nothing more than a drop in the ocean. But if the drop were not there, the ocean would be missing something." Thanks Mom, for the guidance and advice, as usually you were right.

There are times I think back to the amazing work this group accomplished in Rwanda. Seeing well over 22,000 patients in the seventy days we were in operation, including patients in our field hospital and the clinics we ran in Kora and Ruhengeri. While we were caring for the refugee's medical needs, the engineers purified over a million gallons of water for locals and those travelling back from Zaire, educated well over 30,000 children in mine awareness for unexploded grenades and land mines, helped to repair schools, churches, and the local orphanage. The electrical engineers helped by constructing a much-needed incubator for our hospital, which saved many babies lives. They would go on to repairing the generators at a local orphanage, getting them running and supporting the rebuilding of local infrastructure. The military Padre with us, Father Whelan Bosse, was instrumental in assisting local churches and schools being reopened. During this time, he also helped to move a mass grave with the religious meanings respected, as the community watched our every move in relocating the grave, thereby comforting an already suffering population. The platoon from the Canadian Airborne Regiment and Military Police provided our security both at camp as well as travelling outside of camp, and when off duty, many of the troops would turn their hand to helping us with patient care in the hospital and our triage area. Our signalers, supply and administration staff would ensure the flow of supplies and equipment and keep the lines of communication open between us and our superiors back in Canada.

Operation Passage was a Canadian offering to a country coming through a savage civil war and subsequent genocide, our group deployed with a naive understanding of what had taken place, with little understanding at the time the impact it would have on so many of us while deployed and into present time. It was supposed to be a one-time deployment and that was to be it, however the two years following our return, there was much studying, dissecting, and analyzing this deployments missions' successes and failures, from this emerged the Disaster Assistance Response Team (DART). The DART was created with some innovative policy and command initiatives at the time. All this policy development was made possible from the experiences, sacrifices and hard work, and difficult experiences the soldiers deployed on Operation Passage went through.

Reflecting on my time in Rwanda, with the benefit of 20/20 hindsight, I now have a clearer understanding of what took place twenty-five years ago. I have come to understand the mission was nothing short of a leading-edge humanitarian deployment, which two short years later would lead to the creation of a rapidly deployable military humanitarian medical team. This capability over the past twenty-five years has grown and morphed into a science, which can be expanded to include a surgical team, combat team and other medical and support elements.

There are those soldiers from our time in Rwanda whose lives, as has mine, have been forever altered since their return from this grim tour. My hope in publishing these journals is this will lead to a more comprehensive understanding of what this incredible group of men and women accomplished during our time in Rwanda despite the austere and adverse conditions. There is so much that all Canadians should be proud of with what our men and women do in Canada's name, this mission is but one of those achievements. While Operation Passage has gone largely unrecognized for far too long, it is time to let Canada, and the world, know of the amazing care provided to the people of Rwanda in the aftermath of the Rwandan War and Genocide.

Nearing family photo Summer 2019 – Photo Sandra Eis

GLOSSARY OF ACRONYMS/ ABBREVIATIONS

AAR – After Action Report

Americares – Disaster Relief and Medical Aid organization

Capt -Captain, an Officer rank

CDHSR - Canadian Division Headquarters and Signal Regiment

CDS - Chief of Defence Staff

CDO - Commando

CO - Commanding Officer

CSG - Canadian Support Group

CSM – Company Sergeant Major

D and S Platoon - Defence and Security Platoon

DAG – Departure Assistance Group

DART - Disaster Assistance Response Team

ICRC – International Committee of the Red Cross

IMC – International Medical Corps

LCol - Lieutenant Colonel

MEMISA – Belgian medical NGO organization working for development aid and cooperation

MLBU – Mobile Laundry and Bath Unit

MLVW – Medium Logistics Vehicle Wheeled. A military cargo truck

MSF - Médecins Sans Frontières / Doctors Without Borders

NDHQ – National Defence Headquarters

NDMC - National Defence Medical Centre

NGO's - Non-Governmental Organizations

OGrp - Orders Group where important information is passed on

OR – Orderly Room

PA – Physician Assistant

PSF - Pharmacie Sans Frontier / Pharmacists Without Borders

PTSD – Post Traumatic Stress Injury

Recce – Reconnaissance

ROWPU - Reverse Osmosis Water Purification Unit

RPF - Rwandan Patriotic Front

RQ - Regimental Quartermaster

RSM - Regimental Sergeant Major

Snr NCO - Senior Non-Commissioned Officer

UMS - Unit Medical Station

UNAMIR - United Nations Assistance Mission for Rwanda

UNHQ – United Nations Headquarters

UNICEF – United Nations International Children's Emergency Fund

WO – Warrant Officer, a Snr NCO rank

ABOUT THE AUTHOR

Derrick Nearing is a retired Petty Officer who served 13 years as a Field Engineer in the Primary Reserves, followed by another 22 years in the Canadian Forces Medical Branch as a Medical Technician and Physician Assistant. His military career included missions to Somalia, Rwanda and Bosnia where, as a Medic, he witnessed the brutal results of war and its impact on local civilian populations. As a Physician Assistant, he would deploy to Afghanistan as medical support to front line combat troops, caring for the deadly and devastating injuries resulting from improvised explosive devices. Two decades of bearing witness to trauma and suffering saw Derrick eventually leave the military with PTSD, depression and other physical injuries. In *Walking Them Home: A Soldier's Journey in Postwar Rwanda*, he attempts to share personal and intimate details from the journal he kept throughout his time deployed. His first book, Anchor of My Heart: Memories of a Cape Breton Childhood was published in 2017. He presently lives with his wife, Maureen, and their children, Hannah and Reilly, in Pembroke, Ontario.

CPSIA information can be obtained
at www.ICGtesting.com
Printed in the USA
LVHW100341030123
736333LV00005B/217

9 781525 554551